MW00963421

Olympics 100

Canada at the Summer Games

Cleve Dheensaw

ORCA BOOK PUBLISHERS

For Pam, whose patience and support was truly Olympian

Canadian Cataloguing in Publication Data
Dheensaw, Cleve, 1956 –
Olympics 100

ISBN 1055143-068-1
1. Olympics—History. 2. Sports—Canada—History. I. Title.
GV585.D53 1996   796.48   C95–911169–7

The publisher would like to acknowledge the ongoing financial support of
The Canada Council, the Department of Canadian Heritage, and the British Columbia
Ministry of Small Business, Tourism and Culture.

Cover design by Christine Toller
Interior photographs courtesy: Canadian Sports Hall of Fame, B.C. Sports Hall
    of Fame, Canadian Sporting Images, Canadian Press, and Sporting Spotlights
Front cover photographs *(clockwise from top right)*: Percy Williams, Lennox Lewis,
    Ben Johnson, Angela Chalmers, Silken Laumann
Back cover photos: Mark Tewksbury *(right)*, Carolyn Waldo *(left)*

Printed and bound in Canada

Orca Book Publishers   Orca Book Publishers
PO Box 5626, Station B   PO Box 468
Victoria, BC Canada   Custer, WA USA
V8R 6S4   98240-0468

10 9 8 7 6 5 4 3 2 1

TABLE OF CONTENTS

ATHENS 1896

April 6 to 15
311 Athletes from 13 Nations

In Francis Ford Coppola's 1988 film *Tucker: The Man and His Dream*, about a visionary and his ill-fated automobile design, the lead character says: "They'll say we only made fifty of them, but fifty or fifty million, what does it matter? That's just machinery. It's the idea, the dream, that counted." Baron Pierre de Coubertin dared to dream the greatest sporting dream of all time. He didn't have the might of the Big Three automakers against him like Preston Tucker four decades later, but the Baron faced something worse — indifference and skepticism. Yet he managed to put into place the machinery that brought his vision to reality.

And his dream was a full-blown, wide-screen Technicolor monster with a cast of thousands. De Coubertin envisioned a revival of the ancient Greek Olympics, which ran uninterrupted every four years from 776 B.C. to 393 A.D. and provided a physical, social and moral framework for sport, fitness, victory and manhood that profoundly affected and shaped the modern athletic world.

The Olympic champions of ancient Greece were put on a pedestal above that of generals, merchants, teachers or philosophers. To wear the olive wreath of an Olympic champion was to be a national hero — to have odes and poems written, statues erected and massive parades marched in your honour. Two thousand years later, sporting heroes like Wayne Gretzky and Michael Jordan are again bigger and more famous than presidents and prime ministers, and hundreds of thousands of citizens line city streets for parades honouring the World Series or Stanley Cup champions.

The site of the ancient Olympics was the sacred valley of Olympia, the sanctuary of Zeus at the foot of Mount Kronos near the Ionian coast of the Peloponnese. On its wide and fertile plain grew olive and pine groves and amid this earthly beauty were held foot races, wrestling matches and javelin throwing contests as man competed against man in what became a test of human speed, strength and stamina known as the Olympic Games. When German archaeologists began a six-year excavation of the site in 1875, they unearthed remnants of the Temple of Zeus, the sacred olive grove, the Olympic stadium, the Hippodrome where chariot races were contested, the gymnasium and the baths. It was awe-inspiring to think that humankind, which was capable of brutal war, was also capable of laying downs its arms once every four years during the reign of the Greeks for the month of the Olympic competitions.

Thousands were attracted to this excavated site and deeply moved by it. But none more so than de Coubertin, who was grabbed by a dream that began to consume him: Why not revive the Olympic Games? Would not the pursuit of sport through a strict code of amateurism — sport just for the sake of sport — be a way of bringing the youth of the world together in peace rather than war?

De Coubertin was born a nobleman in Paris on January 1, 1863, and educated at the military academy at St. Cyr before resigning his commission to pursue a career in education. Physical activity and sport were frowned on in France at the time. They were thought to be meaningless distractions for the youth of the ruling classes, distractions from really important matters like reading and studying.

But the tide was shifting and in 1889 de Coubertin was appointed by the French government to study physical culture in other countries. He noticed a different attitude in the English-speaking world. He was heavily influenced by the Thomas Hughes novel *Tom Brown's School Days*, in which the mysterious and binding connection between sport and British public schools is explored. De Coubertin also became a big fan of Thomas Arnold, the legendary headmaster of Rugby School in England, who pioneered the concept of linking body and mind in the education process.

Although de Coubertin was definitely the catalyst for the birth of the modern Olympics, there are clues that an evolutionary process was also at work. J.C.F. Guts-Muths, a gymnastics innovator in Germany, first put forward the idea of reviving the ancient Olympics more than forty years before de Coubertin thought of it. Ernst Curtius, picking up on the idea, lectured on the ancient Greek Games at Berlin in 1852.

But it was de Coubertin whose passion was the most feverish. He lived, breathed and slept with this idea eating away at him. He finally publicly put forward his proposal for reviving the Olympics at a meeting of the Athletic Sports Union, held November 25, 1892, at the Sorbonne in Paris. "Let us export oarsmen, runners and fencers," he said at the meeting. "That is the free trade of the future. On the day when it shall take place, the cause of peace will have received a new and powerful support."

Initially, at least, there were few takers. But his enthusiasm began to win converts and at a meeting of seventy-nine sporting representatives from thirteen countries at the Sorbonne's Hall of Sciences in June of 1894, the little Frenchman won over hearts and minds. A resolution was passed: "In order to maintain and promote physical culture, and particularly to bring about a friendly intercourse between nations, sports competitions should be held every fourth year on the lines of the Greek Olympic Games and every nation should be invited to participate." Athletic representatives of twenty-one more countries sent letters of support. Some basic principles were agreed to: the Games would move to different cities every four years, modern sports would replace the ancient sports and the Games would adhere to a strict code of amateurism and be open only to adults (the implication being male adults).

De Coubertin wanted the first modern Games to be held in Paris. But the other delegates knew that such a choice for the first site was a non-starter. Greece was chosen as the host instead, and the conference voted to approve the modern revival of the Olympic Games for April of 1896. Although Olympia was the preferred venue, the ancient stadium there was beyond repair. The capital city, Athens, was the next best thing. However the Greeks were not all that excited that this small group of men, who proclaimed themselves the International Olympic Committee, was suddenly so interested in them. The Greek government was broke and had no money for such an Olympian undertaking.

The whole idea might have been dashed then and there were it not for the enthusiasm of the Crown Prince of Greece, a rich benefactor with intense enthusiasm for the idea. Crown Prince Constantine saw the revival as a magnificent link to the past and headed a fund-raising committee. The dream also fired the imagination of Greek business tycoon Georgios Averoff, who donated one million drachmas to the enterprise. The rest of the money came from the sales of commemorative stamps and coins. The Greek people were soon persuaded.

The horseshoe-shaped marbled Stadium of Herodis, built in 330 B.C., was restored for the occasion, and at 3:05 P.M. on April 6, 1896, King George of Greece melted away fifteen centuries by proclaiming open the first Games of the modern era. Sitting beside the King was the diminutive de Coubertin, who certainly must have felt a tingle go up his spine. More than 70,000 people crowded into the stadium and thousands more congregated on the surrounding hillsides to catch a glimpse of history being made. There were no formal national Olympic associations and the athletes paid their own way to Athens. The selection process was quite simple. If you were an athlete and got to Athens, you got to compete.

John Boland, an Irish tourist who came to Athens as a spectator, was allowed to enter the Games tennis competition on a whim because he knew the secretary of the organizing committee from their Oxford days together. Boland ended up winning the gold medal in men's singles and doubles. That's what you call a vacation. But distance was a tyrant and only 311 athletes from thirteen countries answered the call for those first modern Games, which featured track and field, cycling, fencing, gymnastics, lawn tennis, shooting, swimming, weightlifting and wrestling. No Canadian competed in the first Games. There was one athlete each from Australia, Bulgaria, Chile, Sweden and Switzerland; four each from Austria and Denmark; eight each from Britain and Hungary; fourteen from the US; nineteen each from Germany and France, and 230 from Greece.

In the first event on the first day of competition of the first modern Games in 1896, triple jumper James B. Connolly of the US became the first Olympic champion in 1,527 years. Connolly was a student at Harvard University and asked his dean for some time off to compete in the Olympics. The dean thought the request absurd and turned it down. The Olympics? Weren't they some Greek thing thousands of years ago? So Connolly quit school and went to Athens anyway. Like most of the first modern Olympians, he paid his own way. For his trouble, he went into the books as the first Olympic gold medallist of the modern era and received, like all the 1896 winners, a medal, a diploma and a crown of olive branches. When he got home from Athens, nobody was there to greet him.

That the rebirth of the Olympics failed to stir a great deal of fervour in North America is a bit of an understatement. Connolly had two nickels left in his pocket when he got to the train station in Boston. So he used one to buy a Coke and toasted himself in lieu of champagne. The twenty-seven year old then used his final nickel to catch a streetcar to his home in South Boston. Connolly later became a famous war correspondent and wrote several novels and hundreds of short stories. When, in 1953, Harvard wanted to present him with an honourary degree to make up

The runners at the start of the first 100m final of the modern Olympics.

for the lack of recognition he received in 1896, Connolly flatly refused.

The marathon has long been an event dear to Greek lore. In legend, a professional runner named Pheidippides is said to have carried the news of the Greek victory over the Persians from the battlefield of Marathon to the capital, Athens, in 490 B.C. Upon delivering the glad tiding "Rejoice, we conquer," Pheidippides supposedly dropped dead. So the legend goes.

After de Coubertin held his famous meeting in 1894 at Paris and the revival of the Olympics was agreed upon, there was unanimous approval of a suggestion to conjure up the legend of Pheidippides during the first modern Games at Athens. And so a marathon race was added to the sporting agenda for 1896. The longest race of the ancient Olympics, however, had been only about 5000m. Not that this mattered much to the Greeks, nor the very distinct possibility Pheidippides was just faux Greek history. This was the very stuff of myth — and Greek myth, which made it even better. So the Greek populace took a special interest in the Olympic marathon of 1896 and it quickly became labelled the most important event of the Games. Greek national rundowns and elimination trials were held in the months before the Games to pick the cream of Greece's youthful runners. Thirteen Greeks were chosen to start the Olympic race, alongside four foreigners.

Despite having by far the most athletes at the first modern Games, the Greek citizens were disappointed that most of the medals were going to the foreigners. Winning the marathon was seen as a must to salvage national pride. Close to 200,000 Greeks lined the route for the course as the seventeen runners took off from the starting line in Marathon. Messengers on horseback and bike rode back and forth delivering word to the stadium crowd about what was transpiring along the marathon route. There was a groan when the crowd in the stadium heard Edwin Flack of Australia, an accountant, was leading. But it soon became apparent by the swell of noise from outside the stadium that things had changed. Flack, who won the 1500m, had crumbled to the ground in exhaustion along the route. Running into the stadium, whose occupants were now delirious with joy, sped a tiny little Greek named Spiridon Louis. The Greek king and prince rushed down to greet him and ran with him to the finish line. Forget about Pheidippides, the Greeks had a new marathon hero and Louis' name has since been carved in granite on the Olympic pantheon of legends.

Louis was a letter carrier who had finished his service in the army. And yes, true to legend, he was a shepherd before that. But unlike the Louis of lore, he wasn't just some hick who left his flock of sheep and stumbled down from the hills and suddenly entered the marathon. He had a much more organized plan of attack and managed to finagle the Marathon-to-Athens mail gig. He would run beside his mules while delivering letters and water to villages along the route. So he managed to make a living while training daily on the actual Olympic marathon course. Already the envelope was being pushed on the strict code of amateurism to which de Coubertin so zealously clung.

And what about all those rewards that Louis was offered after winning the marathon? It might have been enough to make the good Baron gag. Greek citizens offered Louis free everything for life, from haircuts to wine. The first of the many nagging problems of money versus amateurism, which were to dog the Olympics for so many years until the 1992 US basketball Dream Team blew the lid off this sham, was already taking shape. Averoff, the merchant whose money helped sponsor the Games, had even offered the hand of his daughter in marriage to the marathon champion if he was Greek. However, Louis had a wife and two children.

Louis turned down most of the freebies that came his way, but did accept a horse and cart from the king himself in order to bring water to his village of Marusi and to better do his postal job. He lived simply after the Games but was showered with enough perks as a genuine Greek folk hero that he lived quite comfortably for the rest of his life.

The 1896 Athens Games and boycotted 1980 Moscow Games are the only Summer Olympics in which at least one Canadian did not compete. As for de Coubertin, he headed the International Olympic Committee until 1925 and loved the Olympic Games so much that when he died in 1937, his heart was taken out of his body and put into a marble column in front of the eternal Olympic flame in Olympia.

PARIS 1900

May 20 to October 28
1330 Athletes from 22 Nations

The 1936 Olympic marathon champion Kee-Chung Sohn of Korea —
forced to compete for Japan and salute the Rising Sun atop the victory
podium by his nation's conquerors — made a heart-wrenching entry
into the opening ceremonies of the 1988 Seoul Olympics as a torch bearer.

There were no such belated and emotionally triumphant homecom-
ings into a Canadian stadium for George Orton. Maybe there should
have been. Orton was the first Canadian to win an Olympic gold medal
and the first to win an Olympic medal of any colour. But there's a twist,
and perhaps a harbinger, of the American cultural imperialism that would
one day infiltrate every aspect of Canadian life. The trouble was Orton
did his Olympic medal winning as part of the US Olympic contingent
at Paris in 1900. An outstanding athlete at the University of Toronto
and for the Toronto Lacrosse Club, Orton became one of the top
middle-distance runners of the 1890s and even captured the US mile
championship at New York in 1892. His style and grace didn't go unno-
ticed by the Americans.

If you thought the problem of the US National Collegiate Athletic
Association (NCAA) skimming off the cream of this country's athletes

is a relatively new phenomenon, guess again. After winning virtually every Canadian intercollegiate race he entered, Orton was enticed to join the University of Pennsylvania track team upon graduation from the U of T. Orton captained Penn and won fifteen US championships. But he remained a Canadian citizen despite being picked by the Americans for their mostly university team heading to Paris for the Olympics. At the Games he trailed badly in the 2500m steeplechase (contested over 3000m since 1920) but found his form just in time to make Canadian sporting history. He sprinted and jumped past four startled competitors on his last lap to capture the gold medal by three metres. He finished in 7:34.4, nearly four seconds ahead of silver medallist Sidney Robinson from Britain.

Mark Tewksbury may have given Canada the kick-start it needed at the Barcelona Olympics, but an American namesake beat him to gold ninety-two years earlier — and also denied George Orton a second gold medal in the 400m hurdles. Leaping over sawed-off telephone poles in lieu of actual hurdles, and facing an arbitrarily added water jump near the finish line, Orton bounced his way to bronze (no time listed) behind Penn teammate John Walter Tewksbury (57.6 seconds) and the previously undefeated Henri Tauzin of France (58.3) in the field of five.

Orton's hopes of a third medal went down the toilet — literally. He was fifth in the 4000m steeplechase, won by John Thomas Rimmer of Britain, after not getting any sleep the night before because of constant trips to the washroom caused by a nervous stomach.

Although Orton entered the Games as part of the US team, present-day Olympic rules and common sense dicate only actual citizens of a particular country may compete for its team at the Games. That has left recent Olympic historians with a dilemma about how to list Orton's achievements from Paris. All references before 1972 credit his medals to the United States. But that tune has changed. American David Wallechinsky lists Orton as USA/Canada in *The Complete Book of the Olympics*. Stan Greenberg of Britain, like a true Commonwealth buddy, lists Orton as a late discovery for Canada in *Olympics Fact Book* and credits his Paris medals to this country. Lord Killanin and John Rodda, editors of the authorative *The Olympic Games*, also give Orton's medals to Canada. And the International Olympic Committe, the final arbitrator, has officially listed Orton's two medals as being for Canada and changed the medals table accordingly.

The 1900 Games, spread from May 20 to October 28 and attracting 1330 competitors (including twelve women) from twenty-two nations, were indifferently organized and a mere adjunct to the massive Exposition Universelle. The Greeks made a strong pitch to be the permanent

Wearing the colours of Penn, George Orton crosses the line at Paris to become the first Canadian to win an Olympic medal.

Olympic hosts, but de Coubertin envisioned his baby as a moveable feast. Unfortunately, the idea of twinning the Games with the World's Fair proved disastrous. The Exposition organizers didn't want the Games and treated them like excess baggage. De Coubertin was pushed aside and not allowed to have a hand in their organization. Sport was considered with bemused uninterest at best and contempt at worst by the Exposition organizers who felt they had been saddled with the Olympics by the French government. After all, these people were running a Fair heralding the start of the twentieth century.

The thought of profusely sweating people huffing and puffing around the city seemed to disgust them. But de Coubertin had managed to convince a reluctant French government to sponsor the second Olympics of the modern era and the World's Fair organizers were stuck with it. They responded by botching almost everything, from the name on down. They didn't even call it the Olympics. That would have been too common and beneath them. Instead it was called the Championnats Internationaux and there is no mention that entire summer of the word "Olympics" in any Paris newspaper. So, many of the competitors in Paris thought they were in an international championship athletic meet associated with the World's Fair and didn't even realize they had competed in an Olympic Games until many years later.

Orton won his medals on a wildly uneven and oddly shaped oval grass track at Croix-Catelan in the Bois de Boulogne, which was Paris' largest park. The thought of tearing up the park for a cinder track was an unspeakable horror Paris officials wouldn't even consider. The jumpers and throwers returned the favour by digging their own pits, giving new meaning to the term replace your divots. Trees and shrubbery were as much a hazard as the unleashed dogs and cats that roamed the park.

You could call the Paris organizers "in-Seine," since that's where the swimming competition took place. The strong river currents made the times recorded virtually worthless to Olympic historians. Professional riders competed with amateurs in cycling, meaning the results later had to be expunged from the official IOC records. The fencing competition was listed as part of the World's Fair cutlery exhibit! De Coubertin himself felt like shouting, "Here, cut this." He had envisioned a grand celebration of sport and sporting culture — complete with curving dioramas on the history of sport and replicas in the park of Greek statues, temples and columns. Instead he got a sad sideshow to a World Exposition. "We have made a hash of our work and the Paris Games are better left forgotten," a dejected de Coubertin said after the 1900 effort. But they did provide Canada with its first Olympic hero, even if he was entered as a faux American.

ST. LOUIS 1904

July 1 to November 23
625 Athletes from 13 Nations

Etienne Desmarteau, the second Canadian to win an individual Olympic gold medal, serves as a telling example that this self-effacing country will often go out of its way to deny (if not devour) its cultural and sporting heroes. All Desmarteau wanted from the Montreal Police Department was a two-week leave during the last week of August and first week of September in which to compete at the 1904 St. Louis Olympic Games. He was denied his request. Desmarteau was a quiet and gentle man not known as a boat-rocker. But this snub was too much. This was the Olympics, after all; the third modern installment of the glorious ancient Greek Games and a connection to one of the nobler inventions of human civilization. So what if the St. Louis Games were just a shabby, mostly ill-concieved sideshow to the 1904 St. Louis World's Fair commemorating the centennial of the Louisiana Purchase? So what if the Games had only the most spartan and spare facilities at Washington University and were clumsily strectched out from July 1 to November 23? So what if nobody in St. Louis, or anywhere else, seemed to care a lick about the 1904 Games and that most of the eighty-five events in fourteen sports attracted only small knots of fans? So what if distance and expense made the Games an almost all-American show, with only 625 athletes (eight female) from thirteen countries? In fact it was in some ways really nothing more than a glorified US club championship, with the cream of athletic clubs from New York City, Chicago, Milwaukee, Missouri, Boston, Pennsylvania, Missouri and St. Louis competing for an American-only championship trophy donated by the A.G. Spalding Sporting Goods Company. Even the Americans didn't have all their best athletes at the Games, as most of the powerful eastern universities didn't bother to send contingents. Regardless, the host US still accounted for 85 percent of the athletes and 84 percent of the medals. The cycling, boxing and wrestling events had only American competitors.

For all these shortcomings, these were still the Olympics — and on the same continent. For the cop from Montreal, that was too good to pass up. The handsome and mustachioed Desmarteau, who held the world records for distance and height in the 65-pound weight throw, bolted to the Games and was sponsored by the Montreal Amateur Athletic Association. For that, he was fired from his job as a police constable. And this after he led the Montreal cops to numerous victories over the police departments of cities all over eastern North America in throwing, running, jumping and lifting contests. Some thank-you. The strapping Desmarteau was specially recruited to the Fifth Precinct from a CPR foundry because of his height (6' 2") and bulk (225 pounds) by the Irish precinct captain who was fond of winning interpolice department contests of lifting, throwing and tug of war. When word reached home the errant Desmarteau had won Olympic gold at St. Louis by throwing the 65-pound weight 10.46m and Montreal newspapers trumpeted his victory as one that honoured all French Canadians, his notice of dismissal was somehow misplaced. Not a word was mentioned about it when he came back to Montreal and resumed his duties with the police department. A nation that eats, or ignores, its heroes sometimes has second thoughts.

The US was expected to dominate the throwing events through a burly group of Irish-American cops from New York City known collectively as the "Whales." But Desmarteau's throw was well ahead of the 10.16m effort launched by thirty-six-year-old silver medallist John J. "Whale" Flanagan, who was also the Olympic 1900, 1904 and 1908 hammer throw gold medallist and an individual who would routinely consume three steaks and a chunk of roast beef at noon in between even larger meals at breakfast and dinner. Unlike Desmarteau, Flanagan had been granted a three-month leave without pay by the New York Police Department to prepare for and compete in the Olympics.

Just six competitors — Desmarteau and five Americans — competed in the 56-pound weight throw, an event held only in the 1904 and 1920 Olympics. Desmarteau's win denied the US a sweep of the track and field gold medals and was one of only five of the seventy-five gold, silver or bronze medals in track and field not won by an American. And just as quickly as he had struck for gold in 1904, Desmarteau was gone — the tragic and fatal victim of typhoid the following year at age twenty-eight. A park in Montreal is named in his honour. And fittingly, for one of Canada's first gold medallists, Olympic events (men's and women's basketball preliminaries) were held at Etienne Desmarteau Centre in 1976.

Desmarteau and a Cuban marathon runner perhaps best exemplified the elusive Olympic spirit which modern Games founder Pierre de Coubertin envisioned. Like Desmarteau, Felix Carvajal quit his job to go to the St. Louis Olympics. And in order to have enough money to get there, this Havana mailman used to finish his mail route and then run around and around the centre square of Havana until an inquisitive crowd gathered. Carvajal then announced his Olympic intentions and asked for donations. He also begged money from his friends and bought passage to New Orleans, hoping to turn a profit in the Quarter playing craps. Instead he lost everything. So he ran and thumbed his way to St. Louis, arriving tired and unkempt. He trained in long slacks and dress shirt until some helpful American athletes cut his pants and turned them into shorts and sliced his long shirt sleeves for comfort.

Carvajal had never before run in a marathon. Along the dusty and hilly backroads Missouri route, he stopped to chat with citizens and try out his English. He finished fourth. The apparant winner, Fred Lorz of New York, ran to the finish line very sprightly indeed, looking none the worse for wear. There was good reason. He grabbed a lift in a car the last eleven miles after experiencing stomach cramps. He claimed he only ran into the stadium as a joke after the car broke down near the finish. He was getting his picture taken with Teddy Roosevelt's daughter, Alice, when a pained and zombie-like Thomas Hicks from New England strode uneasily into the stadium at 3:28:63. Nearly spent along the route and twelve pounds lighter, Hicks had been sustained by ample doses of strychnine, which then was not illegal. Officials were not amused by Lorz's automobile stunt and banned him for life. But Lorz said it was just a lark and he didn't mean to take anything away from Hicks. Lorz was reinstated the following year and won the Boston Marathon.

Conducted as if a junior high school meet or Sunday School picnic at best, or an afterthought at worst, the St. Louis Games came into being when favoured Chicago (a much more bustling and robust city that may

Etienne Desmarteau throwing the 56-pound weight at the St. Louis Olympics to win gold for Canada.

have presented an interesting set of Games) bowed out because of lack of funds. It was a regrettable decision. The Games played little brother to the big World's Fair and did little to enhance the lustre and allure of the fledgling Olympics. The St. Louis Games were actually much more efficiently and effectively organized than the messy Paris Olympics of four years earlier. But most citizens of St. Louis were too busy with World's Fair attractions to notice or care about the Games. And Europe was still the centre of the world in 1904, so most nations gave them a pass.

The entry list was so barren in some events that Canada won the easiest silver medal it will ever take: all the men's eights had to do was show up. There were only two entries. The Argonaut Rowing Club of Toronto placed behind the Vesper Boat Club of Philadelphia. Somewhere there is an un-awarded Olympic bronze medal floating around. In the hardly impressive fashion the second and third modern Olympics turned out, if you now claim to have been there in 1904 with eight of your buddies paddling along the Mississippi as the third boat in the eights, the IOC just might mail you that bronze.

Imagine not playing a sport until the age of thirty-eight and then going on to win an Olympic gold medal in it eight years later at age forty-six. Welcome to the wonderfully cockeyed world of George Seymour Lyon of Toronto. Golf was held in the Olympics in only 1900 and 1904. (A proposal by the Atlanta organizers to reintroduce it for 1996 was rebuffed by the IOC.) Lyon was no early admirer of the sport, only picking it up after successful stints in baseball, cricket, lacrosse, lawn bowling, curling, football, soccer and tennis. In fact, having once held the Canadian pole vault record, he might have been a better bet to compete in the field events. Some certainly thought he should have stuck to other endeavours. Because of his background in other sports, Lyon had a bizarre, if not downright brutal, golf swing that resembled a cricketer wielding a bat. Which was okay since he was one of Canada's top batsmen in the wicket and capped eleven times. It was his cricket-like swing that enabled him to wallop the golf ball a ton off the tee. But even technical purists can't argue with success. Having never swung a golf club until dared by a friend in 1896, Lyon pieced together his game with relative ease and won the Canadian amateur title eight times and the Canadian senior championship on ten occasions.

Unlike many of the other events at the St. Louis Olympics, the competition in golf was intense with seventy-five competitors. Lyon placed seventh in the match-play elimination round and advanced to the championship flight of thirty-two. He was a gregarious man who barked out one-liners and laughingly played practical jokes while competing. This seemed odd to many of his competitors, all the rest of whom were American. They didn't quite know what to make of this offbeat Canadian, who wasn't averse to doing cartwheels or handstands on the fairways. Lyon was the victor on the last of thirty-six holes, besting pacific coast champion Francis Newton of Seattle in the semifinals. In the gold medal final on September 24, Lyon beat the US amateur champion, H. Chandler Egan of Chicago, 3 and 2. Lyon "walked" to the victory podium on his hands. Yes, his hands. Try that, Sylvie Frechette. Lyon became not only Canada's third-ever individual Olympic gold medallist behind 1900 steeplechase champion George Orton and Desmarteau (who won his 1904 gold on September 1) but he also received an ornate sterling silver cup from the St. Louis organizers valued at about $1500.

Lyon went to London for the 1908 Olympics as a fifty year old. But internal bickering caused the British golfing entrants to boycott the event, leaving the Canadian as the lone participant. Lyon was offered the Olympic gold medal by default but he refused, saying it would be a mockery to take it on those terms.

There are many great names in Canadian Olympic history, but none as interesting as the man who helped this nation garner a medal in field lacrosse at St. Louis. Man Afraid Soap was part of the Mohawk team from the Six Nations Reserve near Brantford, Ontario. He may have been averse to the 1904 equivalents of Dial or Irish Spring, but Man Afraid Soap wasn't Man Afraid Medal as the Mohawks were awarded the bronze. All they had to do was show up since there were only three teams in the competition. The Mohawk team also had the second and third best names ever for any Canadian Olympians — Snake Eater and Rain in Face. That must have been quite a line for the sportscasters to announce: "Man Afraid Soap to Snake Eater to Rain in Face and he scores!" The other Mohawk bronze medallists were Black Hawk, Black Eagle, Almighty Voice, Flat Iron, Spotted Tail, Half Moon, Lightfoot, Red Jacket and Night Hawk. The championship went to the Shamrock Lacrosse Team of Winnipeg, one of only three Canadian sides to win gold in a summer team sport at the Olympics to this day (the 1904 soccer team and 1908 lacrosse team are the others).

After the Mohawks were eliminated, the Winnipeg crew defeated the US representatives from the St. Louis Amateur Athletic Association 6–1 and 8–2 in the best-of-three gold medal final. Winnipeg team members were George Cloutier, George Cattanach, Benjamin Jamieson, Jack Flett, George Bretz, Eli Blanchard, Hilliard Laidlaw, H. Lyle, W. Brennaugh, L.H. Pentland, Sandy Cowan, William Laurie Burns and William Orris. Lacrosse was included only in 1904 and 1908 and is on the eclectic list of discontinued Olympic sports that includes cricket, croquet, golf, jeu de paume, motor boating, polo, roque, rugby, tug-of-war and live pigeon shooting.

There is debate whether the soccer competition at St. Louis was classified exhibition or official. Some sources list it as the former and others the latter. But who's counting? The lax nature of the 1900 and 1904 Games renders much of the competition at Paris and St. Louis suspect, anyway. So why deny the Galt Football Club of Ontario its moment of golden glory? It was about as official as anything else in 1900 or 1904. Again, about all you had to do to claim a prize was show up. There were only three soccer teams entered at St. Louis. Galt won both its games, outscoring the opposition 11–0, to claim first place. The two American teams, Christian Brothers College and St. Rose School, played one more game each and finished 1–1–1 and 0–2–1 for second and third places, respectively. St. Rose managed only one goal. Unfortunately it was into its own net. So much for Olympian feats of greatness.

The most disgusting event at St. Louis was Anthropology Days at the Games on August 12–13. It made many people uncomfortable, even by the standards of 1904. So-called "savages," such as Native North Americans, Filipinos, Syrians, Turks, Patagonians from Argentina, pygmies and "Kaffirs" from Africa, the Ainus from Japan and the Coropas from Mexico were culled from the World's Fair exhibitions to demonstrate their native sports and compete in Olympic-style events. When the bewildered and untrained aboriginals did poorly in the sporting events, the smug American organizers pointed to how that was again proof of the superiority of certain races over others. De Coubertin, who did not attend the Games, was reportedly appalled by the display but muted his distaste by blaming it on the "youthful exuberance" of the US and called for the "indulgence of the ancient Greek ancestors" if they were watching from atop Olympus. But then de Coubertin is quoted as saying: "The outrageous charade will lose its appeal when black men, red men and yellow men learn to run, jump and throw and leave the white men behind them." Some astute seer, this good baron.

ATHENS 1906

April 22 to May 2
884 Athletes from 20 Nations

A special set of Intercalated Olympics were held in Athens in 1906 to mark the tenth anniversary of the birth of the Modern Games and as a consolation for denying the pouting Greeks their dream of being permanent Olympic hosts. These Games are now listed as unofficial. Regardless, one of the great moments in Canadian Olympic history occurred at them. Marathoner Bill Sherring, twenty-nine, was an elfish man in a white fedora, green socks and Hamilton St. Patrick's Athletic Club singlet bearing a massive emerald green shamrock and he proudly waved a tiny Union Jack as he ran the course from the ancient town of Marathon to the marble stadium. Fifty-seven runners from fifteen countries began the trek in hopes of replicating Spiridon Louis' historic victory of a decade before. But probably none were as determined as the little CPR brakeman Bill Sherring. With little money to get to the Games, Sherring put what he had on a longshot horse named Cicely. The nag came through and Sherring was off to Athens. Of such twists of fate are Olympic legends created. While in Greece, Sherring supported himself on tips from carrying bags at the Athens rail station. Athens merchants offered the 1906 Olympic marathon champion a five-foot statue of

Hermes, free bread and coffee for a year, free shaves for life and opulent dinners for the victor and his family for the next ten Sundays. They didn't count on a diminutive Canadian winning. Disappointed or not, Crown Prince George lept out of the stands and accompanied Sherring as he made his final lap of the stadium. Spiridon Louis and now Bill Sherring. The little-known little man from Canada, who had won only local Hamilton races before, had won Olympic gold on Greek soil. During the race, he lost fourteen pounds from his already-slight 112-pound frame. Sherring didn't get all the goodies promised if the winner had been Greek but received a statue of Athena and a lamb. He kept the statue but gave the lamb to a farmer he had befriended in Athens. Hamilton city council voted Sherring a prize of $5000.

Vaulter Ed Archibald of Toronto lost his pole in transit. He was given a replacement by the Greeks but it snapped and almost impaled him. Shaken, he crapped out tenth in the field of eleven. But Archibald recomposed himself and two years later won the bronze medal at the London Olympics.

Donald Linden of Toronto finished second to George Bonhag of the US in the 1500m walk but some claimed the American had broken into a gait. A re-race was ordered between Bonhag and Linden. The Canadian and Greek Crown Prince George, who was to oversee the re-run, showed up at the marble stadium the next day but Bonhag was a no-show. Instead of awarding the gold medal to Linden, organizers let stand the results from the previous day.

LONDON 1908

April 27 to October 31
2056 Athletes from 22 Nations

Dismissed by Napoleon as "a nation of shopkeepers," the undeterred English managed to create the greatest Empire the world has ever seen. Yet London's right to stage the 1908 Olympics came only in the "runner-up" category. Ever the romantic, Pierre de Coubertin wanted the fourth Olympics of the modern era awarded to Rome, and they originally were. After what he described as the 1904 "excursion to utilitarian America," de Coubertin longed for the classical elegance of centuries past. He wanted the Olympics to "don once again the sumptuous toga, woven of art and philosophy, in which I had always wanted to clothe them." That had always been his ideal for the Games. But again it was undermined, this time by economics and nature. When Mount Vesuvius erupted in 1906, it did more than just bury two thousand people. The natural disaster was of a sufficient magnitude to destroy any hope of de Coubertin's goal to hold the 1908 Games in Rome. Reluctantly, de Coubertin looked elsewhere. The British stepped forward and took on the Games. They were certainly the second choice, but many people have been undone by underestimating the British. Formal and aloof, yet deceptively powerful people that they are, they managed to save the wavering modern Olympics by providing a watershed set of Games. The same stiff upper lip that went into creating their Empire went into organizing the Olympics. As the strait-laced Victorian age slipped into the past, it was a smart and snappy London that greeted the Games during the height of the fashionable Edwardian era. Although now more stylish, the British were still the British and went about their task with the same sort of almost emotionless and sober ethic that had helped them claim dominion of one quarter of the globe.

The British were ready for the challenge. The portly monarch King Edward VII commanded a magnificent empire of such variety and scope that it staggered the imagination. It was in this time of imperial grandeur that the British constructed a new 70,000-seat stadium for the Games in the west of London at White City in Shepherd's Bush for £40,000 sterling. It contained not only a running track but also a banked, concrete cycling track which encircled it. The 100m pool was located on the stadium infield. This all-inclusive stadium also hosted the gymnastics, wrestling and fencing competitions.

Perhaps it was not surprising that nationalism, one of the major blemishes on the Olympic movement over the years, first became noticeable at London. Here you had the British, defending imperial champions from the nineteenth century, and the cocky and rising Americans, to whom the twentieth century would eventually belong. The rivalry between Britain and the United States at times got nasty. The 122-member American team failed to see their national flags flying among the twenty others that ringed the stadium during the opening ceremonies and were highly upset by this breach of protocol. Some of the Americans, a healthy dose of whom were of Irish descent, were also upset the athletes from Ireland were lumped as part of the British team and forced to march behind the Union Jack.

The Canadians were caught between their British masters and American continental neighbours. Although Canada was destined to come increasingly into the American sphere of influence as the century wore on, most of the Canadian team sided with the British in the bitter Olympic war of words with the Americans. Someone who didn't really understand all the fuss about the Irish having to march with the British team was sprinter Bobby Kerr of Hamilton, Ontario. Born in Enniskillen, Ireland, Kerr didn't think anything of competing in the British championships at Stamford Bridge before the Olympics and winning the 100 and 220 yards — good old imperial distances. Only the heat winners advanced in the Olympics, and the speedy Kerr survived round after round in the field of fifty-seven competitors from sixteen nations, reach-

Dorando Pietri vainly tries to reach the finish line of the 1908 Olympics.

ing the four-man final on July 22. Two runners from the British Empire, Kerr and Reginald Walker of South Africa, were pitted against Americans James Rector and Nathaniel Cartmell. Predictably, it created tremendous interest at the Shepherd's Bush Stadium and 48,000 fans showed up to watch "our colonials" put the upstart Americans in their place. Walker was not orginally selected for the South African team but his friends and family in Durban raised enough money on short notice to send the nineteen-year-old bank clerk to London. The twenty-six-year-old Kerr had beaten Walker handily in taking the 100-yards title in the British championships at Stamford Bridge just two weeks before and felt comfortable heading into the final. Kerr was more worried about the American speedster Rector, who hailed from the University of Virginia. But what the Hamilton-bred runner didn't know was that Walker had been noticed at Stamford Bridge by famed sprints coach Sam Mussabini, who gave the young man from Natal province a two-week cram course in the finer points of starting a sprint race.

Mussabini's tutoring paid off for Walker. Walker used his new-found starting skills to jump into the lead on the inside lane. Rector pulled ahead at 50m but Walker retook the lead and held on to win in 10.8 seconds. In one of the few judging decisions to go in favour of the Americans — and it was Kerr's unluck to be the victim of it — Rector was awarded the silver medal ahead of the Canadian. Three judges ruled Kerr had pipped Rector at the line to take the silver. But the referee, many believe erroneously, ruled in favour of the American and overturned the judges. A furious Kerr wasn't going to leave London with just a bronze for his troubles. And the next day he pounded out his frustrations on the track, winning gold in the 200m. He had earlier swiftly survived the field of forty-three competitors from fourteen countries to slip into the four-man final. Again it was an Empire/US split with Kerr and George Hawkins of Britain up against Americans Nathaniel Cartmell and Robert Cloughen. It was Kerr's sixth race in three days. This time it was Kerr who got the killer start. Pulling his square-built body down the track on powerful legs, he was first around the bend and never headed. Cloughen pulled up close enough to make it a race, but Kerr stretched across the line to win gold in 22.6 seconds. But even the work ethic has its drawbacks. Kerr felt perhaps he had worked too hard in getting ready for the 100m. He believed that may have been why he 'only' took the bronze. So he went out to unwind and sample some of London's nightlife the evening before the 200m final. "I went out last night and got nicely drunk and danced until the early hours of this morning," he told a shocked group of reporters after winning gold in the 200 final.

It was considered a huge boost for the British Empire when the Canadian Kerr scored gold in the 200m and bronze in the 100m at the London Olympics: the crowd loudly cheered the Canadian victory over the Americans. The crowd roared even louder when Kerr was lofted atop the shoulders of this teammates and carried around the track while the Union Jack was raised in honour of his victory. Kerr received a tumultuous reception when he returned to Hamilton on August 11. He was mobbed as he moved his way from the docks to Victoria Park atop an open-air float with his parents and two sisters. Bands played, fireworks exploded, buildings were decorated in bunting, Kerr was laden with gifts and a Bobby Kerr Day was announced to honour the returning hero in an uncharacteristic display of Canadian patriotic emotion. Kerr, who died in 1963, became a dynamo as an administrator for amateur sport at the Hamilton, provincial and national levels.

In the early morning of July 24 outside Windsor Castle, representatives from sixteen countries prepared to begin running the marathon. Little did those fifty-six men, including twelve from Canada, know that one of the most dramatic moments in Olympic history was in the offing. Among them was Tommy Longboat of Ontario and Dorando Pietri of Italy. Cool temperatures and rain were the order for most of the 1908 Olympics. But this day would turn out to be uncharacteristically hot and humid by British standards. The royal family requested the race start on the greens of Windsor Castle so King Edward's grandchildren could watch the start. The distance from that point to the finish line at Shepherd's Bush Stadium was 26 miles, 385 yards — the identical marathon distance used to this very day. Pietri and pre-race favourite Longboat limbered up beneath the balcony of the castle, as the royal grandchildren watched and chattered with amusement and anticipation. Among the excited royal tykes were the future kings of England and the Commonwealth, Edward VIII and George VI.

Pietri was a wisp of man from the village of Carpi and not given much thought by the press, officials or other runners. Longboat came into the race with a huge and richly deserved reputation. An aboriginal Onondaga from the Six Nations Reserve near Hamilton, Longboat had won the 1906 CNE Toronto Marathon and the 1907 Boston Marathon in record times. He was virtually unbeatable on road circuits all around Ontario and the northeastern United States. He came under the mentorship of Tom Flanagan, a shrewd Toronto promoter who entered Longboat in races that had prize purses. A promoter for an Olympic athlete? The US Amateur Athletic Union saw through the charade and labelled Longboat a professional and ineligible for the Games. Longboat was installed as the operator of a cigar store in downtown Toronto to put up a front as to how he supported himself. Despite his fancy clothes and free accommodation at Grand Central Hotel in Toronto, Longboat saw little of the money he won by running. The IOC was convinced and Longboat was declared eligible for the Olympics. Flanagan saw visions of dollar signs dancing in his head — but first his runner had to come home with the Olympic gold medal.

Longboat grabbed the lead as the runners escaped the shadow of Windsor Castle and wound their way through the streets of London en route to Shepherd's Bush. By the ten-mile mark, the favoured Canadian was behind a trio of British runners — Tom Jack, Fred Lord and Jack Price — and was starting to tire. He gamely pounded the pavement but the mugginess was proving too much. He made one more attempt to challenge at fourteen miles and moved into second place behind Charles Hefferon of South Africa. When Pietri overtook him for second, Longboat responded by passing the Italian in turn. But at nineteen miles and just after passing through Harrow, Longboat was done for and pulled to the

Favoured Tommy Longboat failed to reach the finish line of the 1908 Olympic marathon.

side of the road. He tried grimly to move forward but was unable to take another step. He was shoved into a car by medical attendants and his Olympic odyssey was over.

Immediately the wild rumours began. Had he been drugged by his handlers so they could collect huge gambling sums on his loss? Canadian team manager J.H. Crocker, in his report, wrote that he found it odd that Longboat dropped like a log when he was in second place. "It is highly unlikely that Longboat was told to take the marathon equivalent of a dive since he would have been worth a lot more as an Olympic gold medallist. It was just a combination of poor coaching and too hot a day.

With Longboat out of the way, the race was for the taking. But nobody could imagine the drama that was about to unfold as the lead runner — that little man from Carpi — entered the stadium. Pietri was in a daze. The sun had wilted him and his brain was scrambled. He stumbled down the track in the wrong direction before being told to turn around. Confused, he retraced his steps in a staggering fashion before collapsing in a heap as the crowd gasped. Pietri managed to pull himself up, only to fall again. It was an act repreated three more times and stadium crowd cried out for someone to help the tiny and unknown Italian. The crowd and officials believed the South African Hefferon was due next into the stadium. If the victor wasn't to be British, then a subject of the British Empire was the next best thing. With Longboat out, Hefferon would do. But there was immediate disappointment when American John Hayes, who had passed the South African just outside the stadium entrace, unexpectedly appeared.

This was just too much for the British to take. As the brave Pietri began to fall to the track for the fifth and final time in his futile attempt to complete the race, he was grabbed by the chief marathon official Jack Andrew and a few others and dragged across the finish line. Although this was an understandable reaction to a noble attempt by Pietri, it was a flagarant abuse of the rules. The Italian was quickly declared the winner in 2:54:46.4 by the British organizers and the flag of his nation hoisted instead of the Stars and Stripes. The Americans immediately launched a protest, which they rightfully won, and Hayes was declared the gold medallist in 2:55:18.4. The twenty-two-year-old American was a clerk at Bloomingdale's and had been beaten in the 1907 Boston Marathon by Longboat.

But it is Pietri who is best remembered from that gripping drama at the finish line, with Irving Berlin writing a song about him and Arthur Conan Doyle penning an essay about his deed. The fiesty Pietri was okay the next day and complaining about how he would have won the race legally if the British hadn't intervened in the race and carried him across the line. But that seems unrealistic, considering he was carried unconscious from the track on a stretcher and people feared for his life. He did a lap of honour the following day and the crowd gave him a tumultuous ovation. Queen Alexandra presented him with an engraved gold cup. Unfortunately, the engravers transposed the Italian's first and last names on the cup and it reads: "To Pietri Dorando."

Longboat was devastated by his failure at the London Olympics and vowed he had run his last race. But he couldn't afford to stay away from the sport. The dramatic events in Shepherd's Bush kick-started a world-wide marathon mania, with Pietri, Hayes and Longboat going on to run in big-money professional races. Pietri twice beat Hayes in match races at Madison Square Garden on November 25, 1908, and March 15, 1909. Longboat defeated Pietri in a match race at Madison Square Garden on December 15, 1908, when the Italian collapsed near the finish line. Longboat went on winning races for four more years and established himself as the best runner of his day. Years later, his winnings long gone, he drifted through different jobs and died in 1949 back on the reserve. Pietri also lost all his money when his brother stole it. He ended his days driving a cab in Rome, but continued to receive a stipend from the Italian government for his 1908 heroics.

Walter Ewing from Montreal's upper-crust English enclave of Westmount, a twenty-eight-year-old executive of the Lackawanna Coal Company, was the embodiment of the gentleman athlete. A man with dashing Errol Flynn looks, he gravitated to the country club sport of trap shooting. Over three days from August 9–11, he proved he was the best in the world by scoring seventy-two out of a possible eighty to take the Olympic gold medal in a field of sixty-one competitors from eight nations. Ewing was untouchable and clearly the class of the field. George Beattie finished twelve points behind with a score of sixty to give Canada the silver medal. Alexander Maunder of Britain and Anastasios Metaxas of Greece tied for bronze with fifty-seven points each. But the sharp eyes and steely nerve of Ewing and Beattie weren't golden enough in the the trap shooting team event. The Canadian squad of Ewing, Beattie, A.W. Westover, Mylie Fletcher, George Vivian and D. McMackon finished two points off the gold standard at 405 to settle for the silver medal. Beattie stuck with his gun a long time. Sixteen years later, he won silver in the team trap event at the 1924 Paris Olympics. The shooters, although garnering little press or national attention, have provided Canada with some of its finest moments at the Olympics. The military rifle team of William Smith, Charles Robert Crowe, B.M. Williams, Donald McInnis, William M. Eastcott and S.H. Kerr rounded out the 1908 medal parade. Their score of 2439 reeled in a bronze medal.

Ed Archibald's dreams of gold at the Intercalated Games of 1906 ended when his pole was lost en route to Athens and he nearly impaled himself with a borrowed one that snapped. This time, he made sure his pole arrived with him in London. Man and pole were rewarded with a vault of 3.58m. Archibald, Charles Jacobs of the US and Bruno Soderstrom of

Sweden all achieved that height and were awarded bronze medals behind Americans Edward Cooke and Alfred Gilbert, who tied for gold at
3.71m. Gilbert went on to affect the toy-playing lives of millions of Canadian and American children by inventing the Erector Set.

Canadian J. Garfield MacDonald submitted a 1908 silver medal performance of 14.76m in the triple jump. Cal Bricker took the bronze medal
in the long jump at 7.08m but was well off the standard set by tiny American Francis "Frankie" Irons, who lept to gold at 7.48m. Bricker was the
only non-American to crack the top six in the event. Cornelius Walsh
was born in Woodstock, Ontario, but competed for the US and took
bronze in the hammer throw. Thirteen wrestlers, from the US, Britain
and Canada, went to the mats in the bantamweight class, with Aubert
Cote winning bronze. Squads from five nations contested the first cycling team pursuit event ever held in the Olympics, with Canadians
William Morton, Walter Andrews, Frederick McCarthy and William
Anderson travelling the 1810m course in 2:29.6 for the bronze medal.
That Canada was going to win at least a silver medal in the field lacrosse
competition was a foregone conclusion since there were only two teams
entered. But the Canadian team went one better, breaking open a tense
9–9 game to win the contest and the gold medal with a 14–10 decision
over Britain. Team members were Frank Dixon, George "Doc" Campbell,
Angus Dillon, Richard Louis Duckett, George Rennie, Clarence
McKerrow, Alexander Turnbull, Henry Hoobin, Ernest Hamilton, John
Broderick, Thomas Gorman and Patrick "Paddy" Brennan.

The American complaints against the organizers of the 1908 Olympics were so great the British were moved afterwards to publish a
sixty-page defence of the Games, *Replies to Criticism of the Olympic Games*.
Despite the rancor, the British had delivered on short notice a watershed
set of Games that greatly enhanced the Olympic movement. In them
was joy for Kerr and heartbreak for Longboat. And Longboat's failure,
despite an otherwise legendary career, is a reminder that when it comes
to the Olympics, there is no next season. There is only that day.

STOCKHOLM 1912

May 5 to July 22
2546 Athletes from 28 Nations

These are the Games remembered for the remarkably versatile native American Jim Thorpe, one of the classic Olympic victims of all time. There was also a then-unknown young American army Lieutenant from West Point named George S. Patton Jr. who finished out of the medals in fifth place in the modern pentathlon because — if you can believe it — his shooting aim was poor. Lost in all this over the years have been the swimming exploits of a Canadian about whom, typically, most Canadians don't know much. Alas, it is the mark of this country that the names of American heroes like Thorpe and Patton are instantly recognizable while George Hodgson remains George Who?

In one week of Olympic competition in 1912, the nineteen-year-old Hodgson of the Montreal Amateur Athletic Association won two gold medals and broke three world records — feats that would go unequaled by any Canadian swimmer until Alex Baumann of Sudbury took Olympic golds in world record times at Los Angeles in 1984. Hodgson swept to the 400m freestyle gold in an Olympic record 5:24.4 in a field of twenty-six competitors from thirteen countries, with John Hatfield of Britain in the silver position at 5:25.8 and Harold Hardwick of Australia getting bronze for placing at 5:31.2. But Hodgson's best in Stockholm had come four days before in the 1500m final. A year earlier at the 1911 Festivial of Empire in London, which in some ways was a forerunner to the Commonwealth Games, Hodgson splashed his way to the one-mile title. Eighty-three years later at the 1994 Commonwealth Games in Victoria, a predominately Canadian crowd rose as one in the jammed pool to create a deafening din as '92 Olympic champion Kieren Perkins of Australia stroked to the wall in a world record 14:41.66 in the men's 1500m.

Few of those people in the Saanich pool that night probably even knew that a Canadian had done the same in 1912 at the Olympics — and without benefit of a coach. Not only that, Hodgson had done much more. He set no less than three world records during one race. He told the judges before the final he wasn't going to stop at 1500m but would keep churning for a full mile. He touched at 1500m in twenty-two minutes flat for a world record, and the gold medal, and then splashed on to set the world mile mark of 23:34.4. He lowered Henry Taylor's world standard for the 1500m by a whopping 48.4 seconds, and eclipsed Englishman Thomas Battersby's world mile mark by 26.9 seconds. Just for good measure, Hodgson threw in the 1000m world record of 14:37.0 as well in the same swim. Hodgson's 1500m world record lasted for eleven years. He went from Stockholm to win the Kaiser Prize by taking the 500m at a meet in Hamburg. Two years later, Hodgson was fighting the Germans. It, too, was a medal-winning performance: he was decorated for outstanding service during the First World War and was awarded the King's Medal and Air Force Cross. George Hodgson was a self-taught swimmer who learned the water craft in the Montreal AAA pool — then one of the few pools in the country and the only one in Montreal — and during summers on lakes near the family cottage in the Laurentians. Hodgson, later the founder of a Montreal brokerage firm, competed in the 1920 Antwerp Olympics as well, but his best days were behind him and he placed well out of the medals. But his greatest work had already been completed. He set a Canadian medal/record standard in the Olympic pool that couldn't be touched until 1984.

Canada had only thirty-six athletes competing in five sports in 1912 but came away with three gold medals, two silvers and three bronze. The other great Canadian at the Stockholm Games was the twenty-seven-year-old, English-born George Goulding of the Central YMCA in Toronto, who immigrated from across the Atlantic when he was nineteen. He was a converted runner who had finished twenty-second in the 1908 Olympic marathon at London, where a confused and exhausted Dorando Pietri of Italy made his famous but ill-fated attempt to reach

*George Goulding en route
to the 10,000m walk gold
medal at the 1912 Stock-
holm Olympics.*

the finish line. Goulding came back four years later to accomplish something that eluded both he and Pietri in London — gold. For Goulding, it
was in the 10,000m walk in a world record 46:28.4. The temperature was
a stifling 34 degrees when thirty-seven competitors gathered for the event
at Stockholm. Goulding, world record holder in the mile, won his heat
over the British and European champion and eventual three-time Olympic silver medallist Ernest Webb and advanced to the ten-man final. He
was less than impressed by the officiating. "The judges had everybody
nervous," said Goulding. "In my heat they lay down on the grass to rest
and sometimes held up newspapers to cover the walker's body from view,
leaving only the feet visible. They then got in behind or in front of the
walkers. It was a wonder to me that anybody finished."

Goulding had rubbed the skin off his toes in the heats because of
ill-fitting new shoes and his feet were burning and painful. But he was
clear of the pack in the final. However, he again experienced trouble from
the officials. "When I was about forty yards ahead of Webb, I thought
the judges were after me," Goulding later said. "One of them said something in Swedish, which I did not understand. But when I turned to look
at him I saw a broad grin on his face and concluded he must have said
something nice. Still, it was a ticklish moment, for the judges had the
right to pull anyone off the track without previous warning." Three of
the ten finalists had already been disqualified for lifting. Goulding was
spooked and played it conservatively from there. He could afford to. He
set such a punishing pace that three other finalists pulled out of the race,
leaving just four at the end. Leading by about eighty yards heading into
the last mile, he slowed his walk. He wanted to make sure the spectre of
disqualification, from what he feared was fickle judging, wouldn't be his
sorry fate. It wasn't. He had been fourth in the 3500m walk at the 1908
Games, an event won by a thirty-three-year-old Brighton constable who

came out of retirement. But July 11, 1912, was to be Goulding's day. "In the final my feet were really torturing," he said. "However, in winning, I soon forgot the pain and remembered only the pleasure."

A man of few words, Goulding cabled his wife in Toronto: "Won — George." He was presented with his gold medal, an oak leaf and silver cup by King Gustav of Sweden. George Goulding was an Olympic champion. He returned home to a tumultuous welcome and was paraded down Yonge Street while thousands cheered and waved. He was presented with a tea service at Toronto City Hall. Goulding later became physical education director of the Central YMCA. Almost all his walking distances, including those from the 1908 and 1912 Olympics, are now discontinued. But the man won 335 races, from one mile to nearly fifty miles, during his career. He later took part in novelty races, walking while various forms of buggies or animals tried to outrace him.

Charles Perry, the English groundskeeper responsible for laying out the stadium competition area for the first Games stadium at Athens in 1896 and then also at London in 1908, had designed the 383m cinder track at Stockholm. And inside that oval, on Perry's meticulously kept jumping pits and throwing areas, Canada won the volume of its medals. Cal Bricker of Winnipeg improved on his 1908 London performance by thirteen centimetres and lept to silver in the long jump at 7.21m, behind the American Albert Gutterson, who iced Bricker and the rest of the field by reaching the winning 7.60m on his first jump. Bricker's friends recalled a summer when he was a University of Toronto student and had missed arriving on time for an outing on a paddle wheeler to Hamilton. He raced down the gangplank and lept across twenty feet of water to land on the departing vessel. That kind of jumping ability, not to mention chutzpah, held him in good stead at Stockholm. Duncan Gillis of Vancouver threw the hammer 48.39m for silver behind American policeman Matthew McGrath's 54.74m, which stood as the Olympic record until 1936. Frank Lukeman took bronze in the athletic pentathlon, an event that only appeared on the Olympic program three times. William Happenny of Toronto was awarded bronze in the pole vault at 3.80m even though three Americans finished ahead of him (Harry Babcock gold at 3.95 and Frank Nelson and Marcus Wright tied for silver at 3.85). Everard Butler of Toronto captured bronze in single sculls.

Jim Thorpe was the most famous figure of the Stockholm Games. "Thanks, King," he enthused after King Gustav said to him: "Sir, you are the greatest athlete in all the world." The Czar of Russia also was so taken with Thorpe's brilliance that he presented the athlete with a model of a Viking ship made from silver. The native-American Thorpe, who

Hammer thrower Duncan Gillis carries the flag for Canada during the opening ceremonies of the 1912 Stockholm Games.

also had Irish and French blood, was named Bright Path by his Potawatomi mother and Sac and Fox tribe father. He annihilated the competition in winning the decathlon and athletic pentathlon golds (the Canadian Lukeman got a bronze in the latter). But when Roy Johnson, a sportswriter for the rather insignificant *Telegram* newspaper in Worcester, Massachusetts, reported that Thorpe had played minor league baseball for $60 a month, the world's greatest athlete of the time was stripped of his gold medals. When you see the NBA Dream Teamers in the Olympics now and even Canadian Olympic medallists such as Angela Chalmers winning thousands of dollars in track meets, it all seems ludicrous. But that's how strict the Olympic amateur code was from 1896 to as late as the 1980s — although it was often easily breached in the later years.

Thorpe never denied playing professional baseball but, ironically, the money was irrelevent, he said. "I did not play for the money, I played because I liked baseball. I was not very wise to the ways of the world. I hope I will be partly excused by the fact that I was an Indian school boy and did not know that I was doing wrong." At the 1932 Olympics in Los Angeles, Thrope was too poor to buy a ticket for any events. In 1953, after he died alone and in poverty, the American Athletic Union reinstated Thorpe's amateur status. But then-IOC president Avery Brundage, who had finished fifth behind Thorpe and Lukeman in the 1912 athletic pentathlon and who many believe harboured a long-standing grudge against his former American teammate, was adamant that "the Olympic ideal be upheld;" he refused to reinstate Thorpe's Olympic titles. It wasn't until 1982, ten years after Brundage's stern and unbending twenty-year stint as president had ended, that the IOC reinstated Thorpe and handed the gold medals over to his family. Thorpe and Hugo Weislander of Sweden are now listed as co-winners of the 1912 gold medal in the decathlon and Thorpe and Ferdinand Bie of Norway as co-gold medallists in the athletic pentathlon.

The most unusual award winners at the Stockholm Games were the Canadian rowing eights. The Toronto Argonaut crew was a powerful one, as usual, but something strange happened on the way to the Forum — or, in this case, the victory podium. The crew couldn't understand why it was trailing by so much in the final. They knew they were in a class with the eventual British 1–2 finishers from the Leander Boat Club and New College of Oxford and the eventual bronze medallists from the Berliner Ruder-Gesellschaft club in Germany. The Canadians placed last in the final and left it at that, even though they were perplexed. It was later discovered the Canadians had rowed about 300m farther than the other crews because of a mistake in measuring the course. Canada did not protest. The Swedish King Gustav was so impressed by that magnanimous gesture that he presented the Canadian eights with a special trophy for good sportsmanship.

The thirty-six Canadian athletes at Stockholm were among 2546 competitors (including fifty-five women) from twenty-eight countries. King Gustav laid on a banquet with the athletes seated along a table that ran end-to-end on the stadium infield. High jumpers threw salad at each other from across the table. Jokes and happy chatter filled the summer air. Little did this happy throng of young competitors, who were speaking the emerging international language of sport, know then that many of them would be shedding their blood in the convulsions of war that lay just ahead. As was customary at the close of the Games, Baron Pierre de Coubertin mentioned the next host of the Olympics: "A great people [referring to the Germans, the anticipated next hosts] has received the torch of the Olympiads from your hands, and has thereby undertaken to preserve, and if possible, to quicken its precious flame. May the Sixth Olympiad contribute, like its illustrious predecessors, to the general welfare and to the betterment of humanity. May it be prepared in the fruitful labours of peaceful times. May it be celebrated, when the day comes, by all the peoples of the world in gladness and concord."

The 1916 Games in Berlin were never held, pre-empted by the First World War. The Germans went ahead and built their stadiums and arenas anyway, showing the naive hope of many Europeans that it would be a short war. The next Olympic Games weren't held until 1920.

ANTWERP 1920

April 20 to September 12
2692 Athletes from 29 Nations

Many of the trenches weren't yet infilled and *bodies* were still being reclaimed from war-scarred landscapes when the decision was made in 1919 to go ahead with the Games in the following year. Amsterdam, Rome and Budapest all wanted to host the event, but the Olympic committee's choice of the rather unexciting city of Antwerp was dripping with symbolism. Belgium, a hairless chest resting between powerful arms on each side, had been the battleground of Europe. It was where the British and Prussians fought the advancing French army during the Waterloo campaign. And its flat fields were the scene of some of the nastiest trench fighting of the First World War, with Canadian soldiers hit by lethal chlorine gas at the tiny medieval towns of Ypres and Passchendaele while blocking the Germans from advancing to the Channel ports. But no sooner had the guns fallen silent than the determined Pierre de Coubertin decided it was time to bring the youth of the world, at least those from nations rich enough to afford it, to Belgium to confront each other via sport. Just a few years before, the young men of Canada, Britain and other Empire nations came to Europe to fight, and many to die, after neutral Belgium had been invaded by Germany. So de Coubertin was determined the Games should be revived in Antwerp, a work-a-day industrial Belgian port that had seen the pain of the past half decade.

Germany and the other Axis countries were not invited by the IOC. Olympic historians decry this as a complete repudiation of the Olympic ideal — which it was — but who can be surprised by the move? Antwerp and Belgium, themselves weary and recovering from the war, were hardly overjoyed and the Games were poorly attended. But the Olympic movement was revived, which was what really mattered.

The now-familiar five-ring flag was unfurled for the first time during the opening of the Antwerp Games. Symbolizing the spirit of international cooperation, the five interlocking rings represent Europe, Asia, Africa, Australia and the Americas. The rings are red, blue, black, yellow and green. At least one of these colours is found in every national flag in the world. Clearly, de Coubertin was a master of symbolism. It was he who insisted the cancelled 1916 Berlin Games be given the Roman numeral VI and the Antwerp Games be the VII of the modern era to keep a sense of continuity. But lacking the money and the spirit, symbolism was about all the Antwerp Games had going for them and they lost 625 millon francs. With the fighting just twenty months over, war rubble was still in evidence on the streets and the Belgians were hardly in the mood for a circus.

The Canadian team received a $15,000 donation from the federal government and another $5,000 from the province of Ontario. Many athletes and officials had to subsidize their own passage. The Canadians left in waves, competed, and came home as soon as they were done. The shooters sailed out of Montreal on July 20, the track and field team and boxers, July 24, the swimmers and divers, August 7, and the rowers, August 13. With the arrangements and setting so crude, hiccups were bound to happen. The Toronto Argonauts Club, the producer of some of the greatest oarsmen in the world, sent a fours crew that experienced a bumpy ride to Antwerp. At least their shell did. Rough handling by a truck hauling crew caused a rigger support to almost snap just as the team approached the starting line and probably cost the favoured Canadians the gold medal. Coach Joe Wright Sr. appealed to the starter for a delay. The unsympathetic offical said no. The Argos started stroking and hoped for the best. They led near the quarter point before the support snapped completely and the crew was left with only three oars. They might as well have had Gilligan, Skipper and the Professor stroking at that point. It was hopeless and the Italians, French and Swiss passed the Argos to take the medals.

The Antwerp Games were among Canada's best, however, thanks in part to a couple of athletes on whom the Americans perhaps felt they

American-raised Earl Thomson hurdled to Olympic Games gold for Canada at Antwerp.

had a claim. The 110m hurdles is a classic, and explosive, Olympic event and Earl Thomson won it for Canada in a world record. The Americans were stunned by this turn of events. Not by the gold medal perform-ance, which was expected from the swift and intense Thomson, but by the country which was credited with the victory. Thomson seemed as American as apple pie, what with growing up in California and playing high school pigskin and baseball in Long Beach when not hurdling. He twice won the US collegiate hurdles title while a star athlete at USC and then Dartmouth. He set the world record of 14.8 seconds and American officials were happily touting him as their big gold-medal hope for the Antwerp track. But it was Thomson himself who pointed out that his family moved to California when he was three and that he was actually born on a farm near Prince Albert, Saskatchewan. He was a Canadian citizen, despite his American background and training.

Thomson trained and hung around almost exclusively with his Ameri-can mates during the Games. When he finished second behind an American in one of the heats, Canadian officials were overheard mum-bling that he may have let the US hurdler win. But Thomson had actually pulled a leg muscle. And it wasn't to the Canadian camp he went for help but instead to US team trainer Billy Morris, who treated him before the final. Thomson, wearing the bright red Maple Leaf on his white singlet, was shoulder-to-shoulder with US team friends Harold Barron and Fred Murray at 50m before the native of Saskatchewan pulled away to win gold for Canada, tying his world record of 14.8 seconds on the soft and rain-sogged track of the unfinished stadium. It can be argued that Thomson, who also competed in the long jump at Antwerp, didn't have much connection with Canada. That's true, unless the small matter of one's birth, military service and Olympic uniform aren't taken into account. Thomson went on to coach track in the US, with a noteworthy thirty-seven-year stint as head coach of the Naval Academy team at Annapolis.

Bert Schneider, the other individual gold medallist for Canada at the Antwerp Olympics, was the flip side of Thomson — an American citizen who grew up in Montreal. Oddly, while track rules forbade Canadian-born Thomson to run for his adopted country of America, boxing officialdom allowed Schneider to compete for Canada. He was nine years old when his father uprooted the young family from Cleveland to take a job in a Montreal steel mill. The young Schneider picked up some rudimentary knowledge of boxing during his days at a technical high school in Montreal before seeing the world via the merchant navy. The fact his father was born in Germany caused Bert Schneider no end of grief. Bert was denied entrance into the Canadian army because of it and even did a brief stint in a British jail as an undesirable alien. After the merchant navy, he returned to Montreal and twice became the amateur welterweight champion of Canada. But the Olympics were the last thing on Schneider's mind because he was American. He later, rather sheepishly, also admitted he didn't even know boxing was an Olympic event. He received the shock of his life one morning when he picked up the *Montreal Star* and read he had been selected to the Canadian team. He won four fights in three days in the welterweight field of fifteen competitors from ten countries. After beating American Fred Colberg in the semifinals, Schneider met Alexander Ireland of Britain in a punishing battle for the gold medal. Schneider used his tremendous upper-body strength and bruising style to move in on Ireland. The bout ended in a draw and the referee ordered the two tired and spent fighters to go another round. Schneider had enough wind left to land two roundhouse lefts in the overtime and that was enough to earn the decision. He later tried the pro boxing game but unfortunately had a rocky — as opposed to Rocky — time of it. He hung up the gloves and joined the US border patrol but returned to Canada upon retirement.

Two other fighters came close at Antwerp, but fell just short in their final bouts. Canada's boxing team at the 1920 Games was quite remarkable, coming away with a gold, two silvers and a bronze. Fiesty little

Chris Graham clubbed his way into the bantamweight final before losing in a decision to Clarence Walker of South Africa. Georges Prudhomme
of Montreal did well to survive a tough field of fifteen from eight countries to reach the middleweight final. But that's where he met his match in the
twenty-eight-year-old London cop Harry Mallin, who won two Olympic golds and sailed through undefeated in his amateur career. Mallin,
who in an infamous Olympic incident was bitten on the chest in the
1924 quarterfinals, easily decisioned Prudhomme for the 1920 middleweight gold medal. Clarence Newton won bronze in the lightweight class.

Norman Ross, later a famous announcer during the golden days of
radio, won three gold medals in the pool for the United States. Unfortunately for George Vernot of Montreal, two of them were in his events.
Ross won the 1500m in 22:23.2 and Vernot took silver in 22:36.4, but
both were way off the world record pace that George Hodgson of Canada
set in winning the same event in 22:00.0 at the 1912 Stockholm Olympics. Americans Ross, Ludy Langer, Fred Kahele and Canadian Vernot
churned furiously to the wall on the last leg of the 400m final of the 1920
Games. Ross touched first, followed by Langer for silver and Vernot for
bronze. The men's 400m freestyle has provided the Olympics with some
legendary winners, including Hodgson in 1912; Tarzan-to-be Johnny
Weissmuller in 1924; future Tarzan, Buck Rogers and Flash Gordon star
Clarence "Buster" Crabbe in 1932; the Aussie "Seaweed Streak" veg-
etarian Murray Rose in 1956 and 1960; and eighteen-year-old American
wonder boy Don Schollander in 1964.

Canada's most unusual gold medal in Summer Olympics history has
to be credited to a hockey team. Not in field hockey, even though that
too would be unusual, since that sport has been the domain of India and
Pakistan but hardly Canada. Four years before the first Winter Olympics in Chamonix, France, ice hockey and figure skating were included
in the 1920 Antwerp Games. Canada sent to Antwerp the Winnipeg Falcons, victors over the University of Toronto Varsity Blues in that year's
Allan Cup final. Hello, world: welcome to Canada's game. The Falcons
— led by Mike Goodman, also the North American speed-skating champion, and future Hockey Hall of Famer Frank Frederickson — skated up,
around and through the Americans, Czechs and Swedes by combined
scores of 29–1 to win the easiest gold medal Canada will ever get in the
Summer Games. The Canadian victories were 15–0 over Czechoslovakia, 2–0 over the US and 12–1 over Sweden. The Europeans couldn't
believe a man could skate as fast as Goodman and were convinced his
skates contained some yet-unheard-of new technological properties.

PARIS 1924

May 4 to July 27
3092 Athletes from 44 Nations

The world had yet to hear of Hollywood's treasured Oscar when Cambridge University student Harold Abrahams and Glasgow divinity student Eric Liddell arrived in Paris for the 1924 Olympics. The first Academy Awards presentations, in 1929 at the Hollywood Roosevelt Hotel, were still five years away. But what these two British runners did in Paris, or in the case of Liddell didn't do on a Sunday, had a dramatic impact fifty-eight years later on March 29, 1982, at the Dorothy Chandler Pavilion in Los Angeles when *Chariots of Fire* scored probably the biggest upset best-picture win in Academy Awards history. There are complaints now the film doesn't hold up well and that tremendous liberties were taken with what actually happened at the Paris Olympics. Slow motion scenes of men running on a beach to synthesized music became almost a Madison Avenue cliché after the film's success, leaving some like film critic Richard Corliss to scoff that this Olympic story was "a hymn to the human spirit as if scored by Barry Manilow." But the overall explanation of what happened in Paris is generally in order, with a few fibs thrown in, and the film still holds a certain inspirational and lyrical appeal.

While Abrahams and Liddell were fashioning their stories of personal struggle, commitment and ultimate glory on the track at historic Colombes Stadium, a Canadian didn't win a gold medal in Olympic track and field for the first time since the inaugural modern Games of 1896 at Athens (in which Canadians didn't compete). Paris was also the first time a Canadian did not win a track and field medal of any colour since 1896. Although nobody is about to make a movie about Canada's involvement in the 1924 Paris Olympics, its seventy-seven athletes and ten officials did leave at least some mark through two silver medals in rowing, a silver in shooting and a bronze in boxing. And the University of Toronto rowing crew did extremely well to finish second behind a legend, although not one of *Chariots* fame, in the eights rowing final. The Yale crew, representing the US, had in its number seven seat a tall and rangy oarsmen named Benjamin Spock, destined later to influence a generation of parents with the publication in 1945 of his *Common Sense Book of Baby and Child Care*. Spock and his Yale buddies weren't shabby rowers, winning Olympic gold in 6:33.4. The Canadians finished second in 6:49.0 for silver. The crew members were Arthur Bell, Bob Hunter, Bill Langford, Harold Little, John Smith, Warren Snyder, Norman Taylor, Bill Wallace and coxswain Ivor Campbell.

With only four entries in the coxless fours, the odds were great the Vancouver Rowing Club crew of Colin Finlayson, Archie Black, George Mackay and William Wood would be coming home with some sort of medal. They beat the heavily favoured European champion Swiss crew in a world record 6:31.2 in the heats, which were redundant since all four crews advanced to the final anyway. The Canadians got off to a bad start because they couldn't hear the verbal start command over the wind. Much to their shock, they saw the other three boats take off. But by the halfway mark at 1000m, the Swiss and French had been passed and only Britain remained to be overcome. Because of poor lane placing, the Canadians had to negotiate a bend in the river the other three crews avoided. But the Vancouver foursome held tough in second. They placed about ten seconds behind the powerful British (7:08.6) in the final, capturing silver in 7:18.0.

The Canadian trap shooting team of George Beattie, James Montgomery, Sam Vance, John Black, Sam Newton and Bill Barnes almost captured gold but finished three points behind the American team at the Issy venue. Canada and Finland tied with 360 points (each team shot at 400 clay birds). The Canucks were awarded the silver medal on tie-breakers.

The welterweight boxing competition at Paris was well attended, with twenty-nine fighters from eighteen countries going for gold. Doug Lewis of Canada slugged his way to the semifinals, losing on points to

*The Canadian coxless
fours from Vancouver
won rowing silver at the
Paris Olympics despite
having to negotiate an
extra bend in the river.*

Jean Delarge of Belgium. Lewis rebounded to crisply outpoint Patrick
Dwyer of Ireland in the bronze medal bout. Maybe it was best that Lewis
didn't get to the final, where a mini-riot broke out after Delarge decisioned
Hector Mendez of Argentina. Irate Argentine fans invaded the ring chanting their man's name. When a Belgian supporter entered the scene with
a flag from his country, he was pushed to the canvas and a half-hour
mélée ensued before the ring was finally cleared. That's one scene they
didn't show in *Chariots*.

The ones they did show were sentimentalized, but wonderfully so.
Harold Abrahams was an aristocratic young Brit who was not averse to
a pint of bitter and a good cigar even while training. But no matter what
appears in *Chariots*, he did not run around the Great Courtyard of Cambridge's Trinity College in the time it took for the clock in the tower to
strike twelve times at noon (Lord Burghley did). The 100m was also not
the chance for Abrahams to redeem himself after failure in the 200 as
indicated in the film, since the 100 was run before the 200 at Paris. And
although Abrahams was Jewish, he was to the manor born and hardly
needing athletic success to overcome subtle societal prejudices as suggested in the film. But regardless of whether or not it is the strict truth,
Chariots of Fire probably did more to repopularize the Olympics in the
Western Bloc after the Moscow boycott than any number of press releases Juan Antonio Samaranch could have churned out. It captured, for
many, the very essence of the Games. To do that, the film's makers didn't
mind fudging a bit. Tom McNab, who coached the British track and
field teams at the 1972 Munich and 1976 Montreal olympics and who
was the script and technical supervisor for *Chariots*, admits the film was
"only loosely based on fact; and that disappoints people when I tell them."

But there are no apologies for portraying Paris '24 with a heightened sense of drama. "If you want to make a film based completely on fact, make a documentary," says McNab. "Otherwise, you take the essence of the truth and enhance it so that it's dramatically captivating."

According to McNab, "If he had been alive, Abrahams wouldn't have allowed *Chariots of Fire* to come out." Abrahams' family, upset at the liberties taken with the story, wanted nothing to do with it and never even attended the film's premier. Porritt went on to have an illustrious career as longtime president of the Commonwealth Games Federation, three-decade surgeon to the royal family and even as Governor General of New Zealand. He too was incensed about *Chariots* and would not allow his name to be used in the film. Until Abrahams died in 1978, he and Porritt met every July 7 at 7:00 P.M. for wine and cigars, it being the exact anniversary of when the 100m final of the 1924 Olympics was run.

In what is now a historic victory, Abrahams streaked across the finish line in the 100m in 10.6 seconds, followed by American Jackson Scholz in 10.7 and New Zealander Arthur Porritt in 10.8. Two days later, Scholz whipsawed his way to the 200m crown in 21.6 seconds. Abrahams was sixth in 22.3. The bronze medallist was Eric Liddell, the Chinese-born devout Christian who gave up his chance for glory in the 100m because the heats were on a Sunday. As any *Chariots* buff knows, Liddell rallied to win the gold medal in the 400m in a world record 47.6 seconds (David Johnston of Canada was fourth in 48.8, less than a stride away from the silver medal). But Scholz did not approach Liddell before the start of the 400 final to give him an inspirational religious message, as shown in the film. Scholz said he wasn't even religious and that scene surprised him. And it caused him no end of inconvenience after *Chariots* was released. Scholz's retirement condo in Florida was flooded with letters by lonely or troubled people asking him to write back inspirational messages for them. Liddell's absence from the 4x400 relay (because it was run on a Sunday), almost became Canada's gain. With the Flying Scot off preaching a sermon in a Paris chapel, the British foursome came third in 3:17.4. But they were still too far in front of the fourth-place Canadian team of Johnston, Bill Maynes, Horace Aylwin and Allan Christie (3:22.8). Liddell returned to China as a missionary and died in a Japanese prison camp just as the Second World War was ending.

Americans Hazel Wightman and R. Norris Williams won gold in mixed doubles tennis. Williams was happy just to be in Paris. He was happy to be anywhere. As a twelve-year-old boy on a moonless 1912 night somewhere off Newfoundland, he watched in dumbstruck disbelief from an evacuated row boat as the *Titanic* sank. There were no *Titanic*

The finish of the Chariots of Fire *race of the 1924 Paris Olympic Games.*

survivors on the Canadian squad but there were some team officials who felt lucky to have survived the gouging they took in Paris from unscrupulous hotel managers.

Finland finished second in the medals table behind the US with fourteen golds, thirteen silvers and ten bronzes for the best per capita performance by far of the 1924 Games. The Finns had a hammerlock on the middle- and long-distance running events, led by the incomparable Paavo Nurmi's five gold medals. The statue of him outside the 1952 Helsinki Olympic Stadium was erected in honour of his mind-boggling Paris performance, where he even managed to win the 5000 and 1500m gold medals less than two hours apart on the same day. As with Kenya's current death grip on men's middle-distance track, many explanations were offered as to why it was possible for one country to be so dominant. With the Kenyans, the plausible theories are a rugged life running to and from school over dusty, potholed roads and chasing over hillsides for stray cattle at high altitude in the Rift Valley. For the Finns, the explanations varied from the effects their sauna baths and harsh climate had on the human body to the dried fish and sour milk they consumed. If anybody ever makes a movie about Nurmi at the Paris Olympics, they can show him sitting leisurely in a sauna before his races and writing down inspirational thoughts while chewing on dried raw fish. It happened. Honest.

AMSTERDAM 1928

May 17 to August 12
3014 Athletes from 46 Nations

If Canada had any political, economic or cultural clout in this world, *Chariots of Fire* would have been about Percy Williams in 1928 at Amsterdam and not Britons Harold Abrahams and Eric Liddell at Paris in 1924. Williams was a sickly wisp of an eighteen-year-old at just 110 pounds when he was discovered at a school meet in Vancouver by high school coach Bob Granger just two years before the Amsterdam Olympics. Williams, who as an adult weighed only 125 pounds, grew up weak and slight because a childhood case of rheumatic fever had left him with a damaged heart. Before the 1928 Olympics, he was virtually unknown outside Canada. He wasn't exactly a household name in Canada, either. "Unrated and unprepossessing ... he looked as frail as a frightened fawn," is how former *Vancouver Sun* sports columnist Jim Kearney described him. Williams is an unlikely choice to be probably Canada's greatest Olympian and someone who may even have influenced what this nation's flag looks like today. His gold medals in the 100m and 200m at Amsterdam so enthused a then-youngster named George Stanley, that Stanley thought of them many years later when he designed Canada's simple but eloquent Maple Leaf national flag in 1964. "I was so impressed with a picture of Percy Williams winning a gold medal in the 1928 Olympics that it always stayed in my mind and inspired me when I was designing the flag," recalled Stanley, the former lieutenant-governor of New Brunswick. "As Williams breasted the tape, you could see the large Maple Leaf on his jersey and there was no doubt everybody knew it was Canada."

If you look at the book ends of his life, from pale and wraith-like youth to pained old recluse, he is indeed an odd choice to be, arguably, this nation's greatest Olympian. But fairy tales do come true, if only for two days at the Olympic Games. Most of Williams' life wasn't *Chariots* stuff. But Amsterdam was. Only two years before that, Williams was a poor bet to become a national hero. That was probably the last thing on his or anybody else's mind. Like Wayne Gretzky, his build hardly suggested the remarkable prowess that lay within. But unlike Gretzky, who was a boy wonder on the ice from Pee Wee, Williams didn't show it early. He was only a casual athlete at King Edward High School, preparing for a few weeks in May before the city all-schools track meet in June. But Bob Granger, who coached several sports at rival King George High School, saw genius one summer day in 1926 and the course of Canadian Olympic history changed. Granger, who coached the Vancouver high school track champion Wally Scott, couldn't believe it when Williams breasted the tape simultaneously with Scott during a challenge race that summer of '26. He took the young Williams under his tutelage and dared to dream the greatest dream of all. Granger believed right from that day in 1926 that Williams would win Olympic gold in the 100m. Granger had some radical training ideas for his time, and Williams was the canvas on which he would lay those strokes. Granger read and studied everything he could about training methods, which was hardly voluminous back then. A rugby player and swimmer in his youth, he began devoting most of his time to devising training and conditioning techniques for high school athletes. Williams was casual and frail, but Granger knew he had the student of a lifetime. Granger wasn't always right, however, and by today's standards of volume training, his methods seemed downright wacko. Granger believed in conserving the body's energy. Just before the 200m final at Amsterdam while the other sprinters were warming up on the track, Williams was made to lay in his dressing room buried under a Mount Everest of blankets. Granger wanted Williams warmed up but without having him expend any energy doing so. It was bizarre but ultimately successful.

In two years, Granger taught Williams the proper way to start and how to move his arms. Modest and quiet, Williams unquestioningly soaked up Granger's words like a sponge. The natural speed of the athlete took it from there. But Williams went to the 1928 national Olympic

Canadian Jimmy Ball glances across at hard-charging American Ray Barbuti at the finish line in the 1928 Amersterdam Olympics 400m final

trials in Hamilton still as a western outsider who nobody really knew much about. A year earlier, the Amateur Athletic Union rep in BC didn't think much of William's chances and decided the young Vancouverite shouldn't get a train ticket for the 1927 national championships. Bob Brown, of Vancouver baseball fame, bought Williams his passage. By the Olympic year the AAU had wised up and Williams got his way paid. Granger wasn't so fortunate. He paid his carriage to Hamilton by working in the galley of the CPR diner en route. But the duo made an impression in Steel Town, to put it mildly, as Williams swept the 100 and 200m. He won the 100m at the national trials in 10.6 seconds to equal the Olympic record set by Harold Abrahams in the *Chariots of Fire* race at Paris in 1924. There was no money in Canadian Olympic Association coffers to include Granger when the track and field athletes, swimmers, wrestlers and rowers left Montreal for Amsterdam on July 11, 1928, on the *S.S. Albertic* or when the cyclists, boxers and lacrosse players departed July 18 on the *Empress of Scotland*. But Williams' mother and friends raised $300 in Vancouver and sent it to Granger, who boarded a cattle boat in Montreal. All he knew was the boat was heading for Amsterdam. But cattle boats ran an erractic schedule, depending on changing pick-up and drop off times, so Granger had no idea when he would arrive in the Olympic city. He fortunately got to Amsterdam just three days after Williams, a little smellier but not too much the worse for wear. Granger still wasn't satisfied with Williams' starts and so took apart his hotel room bed in Amsterdam. He put the mattress against the wall and had the young sprinter explode into it from a crouched position across the room.

Now is where the steely but rousing synthesized music by Vangelis would have started to swell if *Chariots* had been set in Amsterdam '28 instead of Paris '24. Percy Williams, a faceless unknown from Canada in the field of eighty-seven entrants from thirty-seven nations, stepped to the start line for the twelfth preliminary heat in the Olympic men's 100m. He won, leaving the national champions of Czechoslovakia, Portugal, France and Lithuania in the cinder dust. Granger had him sit motionless for the next three hours. In the fourth heat of the second round, the twenty-year-old Canadian had whipsawed through the field and again equalled Abrahams' Olympic record of 10.6 seconds. The chariots were starting to burn bright red.

The next day, July 30, Williams overcame a bad start and went through second in his semifinal and was in the final. At 4:00 P.M., the six fastest men in the world nervously crouched at the start line: the favourite was eighteen-year-old California schoolboy sensation Frank Wykoff, who had tied Abrahams' Olympic record four times; Georg Lammers of Germany; Bob McAllister, a bulky New York cop; Wilfred Legg of South Africa; and the appropriately named Jack London of Britain, a London University medical student from British Guiana who was nicknamed Mr. London of London. And there was the skinny Canadian nobody had heard of before this moment. The gun. And Legg was out too soon. The runners came back to their marks. Again the gun. This time Wyckoff broke too soon. The start, which had always been Williams' Achilles' heel during his development, was instead proving the undoing of others in the field. They appeared unnerved. Williams later said the hotel room bursts into the mattress were rushing through his mind through all this. "Just remember the hotel room, just remember the hotel room."

For the third time the gun went off. Williams anticipated it perfectly. He was off like a gazelle and into the lead. He was never headed. Nobody came close. By 50m, he was well in front. London made a vain attempt to lunge at the line but still finished well off and and two feet behind. In less than eleven seconds, a frail Canadian went from virtual unknown to the fastest man in the world. It was Williams first in 10.8 seconds, London second, Lammers third, Wykoff fourth, Legg fifth and McAllister (who had beaten Williams in the semifinals) sixth. A disbelieving P.J. Mulqueen, chairman of the Canadian Olympic Association, pushed his way onto the track and planted a kiss on Williams' cheek. In *Chariots of Fire*, the ebullient coach Mussabini (played by Ian Holm) punches a hole through his straw boater hat when news reaches him of Abrahams' victory in the 100m at the 1924 Paris Games. In 1928 at

Amsterdam, Granger, sitting in stunned silence in the stands, clasped his face in his hands and cried.

But ahead lay the 200m and the attempt at a sprint sweep — something that hadn't happened at the Olympics in sixteen years. The road to gold lay through two American stars. Charlie Paddock, the two-time Olympic silver medallist over the distance, played a part in the *Chariots* scenario four years before by shunting the bible-reading Scotsman Eric Liddell to third place. Also on hand was another *Chariots* alumnus, Jackson Scholz, the American who won the 200m at Paris in 1924 and placed second to Abrahams in the 100m. The others to be wary of in the field of seventy-eight runners from thirty-three countries were talented American Charlie Borah and the swift Helmut Kornig of Germany. Williams stepped to the line in the fourteenth heat of the first round and won handily. But the unlucky draw for the next round pitted him directly against Borah and Kornig, with only two advancing. The favoured American and German were out quickly and all seemed lost for Williams. He tried to adjust at 100m by quickening his pace but faltered slightly to fall even farther behind the leaders as Borah hung on Kornig's shoulder several metres up the track. But with less than 60m to go, Williams finally shifted to top speed and caught Borah just a metre from the line and slipped past him.

Williams won his semifinal the next day on August 1 and Granger warned him to beware of Kornig's front-running explosiveness in the final later that afternoon. At 3:55 P.M., Williams slipped into his starting slot in lane two. Also in the 200m final was fellow-Canadian John Fitzpatrick of Hamilton. Of more immediate concern were Kornig and Scholz. Williams kept in touch with both of them and it looked to be a blanket finish as the runners rounded the bend. But the spindly Williams squeezed from the pack with 50m left, his ghost white arms and legs pumping furiously and putting air between him and the others. The strain of having run the 100m just days earlier was not showing. Williams was the freshest of the mad dashers in the stretch. All Kornig and Scholz could do was watch his back as he screeched home for gold in 21.8 seconds, two feet ahead of Walter Rangeley of Britain and three feet ahead of Kornig and Scholz. Fitzpatrick was fifth. A swelling Vangelis overture, please. All hail Percy Williams of Canada — who, with Americans Archie Hahn (1904), Ralph Craig (1912), Eddie Tolan (1932), Jesse Owens (1936), Bobby-Joe Morrow (1956), Carl Lewis (1984) and Russian Valeriy Borzov (1972) — pulled off the sprint double, one of the storied achievements of the Olympic Games.

The Olympic world of 1928 was nothing like that of today, where

Percy Williams of Vancouver lunges across the line to win the 100 metres gold medal at the 1928 Amsterdam Olympics.

every stroke of the arm and every raise of the knee by Olympic champions such as Lewis or Britain's Linford Christie is slowed to almost hypnotic slow motion on television and those less-than-ten-seconds are analysed in the minutest of detail. Above all, many of the runners become celebrities and the race a mini-drama where hopes are dashed or fortunes won over just 100m of rubberized real estate. It wasn't like that in Williams' era. "People don't believe me when I tell them, but I didn't know any of those people I ran against," he said. "I didn't even know what they looked like until I saw them on the track. And certainly very few people there could recognize me." Williams recalled that after his races there appeared a large crowd in front of the Canadian hotel. He had no idea what they had gathered for so he just sauntered over and joined them. When he inquired what all the interest was about, a Dutchman turned to him and said: "We're waiting for the Canadian runner, Williams, to come out of the hotel." So Williams, who didn't tell anybody who he was, just hung around with the crowd and waited for himself.

Williams returned home a conquering hero. The train trip to British Columbia was unlike any other ever undertaken by a Canadian sportsman. Travelling with his mother, he was lauded and lionized at every stop. He was presented with a gold watch in Montreal, a silver tea service in Hamilton, a bronze statue and silver cup in Winnipeg and a plaque in Calgary. After the CPR train pulled into Vancouver, thousands lined the streets, sometimes three and four deep, as he paraded in an open touring car with BC premier S.F. Tolmie. They were followed by four Mounties atop horseback in full regalia and drove up Granville to Georgia to Stanley Park. Schools were let out for the day and children in knickerbockers ran up to the car to touch the sudden legend. Men and women on the curbs smiled and waved. People looked out of building windows and shouted down "Bravo." An enterprising Vancouver candy company put out "Our Percy" chocolate bars. Waiting in Stanley Park for Williams was a sparkling new blue Graham-Paige sports car. He also received a $16,000 trust account for his education. Granger was not forgotten and was presented $500 in gold by Vancouver mayor Louis Taylor. Two years later, Williams set the 100m world record of 10.3 seconds, which stood for eleven years. At Hamilton, he was picked to be the the first athlete ever to recite the oath of allegiance at the British Empire (now Commonwealth) Games during the opening ceremonies of the first Games in 1930.

But life would not always be this happy for Percy Williams. His athletic unravelling began at those first British Empire Games. He set the longstanding Games record of 9.6 seconds in the 100 yard heats and was off like a bullet in the final. His pace seemed easily on line to snap the world record of 9.5 seconds. But at seventy yards, something happened. He tore a major muscle in his left thigh and was obviously in a great deal of pain. But he kept his legs and arms pumping and managed to stagger across the finish line before falling in a heap on the track. He had won the gold medal in 9.9 seconds, but his career was all but over. The Canadian team didn't have a doctor at the track and there was little in the way of sports medicine to have the injury properly healed in the months following. Although Williams kept running for a few more years, he was constantly dogged by muscle problems in the leg and was never the same after that rainy afternoon in Hamilton on August 23, 1930. He didn't make it past the semifinals at the 1932 Los Angeles Olympics. Williams turned the first sod in 1953 for the Empire Stadium which was being constructed for the 1954 Vancouver British Empire Games. But getting him to agree to do that was a real chore. When the federal government invited all of the nation's living Olympic gold medallists to Montreal before the 1976 Summer Games, only one didn't attend — Percy Williams. He never married. The man who ran his own insurance business, but wanted his privacy, was eventually wracked by pain in his leg. Tired and alone, he took a shotgun to his head and committed suicide in 1982.

James Ball of Winnipeg made some key mistakes that cost him dearly in the 400m final at the Amsterdam Olympic Stadium, which was built on sixteen hectares of reclaimed swampland and on a foundation of more than 4,500 piles driven into the ground. Ball's mistakes proved the difference between gold and silver — a chasm that only grows larger as the years go by. "James Ball of Canada made all the mistakes it is possible for a runner to make in such a race," winced Philip Noel-Baker, twice British track and field team captain at previous Games and vice-commissioner for the overall British team at the Amsterdam Olympics. It was allowed in the 400m in the 1920s to break out of your lane and go into the curb lane down the home stretch. Incredibly, the twenty-five-year-old Ball forgot. He stayed in his own lane the entire race and ran many yards farther than anyone else in the race. Amazingly, he still was on course for gold — bearing down mercilessly on the leader Ray Barbuti of the United States. But then Ball commited one of the cardinal sins of track — 1920s or 1990s. Just as he was nearing the finish, he glanced to his side to see where his competitors were. Big mistake, as any schoolaged runner can tell you. That sideways glance probably cost Ball the Olympic gold. It was so close that the split second he lost straining and looking awkardly to his left at the line allowed the lunging Barbuti — who crashed to the track in a spray of cinder after breaking the tape — to take gold in 47.8 seconds to Ball's 48.0. It was the American Barbuti, a stocky Syracuse University football player, who inherited the gold won four years earlier in the event by the religious "Never On Sunday" Scotsman Eric Liddell of *Chariots* lore. It is unfortunate Ball had such major mental lapses in the most important race he would ever run. But his talent was self-evident, regardless. Powered by Ball and the ever-present Phil Edwards, the Canadian 4x400 relay team, which also had Alexander Wilson and Stanley Glover, captured the bronze medal in 3:15.4 behind the Barbuti-led US squad (world record 3:14.2) and Germany (3:14.8).

Although Amsterdam will remain synomous with Williams for most Canadians, women from Canada came away with several memorable moments through an explosive group of athletes. It was the first time women had competed in track and field at the Olympics and they only did so after much worldwide controversy and over the objections of Baron Pierre de Coubertin himself. A doctor wrote to the *Times of London* complaining, "Nature made women to bear children and she cannot rid herself of fat to the extent necessary for physcial fitness demanded by feats of extreme endurance." There were also concerns about women not being able to take the roller-coaster emotional rigours of athletics. Several Canadian officials, led by team manager Dr. A.S. Lamb of McGill, also held forth in Amsterdam that sport was too demanding for the female sex and women should be barred from future Olympics for their own protection. But every inch an athlete, and certainly not fat and definitely not unhinged emotionally by the demands of her sport, was the striking eighteen-year-old Ethel Catherwood. Nicknamed the Saskatoon Lily, she won the women's high jump at 1.59m on the last day of the Games, although an official's error denied her the world record. Catherwood was anointed the "most beautiful girl in the Olympics" by *New York Times* reporter

Wythe Williams. It was a different era, folks. The photogenic Catherwood immediately became a favourite of the largely male crowd as she sauntered around the infield on the cold, grey day. It mattered little to the men watching that she wrapped herself in a bulky red Hudson's Bay blanket between jumps. The graceful and talented prairie teenager, who was known for her confident smile and cool demeanor as she approached the bar, didn't even enter the competition until more than two hours and the five-foot mark had passed. She returned home to a hero's welcome as thousands lined the streets and celebrated in Saskatoon. Catherwood was presented with $3500 by a grateful prairie populace to continue her piano and business studies. With her glamour-queen looks, she was rumoured to be headed for the movies. She did move to California in 1930, but hundreds of miles north of Hollywood, in the San Francisco Bay area. Catherwood married a fellow high jump Olympic champion, Harold Osborn, who won gold for the US at the 1924 Paris Games.

Canada's fabulous 4x100m relay team of Fanny Rosenfeld, Ethel Smith, Florence Bell and Myrtle Cook set the world record in its heat at Amsterdam. The Toronto women then bettered that mark by a full second in winning Olympic gold in 48.4 seconds. The Americans were just wannabes in second at 48.8 and the Germans third in 49.2. Rosenfeld set the pace by pulling out to a substantial lead before handing off to Smith, who managed to increase it. Then it was Bell, not only the slowest member of the team but also injured. It would be up to the weakest link. How she went, so would go the entire race. But Bell sucked it up and powered through the third leg with the greatest run of her life. She gave the anchor runner, Cook, a two-metre lead. That was all the gifted Cook needed. With that kind of speed to burn, the Canadians were looking for big things in the women's individual sprints and came through, although not unscathed. In a tough call, Cook was disqualified for twice false starting in the highly contentious 100m. Cook crumpled to a heap next to the start line and began weeping. Officials finally had to ask her to move to the infield, where she sat on some pillows and cried loudly for nearly half an hour. Rosenfeld and Smith captured silver and bronze in the 100m, but it appeared to many that Rosenfeld may have finished ahead of the announced winner, sixteen-year-old Elizabeth Robinson of the US (12.2 seconds). It was as tight as could be and many of the judges also sided with Rosenfeld. The controversy even reached the League of Nations but Canada's pleas went for naught. Canada got the best of the Americans in the 4x100 to wash away some of the sour taste.

This remarkable group of six female Canadians won two gold, one silver and one bronze in the five women's track and field events (100m,

800m, 4x100m, high jump and discus throw) contested at Amsterdam to finish tops in the world in overall team achievement. Two of them became groundbreakers as well in an associated field — sportswriting. Myrtle Cook became sports editor and columnist for the *Montreal Star* as Myrtle Cook McGowan. Rosenfeld, who arrived in Canada in swaddling blankets as the baby daughter of Russian Jewish immigrants, became a sportswriter and columnist for the Toronto *Globe and Mail*. Both were multitalented in their athletic skills. Cook won city, regional, provincial or national titles in track, tennis, ice hockey, basketball, tenpin, cycling and canoeing. Rosenfeld, nicknamed Bobbie, starred not only in track but in field events as well and also becoming an accomplished ice hockey, basketball and softball player, not to mention Toronto city tennis champion and Canadian women's track and field coach at the 1934 London British Empire Games. The sinewy Rosenfeld, of medium-to-skinny build, had a shot that even in the pre-slapshot era made hockey goalies cringe. She didn't know a thing about running the longer distances and was thrown into the 800m at the Amsterdam Olympics as a "rabbit" so her sprint speed could set the pace for teammate Jean Thompson. Rosenfeld finished fifth, one placing behind middle-distance specialist Thompson.

Rosenfeld, the greatest women's all-rounder of her era, in 1950 was named Canada's top female athlete of the half-century in a media poll conducted by the Canadian Press (the men's winner was Lionel Conacher). The annual CP award handed out to Canada's female athlete of the year is named in honour of Rosenfeld. Arthritis ended her athletic career in 1933 and she spent the rest of her years in considerable pain before dying at age sixty-six in 1969. Only 209 of the 3014 athletes at the 1928 Olympics were women and there were such scenes of huffing and puffing and some anguish at the finish line as Rosenfeld, Thompson and twenty-three others contested the women's 800m — won by Lina Radke of Germany in 2:16.8 — that a horrified male sports bureaucracy decreed that long distances were too much for gentle womenfolk to handle and the female 800m was stripped from the Olympic agenda and left off until Rome in 1960. One wonders what they would have thought in 1928 at the prospect of an Olympic women's marathon, something that came to be in 1984.

Sixty-two Canadian men and seven women contested the 1928 Olympics. There was no Olympic Village and the team stayed in a group of downtown hotels allocated for squads from "The Empire." The Canucks were fine just as long as they didn't inhale standing next to the beer-swilling Australians after hours. "The accommodation was not ideal, but it was vastly superior to that of many other countries," reported Canadian team manager Dr. Lamb. Canada won four gold medals, four silvers and seven bronze for tenth spot on the medals table. Away from the track, Don Stockton of Montreal won silver in middleweight wrestling and Toronto "twins" Joe Wright Jr. (who carried the Red Ensign during the opening ceremonies) and Jack Guest (who was born on the same day in 1906 as his scull-mate Wright Jr.) took silver in double sculls rowing on the Sloten Canal. The Toronto Argonauts club of Fred Hedges, Frank Fiddes, John Hand, Herbert Richardson, Jack Murdock, Athol Meech, Edgar Norris, William Ross and cox Jack Donelly were third in 6:03.8 in the razor's-edge men's eights to the gold medallist Americans from the University of California (6:03.2) and silver medallist British from the Thames Rowing Club (6:03.6). Other bronze medals went to Ray Smillie of Toronto in welterweight boxing, and to two wrestlers: Maurice Letchford of Montreal in welterweight and Jim Trifunov of Regina in bantamweight.

Trifunov, the Serbia-born son of immigrants who settled in Saskatchewan, had to begin working at age ten to support his family when his father died in 1913. Too poor to afford even a bicycle, he walked up to eight miles a day in the pre-dawn dark before school to deliver the *Regina Leader-Post* newspaper to bring in money for the family. Trifunov won ten national amateur titles and represented Canada at the 1924 Paris, 1928 Amsterdam and 1932 Los Angeles olympics. Trifunov had no money to get to Paris in 1924, but his co-workers at the *Leader-Post* all chipped in a couple of dollars each and he managed to scrape together the rest. He did the best at Amsterdam four years later, placing in the bronze-medal position in bantamweight (56kg). Two years later at Hamilton, Trifunov pinned Joe Reid of England to win gold in the British Empire Games. The intense little man with the cabbage ears went on to coach the Canadian wrestling teams at the 1952 Helsinki, 1956 Melbourne and 1960 Rome olympics and was manager of the grapplers at the 1954 Vancouver, 1958 Cardiff and 1970 Edinburgh commonwealth games.

Tarzan-to-be Johnny Weissmuller led the US 4x200 relay team to victory at the Amsterdam pool in a world record 9:36.2 to finish his Olympic career with five gold medals, while the Canadian foursome of F. Munro Bourne, James Thompson, Garnet Ault and Walter Spence took bronze in 9:47.8. But in the end for Canada, these will always be the Games that Percy built.

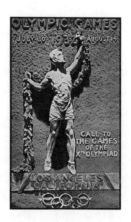

LOS ANGELES 1932

July 30 to August 14
1408 Athletes from 37 Nations

The 1932 Olympics were enough to dispell doubts anyone might have harboured about the true power of the L.A. dream factory. If the emergence of Hollywood's dashing stars and alluring starlets wasn't enough of an opiate for the masses, just give them a circus. At the height of the Depression, La La Land delivered to the world a spectacle unrivalled in sporting history to that time. A magnificent and then-unparalleled stadium of 105,000, which still stands and also hosted the 1984 Summer Olympics, was constructed for $2 million. Seating rose up for seventy-nine rows. As the finishing touch, architect Stanley Gould built an Olympic torch that towered forty-five feet above the stadium peristyle and 120 feet above the infield. Despite a slow start, ticket revenues reached the $1.3 million plateau ten days before the Games — which was double that of the entire 1928 Amsterdam Olympics. A total of 1.25 million tickets was sold — again more than double pre-Depression Amsterdam — and a profit of $213,877 was handed over to the city and county at a time when workers were without jobs and homeless families stood in bread lines. The undaunted Community Development Association organizers sent gold-embossed invitations around the world in 1930, just a year after the stock market crash. But was anybody interested in coming to this Olympic party? Just six months before the Games were to begin, not a single nation had confirmed its attendance. The distances were too great and the money too short (the sixty-nine Brazilian athletes tried to support themselves by selling bags of coffee beans at ports along the way before docking at L.A.). Worried that nations were too strapped to send athletes, the organizers arranged for cheap railroad and steamship passage and brought the price down to $500 per athlete from Europe. The most innovative promise of all had been announced earlier. Thanks to a revolutionary new concept — a village for athletes — every competitor would be housed, fed, pampered and transported for less than $2 a day. Love or hate Americans, you can't deny their marketing sense and know-how. The 1408 athletes from 37 nations in Los Angeles represented a significant drop from Amsterdam in 1928 and Paris in 1924, but they arrived from much farther distances and at a time when the jobless were riding the rails for other reasons.

It was a frantic, eleventh-hour effort that got a Canadian team to Los Angeles. A total of $36,000 was raised, most of it virtually at the last second, to send a team of 130 athletes and twenty officials. "We would like to send a larger team but haven't got the money," said M.M. "Bobby" Robinson, the secretary of the Canadian Olympic Association and a master of understatement. The problem was acute and the COA had only $12,000 in its coffers in early July. When the gravity of the situation sank in, the athletes were told they had little time to beat the depressed bushes for money if they hoped to compete in the Olympics. The 115 athletes rose to the challenge, raising enough from their sports associations, their own pockets and those of their friends to sponsor themselves. The Olympic Special train left Union Station in Toronto for Los Angeles on July 21 with the large Canadian and British teams and those from South Africa, Belgium and Hungary onboard.

Once they got to the land of milk and honey, the men were ushered into the first-ever Athletes' Village. It was a pleasant, landscaped 320 acres laid into the contours of the Baldwin Hills. Cooled by fresh ocean breezes and just ten minutes from the Memorial Coliseum, it offered a stunning vista. The 1281 male athletes stayed four to a dorm in the 550 two-room, white and pink Mexican-style cottages arranged in a semicircle. The Village also featured a hospital, library, post office, barber shop, cinema, five miles of paths and forty-two kitchens serving every imaginable style of cuisine in five dining rooms. The airy Chapman Park Hotel on Wilshire Boulevard was given over entirely to the 127 women athletes. The initial reaction to the idea of Village-style living was lukewarm. But after seeing how well it worked in Los Angeles, not only economically but also in fostering kinship, Athletes Villages have become the norm at every Games since. The Canadians, like the others, took to it immediately. There was only one female in the men's village, a Filipino housekeeper who got more than she bargained for in the job. She walked with her eyes looking ramrod straight, rarely venturing a sideward glance. Well, maybe she peeked once or twice. "It's practically a nudist colony," wrote the *Vancouver Sun*, about the men's Village. "The boys go about, many of them with nothing on. Women are barred from the Village, even as spectators. It is feared that scenes such as these might prove too shocking for feminine orbs. The boys lie about in the sun as brown as Indians. You can't tell a son of Nippon from a Canuck or a fair Swede from a swart Mexican."

Canada was a hit at the opening of the Games, filing into the packed and sundrenched stadium in red blazers with white trim, white hats and white flannel pants or skirts. Hollywood legends Charlie Chaplin, Marlene Dietrich, Douglas Fairbanks, Clara Bow and Mary Pickford entertained the opening crowd (and waived their fees for doing so). In the stands were Gary Cooper, Bing Crosby, Cary Grant, the Marx brothers, countless other film stars and the likes of Ty Cobb and Will Rogers. The Olympics became so big when they returned to L.A. in 1984 that none other than His Confused Eminence himself, Ronald Reagan, opened them. But President Herbert Hoover couldn't be bothered in 1932 and instead sent Vice-President Charles Curtis. Hoover was said to be indignant to even be asked to open the Games when the election race was just heating up. "It's a crazy thing and takes some gall to expect me to be a part of it," he said, of the Olympics. Obviously, no one explained to him the meaning of the term photo-op. Earlier that July, Franklin Delano Roosevelt had been chosen the Democratic nominee and it wasn't hard to see why he brushed aside the aloof Hoover in the US elections later that year.

It was so hot during the opening ceremonies that US track and field head coach Lawson Robertson of USC, an expatriate Canadian, wouldn't let many of his athletes march. But the Canadians weren't about to let something like the sun stand in the way of a good time. With the Olympics on the same continent, there was a large contingent of Canadian fans at the Games: up to 30,000 were estimated to be in the vast opening ceremony crowd of 105,000. Lou Marsh, the legendary Canadian sportswriter, was beside himself. "I tell you folks, what we got was an ovation and when I say ovation I mean a blood-tingling ovation," he wrote. "It was glorious." The Canadian women made an impression. It must be the bracing winter air or something. "The Canadian girls have made a real hit down here with their good looks and their nice mannerisms," wrote the *Vancouver Sun*. "Papers here refer to them as the best-looking girls at the Games." These kinds of sexist comments wouldn't get past any editor today, nor would they even be attempted in print by journalists. But 1932 was a different time and Lou Marsh couldn't have agreed more with the other assesments of the hot lookers from Canada. "We were the first big contingent to swing into the vast bowl and let me tell you something, we had the best-looking contingent of feminine athletes in the whole show," he wrote. But the quote of the Games goes to Maxwell Stiles of the *Los Angeles Examiner*: "The Canadian girls are undoubtedly the prettiest and most wholesome of the Games. They constitute a denial of the general idea that a woman athlete must be built like a Baby Grand Piano and have a face like a hatchet. Their ages range from sixteen to twenty-one, and they are here to show the world that Canada has some splendid young women who are good-looking and who know how to conduct themselves."

On the subject of femininity, no story can possibly beat the punchline to that of the women's 100m at the 1932 Olympics. *Montreal Star* sports columnist Myrtle Cook, one of the heroines of Canada's splendid female track and field team at the 1928 Amsterdam Olympics, began writing about and championing a nineteen-year-old girl whom she noticed had excelled in high school basketball, badminton and swimming and was now a rising softball star in leagues around Montreal. Cook encouraged the youngster, Hilda Strike, to try sprinting and train hard despite her lack of height and size. They worked on her start, which was the only thing that could overcome the inherent disadvantages built into a slight 5' 3", 105-pound frame. Strike was a natural despite her size, and was clearly a star by the time of the 1932 Olympics. She was one of only nine females selected for the Canadian track and field team. Strike's main opponent was Stella Walsh, a Polish-born resident of Cleveland, who was the first woman to break the eleven seconds barrier in the 100 yards. Unable to find a job in the Depression, Walsh approached the Polish consulate in New York for support. The consulate offered her a job the day before she was scheduled to become a US citizen. Walsh tore up the citizenship papers and decided to compete for her native Poland as Stanislawa Walasiewicz.

As expected, both Strike and Walsh/Walasiewicz tore up the track in advancing to the final at the Los Angeles Games. Strike, using her immense talent at starts, was off like a bullet and victory seemed certain in the final. She led all the way to 85m but Walsh/Walasiewicz caught her and then flung herself to the tape and edged Strike by less than an eye-

*Arms raised, Hilda
Strike strikes silver for
Canada in the women's
100m final at the 1932
Los Angeles Olympics.*

lash. Both sprinters were across the line in a world-record-tying 11.9 seconds with little to separate them. Maybe Strike should have used her breasts to advantage in such a close race and pushed out her chest — because that's not an advantage her opponent had. In a shocking post-script decades later, Stella Walsh was shot and killed in 1980 when she strayed into the middle of a bungled robbery attempt in the parking lot of a Cleveland discount store. When the autopsy was performed on Walsh, who set eleven world records and won two Olympic medals, it was discovered "she" had a penis and testicles. Hilda Strike had lost the 1932 Olympic gold medal in the women's 100m to a man!

The first day of competition brought a quick hit for Canada and one of its most astounding, long-shot gold medals ever. The amazing thing was that because of finances, Duncan McNaughton was one of those Canadian athletes who wouldn't have made the final cut of 130 to the Games and would have been left at home. The only reason he competed was that he was already in Los Angeles and so it didn't cost anything to get him to the Games. McNaughton was a geology student at USC, just down the road from the new stadium. Born in Cornwall, Ont., and raised in North Vancouver, nobody gave the tall and slim high jumper much of a chance. In fact, no-cost or not, Canadian officials were reluctant to include McNaughton on the team when he met the incoming train. He pestered the uncertain team managers until they finally relented and allowed him to join the squad in the Village. He had been good in his first two years of competing for USC but still a long way from being anywhere near the best in the world. He fouled out of the competition at the 1930 Hamilton British Empire Games and his best jump to date was 6' 4½", well off the world record of 6' 8¼" held by 1924 Olympic champion Harold Osborn of the United States (the nation which had won this event in eight of the nine previous Games). The competition, held under a broiling sun from 2:30 to 5:45 P.M., was long but dramatic. The crowd of 45,000 sat in tense silence, the still air broken only by their gasps when the men pushed off the cinder and lept. The field of fourteen jumpers from ten countries was whittled to four when only McNaughton, Robert Van Osdel of the US, Simeon Toribio of the Phillipines and promising Los Angeles high school sensation Cornelius Johnson cleared 6' 5½".

McNaughton and Van Osdel were school mates at USC and great friends. Van Osdel had taken the young British Columbian under his wing when he arrived two years before and tutored him on the finer points of jumping. Soon, only the two pals were left after fourth-finishing Johnson (who would win the gold at Berlin four years later) and bronze medallist Toribio were eliminated. Neither McNaughton nor Van Osdel could get over at 6' 7" or 6' 6½" so the bar was lowered to just under 6' 6". At this point, the two approached the track judges and asked if the Olympic championship could be shared between them. The officials said no way. So the exhausted friends headed back to the jumping area knowing there was only room for one of them on the victory podium. They both failed on their first tries at just under 6' 6". Van Osdel walked over to McNaughton and told him to concentrate on his kick. Keeping that in mind and gathering what little strength he had left, McNaughton flung himself over the bar on his second attempt while his buddy and mentor Van Osdel missed. That's all he needed. McNaughton had recorded one of the greatest upsets in Olympic history. The top four finishers were all officially awarded the height of 6' 5½". If the modern tie-breaking rules were in use in 1932, McNaughton would only have won bronze instead of gold. Van Osdel, who had never before lost to McNaughton, would have been given the gold medal and Johnson the silver. But this was 1932 and McNaughton was the Olympic champion.

None of this had seemed in the realm of earthly possibility when he entered his first meet for Burnaby School at Central Park on May 23, 1925 and won the senior high jump title at 4' 8", along with a first in the long jump and a second in the 100 yards. "He was a long, gangling kid with a sunny smile, keen sense of humour and a million dollar disposition, and when we began to look for track and field talent, he immediately attracted attention as a jumper," recalled Burnaby School instructor and coach George W. Sievers. Even when he was leaping 6' at King Edward

*Duncan McNaughton
leaps for high jump gold
at the 1932 Los Angeles
Olympics.*

High School, McNaughton couldn't have imagined that a few years later he would be responsible for the Red Ensign being raised up the central mast during the first medal ceremony of the Los Angeles Olympics. That's not all McNaughton would win. He was awarded the Distinguished Flying Cross while with the RCAF during the Second World War and later fashioned a career as a geologist, getting his doctorate from USC and eventually setting up shop as a well-known oil industry consultant in Dallas. He and Van Osdel remained close friends.

Canada had other days of thunder in the immense stadium, thanks to a trio of swift Montreal runners — Alexander Wilson, Phil Edwards and Hilda Strike. The men's 800m final was a corker, with Wilson missing gold by a heartbeat after a driving battle down the home stretch. Edwards, a McGill medical student whose father was a magistrate in their native British Guiana, set the pace from the start and was through the first lap in 52.8 seconds. But Wilson and then Tommy Hampson, a twenty-four-year-old British school teacher from St. Albans in Hertfordshire, came roaring around the last turn to overtake the tiring Edwards. Now it was down to Wilson and Hampson, the latter the 880 yards champion from the British Empire Games two years earlier in Hamilton. The two thundered down the track while the crowd of 45,000 in the stadium rose in unison. They battled grimly to the tape, with the slim and blond Wilson in the lead. But the Englishman timed his kick to perfection and the Canadian was doomed. Hampson needed everything left in him to storm from behind and pip Wilson by a foot in a world record 1:49.7. Wilson, a Scottish-Canadian who competed in the US for the Fighting Irish of Notre Dame, also ran under the old world record of 1:50.6 by taking silver in 1:49.9. "To win was a question of stamina and courage," noted

Lou Marsh. "Hampson had both but Wilson had only one. The heart of him was big enough, but Hampson had just enough left in his powerful frame to edge his way by, inch by inch." Edwards — it was his fate never to be the golden boy — captured the bronze medal in 1:51.5 for a silver-bronze Canadian finish. "How John Bull and a couple of his sons made Uncle Sammy — and the rest of the world too — take it and like it at the big cement-rimmed saucer," added Marsh, who seemed to be in a sort of British Empire thrall. "Boy, what a spine-tingling thrill when an Englishman, a Canadian and a British Guianian running for Canada, cleaned the works for the cocky Sammies in the greatest event of the track program of this tenth Olympiad — the 800m final — and sent three Jacks up the triple flag mast. And what sheer heart-throbbing ecstasy for the British-born in that mob of 45,000 people when the official band struck up that glorious old hymn "God Save the King" in this fearful orgy. It was a draught of nectar from the mighty gods, the mightiest race and the most glorious victory I ever saw." Hampson credited his win to the love he had for his fiancee, Winnie.

Edwards, who became a medical doctor, was the only man to contest both the 800 and 1500m at Los Angeles. He came within three yards of winning the 1500 for Canada — the classic middle-distance race — and probably would have if the 800m earlier in the Games hadn't taken so much out of him. He again ran to the front of the pack in the 1500 final, as he did in the 800, and set a blistering pace. Edwards and Glenn Cunningham of the US opened up a twenty-two-metre lead on the rest of the pack when the bell sounded for the final lap. But instead of being a two-man battle for gold, Luigi Beccali of Italy and John Cornes of Britain appeared out of nowhere from way back to challenge the two leaders. Edwards opened the throttle and passed Cunnigham in an all-out bid for victory. He pulled five steps ahead and thought he was going to do it. Olympic gold was just 100m away. But the rapidly charging little Italian, Beccali, had caught Cunningham and now had his eyes set on Edwards' back. The man from Montreal could hear the man from Milan approaching but was too tired to respond. Beccali edged past for the gold while a disheartened Edwards saw not only the Italian but also Cornes pass him just before the tape. Beccali, who gave the Fascist salute atop the victory podium during the medals ceremony, won gold in an Olympic record 3:51.2; Cornes won silver in 3:52.6 and Edwards bronze in 3:52.8. Finishing a quiet seventh was the brilliant but troubled New Zealand running genius Jack Lovelock, who would win this event four years later at the Berlin Olympics and become an Oxford-trained doctor before commiting suicide by throwing himself under a train.

As Edwards grimaced in pain and dejection after the 1932 race, he was approached by the English great and 1928 Olympic 400m hurdles champion Lord Burghley, who put his arms around the exhausted runner and said: "Well, we didn't win it but because of you the Empire did jolly well just the same." The gifted Edwards was a fluid, natural runner. He had the stride of an elk and was as versatile as they come. He competed in three British Empire and eight Olympic games events and never failed to finish within the top six. He won five Olympic bronze medals. In 1934 at London, he held off hard-charging William Botha of South Africa to take the 880 yards in 1:54.2 to become the first black man to win a gold medal in the history of the British Empire (now Commonwealth) Games. He did that, amusingly, in a stadium called White City. "I can still see in my mind's eye the beautiful running of the Canadian, Phil Edwards," said Harold Abrahams of *Chariots of Fire* fame, in recalling Edwards' Olympic and British Empire games performances. He has been dubbed the Man of Bronze because of his five Olympic third-place finishes. "Perhaps he is typical for Canada," noted big Jim Worrall, the former longstanding IOC member for Canada and later IOC vice-president. "His [Edwards'] name is known and honoured, but five Olympic medals? One would think he'd be a national byword and yet he isn't. But to me he is one of the finest we have ever had. The gold medals carry the glitter, in every sense, but the silver and bronze are remarkable achievements when one pauses to consider the intensity of competition at the Olympic level."

With all eyes on starry American rivals Ben Eastman of Stanford and Bill Carr of Pine Bluff, Arkansas, nobody was even concerned about Montreal's Wilson in the 400m final, despite his silver medal earlier in the 800. But Wilson gave the Americans a scare by hanging tough with them until the end in the bitterly fought battle. Carr, whose running career came to an end less than a year later when he was badly injured in an autombile accident, took the lead at 100m and kept it to win in a world record 46.2 seconds. Wilson (47.4 seconds) also broke the old world record and finished a yard behind Eastman (46.4) for the bronze medal. The Carr-led Americans set a world record of 3:11.8 in the first heat of the men's 4x400 relay and the outcome of the final was a foregone conclusion. They totally destroyed that new record by going 3:08.2 in the final. The talented Canadian foursome of Wilson, Edwards, Jimmy Ball and Ray Lewis won the bronze medal in 3:12.8, well ahead of fourth-place Germany (3:14.4). The British squad of Hampson, Burghley, Godfrey Rampling (whose daughter Charlotte became a well-known film actress) and Crew Stoneley won the silver medal in 3:11.2. Canada seemed well on its way to gold in the women's 4x100 relay until the final baton exchange. Leading all the way, disaster struck when little Mary Frizzel of Vancouver and Strike got their signals crossed and the Montrealer came to a complete halt to grab the baton. That was just the mistake the trailing Americans needed from Canada. And they exploited it. But barely. With the Canadian lead gone, the Americans forged ahead. Strike fought back and she and Wilhelmina Von Bremen were neck-and-neck coming to the tape on the anchor leg. But again it was silver for Strike by a hair's breadth. This time, however, it was to women. The Americans finished in a world record 46.9 seconds and the Canadian team of Strike, Mary and Mildred Frizzel and Lillian Palmer was second in 47.0 seconds. Britain took bronze in 47.6 as the top three teams eclipsed the old world record of 48.4 seconds established at the 1928 Olympics by the Canadian squad of Fanny Rosenfeld, Ethel Smith, Florence Bell and Myrtle Cook. If Edwards is Canada's man of the Bronze Age, Strike is the Silver Streak. She also won two silver medals, in the 100 yards and 4x110 yards relay, at the 1934 London British Empire Games before getting married and retiring from running in 1935.

Eva Dawes of Toronto took bronze in the women's high jump with a leap of 5' 3". The silver medallist was the legendary Mildred "Babe" Didriksen of Beaumont, Texas, who won gold in the 80m hurdles and javelin and was undoubtedly THE female star of the 1932 Games at age eighteen. She had qualified for five events but was limited to competing in only three because of the old Olympic rules. Didriksen, who later became the world's greatest female golfer, and American teammate Jean Shiley were well ahead of Dawes at 5' 5¼" in the high jump.

Toronto's Horace Gwynne — everybody just called him Lefty — was a boxer living in a jockey's body. Although he eventually went on to make some money in the silks, the Sweet Science was his first love. And he was something of a prodigy, putting on exhibitions as a four year old with his six-year-old brother for the amusement of British army troops in Wales. Gwynne starting hanging around the old Woodbine racetrack at Toronto in 1926 when he was thirteen and took odd jobs around the stables. He was small enough to become a jockey although he didn't meet with much initial success, failing to win a single race in his first season of riding. He was better in the ring at the Central YMCA, where he moulded himself into a bantamweight in the classic style and won amateur bouts throughout Ontario, Quebec and the northern United States. He easily made the cut for the Olympics at age nineteen and was on the train out of Union Station for Los Angeles. Gwynne wasn't very scientific about his approach to boxing and rarely scouted or worried about his next opponent. That was probably just as well. If he knew what he was facing in the field of ten at L.A., he just might have packed it in before his first bout — which was against the tough and crafty Italian champion Vito Melis. But the unperturbed Canadian easily won the decision and even sent the surprised Melis sprawling to the canvas on one occasion. Gwynne outpunched Jose Villanueva of the Phillipines by a wide margin in the semifinals and before he knew it, was in the bout for Olympic gold. Gwynne was decidedly the underdog as he went up against European champion Hans Ziglarski of Germany, who came hard after the Canadian. But Ziglarski's stalking was in vain. The quick Gwynne managed to elude most of the German's looping, roundhouse punches and counter-punched effectively with scoring blows. Living up to his nickname, Gwynne tagged Ziglarski with a solid left that sent the German to his knees in the second round. Clearly ahead on points, Gwynne just rode out the bout and collected his gold medal.

After the bout, Gwynne was invited to a Hollywood backlot and got one of the thrills of his life by meeting movie star Norma Shearer on the set of *Smilin Through*. He returned to Toronto a Canadian hero and received a gold watch at a special city hall reception in his honour. Gwynne turned professional in Toronto and Detroit. Conn Smythe paid him $1000 for five fights at Maple Leaf Gardens and Gwynne thought he had made a "fortune." But in the end, there wasn't much call or bounty for wispy bantamweights in the pro game and Gwynne began to struggle. In 1939, he had to take a job in an automobile factory to pad his meagre boxing income. "Some of these kids coming out of the Olympics now make millions," said Gwynne, in an interview in the 1980s. "If I hadn't worked, I would have starved to death." Gwynne, who in just three quick days under the smogless 1932 California sky had zoomed to the pinnacle of the amateur sporting world, went back to work at the racetrack for fourteen years before turning to the field of recreation as manager of several community centres around Toronto. He never went back to Los Angeles until fifty-two years after the 1932 Games, when the Summer Olympics returned to La La Land in 1984. When they did, so did Gwynne. He watched from ringside as bantamweight Dale Walters won bronze for Canada in '84. The two men shook hands after Walters' final bout. "I could see myself all over again in that young man," said Gwynne.

Danny MacDonald of Toronto advanced from a field of nine competitors to make it to the final of welterweight wrestling. The gold medal eluded him when he was defeated by Jack Van Bebber of the United States. MacDonald assured himself of at least a silver when he beat Jean Foldeak of Germany in the semifinals. Canada was assured at least a silver medal in eight-metre yachting since the US was the only other entry. If only it could always be this easy. The Americans got eight points in the racing to win gold while the Canadian crew of Ronald Maitland, Ernest Cribb, Harry Jones, Peter Gordon, Hubert Wallace and George Gyles took silver with four points. It was almost as easy in the six-metre class, where Canada was guaranteed at least bronze in the three-nation field. And that's what Philip Rogers, Gerald Wilson, Gardner Boultbee and Ken Glass got with their four points. The Swedes won all six of the races for eighteen points and the gold medal while the Americans accumulated twelve points for silver. It was tougher, and much more thrilling, in the Olympic rowing competition on Long Beach harbour as Canada captured the bronze medal in the eights. The Hamilton Leanders crew of Earl Eastwood, Joe Harris, Stanley Stanyar, Harry Fry, Cedric Liddell, William Thoburn, Donald Boal, Albert Taylor and coxswain George MacDonald finished in 6:40.4 to nip Britain (6:40.8) for third place in the field of eight crews. The Americans from the University of California at Berkeley won on the very last stroke in 6:37.6 over the Italian crew from the University of Pisa (6:37.8). Charles "Ned" Pratt and Noel de Mille of Toronto rowed for bronze in the five-entry double sculls competition in 7:27.6 behind the aging Americans Ken Myers, thirty-six, and William Garrett Gilmore, thirty-seven, (7:17.4) and Herbert Buhtz and Gerhard Boetzelen of Germany (7:22.8).

Nobody would or could have blamed Los Angeles if the 1932 Games were humble or scaled back because of the Depression. But never underestimate the Americans' ability to throw a party, which they do with the same fervour and gusto as overthrowing left-leaning governments in countries usually too small to fight back. As they proved again at Los Angeles in 1984, they are the hosts with the most. When the richest dudes in the neighbourhood throw a party, you know chances are it's going to be a pretty good bash. "Some people just thought these Olympics were some real estate racket of Los Angeles and didn't come," said American humourist, entertainer and sage Will Rogers. "You have been badly fooled. You have missed the greatest show, from every angle, that was ever held in America."

BERLIN 1936

August 1 to August 16
4066 Athletes from 49 Nations

Comparing themselves favourably to the ancient Greeks has been an historic conceit of the Germans. So it's hardly surprising that Leni Riefenstahl's landmark film about the 1936 Berlin Olympics, *Olympia*, opens with long and lyrical tracking shots of the Acropolis and Temple of Zeus and nude bodies swaying elegantly in athletic motion. It's also not surprising the film was financed through the offices of Nazi propaganda minister Joseph Goebbels or that it was "Dedicated to the Founder of the Modern Olympic Games: Baron Pierre de Coubertin," who died a year before its 1938 release. For a Nazi regime in love with pageantry and ceremony, the Olympics were the perfect vehicle to bring legitimacy and exposure to National Socialism. The massive rallies at Nuremberg, and then the pomp and spectacular theatre provided by the Olympics, epitomized the controlled public show and fantasia which the Nazis loved and which surrounded the movement from its start. The Nazis and the Olympics were a natural fit. The regime did everything it could to cloak the evil that lay just beneath the shimmering surface of its Games. The ever-burgeoning persecution of the Jews was put on hold while the Olympic festival unfolded. Journalists and fans of all nations and colours were given a warm welcome. Contrary to popular myth, Hitler did not snub Jesse Owens by refusing to shake his hand. The Führer invited three German winners to his box on the opening day of competition but was tired and had left the stadium before the first Afro-American to win, high jumper Cornelius Johnson, had captured his gold. But after being rebuked by IOC president Henri de Baillet-Latour and told to either congratulate everybody or nobody in his private box, Hitler began meeting the German medallists at private German team functions. So he never got the opportunity to accept or ignore Owens' right hand. (If Owens was snubbed by anybody, it was US president Franklin Delano Roosevelt, who didn't invite the black running great to the White House or even send him a note of congratulations.)

Canadians who took part in the 1936 Games remember a remarkable and gilded event highlighted by its excess and precision. But there's no doubt there was a dark undercurrent. That was made abundantly clear when the Greeks, the traditional first entrants into the stadium during the opening ceremony march-in of teams, extended their right arms in the Nazi salute when passing Hitler's box. The German team, perhaps symbolically, was dressed all in white. Berlin was awarded the 1936 Olympics on May 13, 1931, by out-balloting Barcelona 43–16 in the IOC vote. Two years later, Hitler took power and the entire equation changed. The Nazis were against modern sport and its underlying democratic principles which implied that no matter the prejudices in society, all men were equal on the fields of competition. This, of course, was anathema to the Nazis. Fears began spreading through the IOC and international sports organizations that the Nazis would do something extreme and perhaps even declare the 1936 Olympics open only to non-Jewish, white athletes. But Goebbels saw the possibility of the Games as a tremendous propaganda tool and that's how the Nazis approached the project — with smiling faces and within the letter of the Olympic charter.

"We'd heard about Hitler but it didn't mean that much to us at the time," said Doug Peden, who led Canada to the silver medal in basketball at the Berlin Games. "We were just happy to be there. People were waving from the fields as we were driven into town and all the big teams received a large reception when they entered the Athletes' Village. It was a tremendously clean city for the Games and there was no garbage or debris anywhere. We heard that housewives were asked not to hang their laundry out during the two weeks of the Games. There were a hell of a lot of guys in uniform running around ... but all very friendly and helpful. There was no sense at the time that the Olympic ideals were being subverted for Nazi goals. The athletes didn't know. Nothing really detracted from the Games for us. We might have wondered, if some-body had told us what to look for. But I never ever remember thinking I don't feel comfortable being in this country. Other than the Nazi salutes during the opening ceremonies and the Youth Corps, there was no real contact with anything political." Since the basketball team representing Canada at Berlin was the Windsor V-Fords (with four pick-ups from BC), Ford of Germany provided cars to tour the Canadian hoopsters around the Olympic city. "If you wanted anything, a boy all dressed in white would appear at your door in the Village and he would make sure you got what you needed," recalled Chuck Chapman, another star on Canada's silver-medal basketball squad. "I noticed the army ran every-thing. But everything ran extremely smoothly and we really didn't notice anything nasty going on. That's why we couldn't believe what they had in the newspapers about the Games when we got home."

The war of words was being fought at the administrative level, not at the level of the athletes. Jesse Owens told the *New York Times* he experi-enced "absolutely no discrimination at all" in Berlin. But several groups, including those in Canada, labeled the Games a carefully orchestrated charade and called for a boycott. The Nazis promised the German try-outs would be open to all. But they found excuses to cut all Jews good enough to make the German team, including national women's high jump cham-pion Gretel Bergmann. To answer growing criticism from abroad, half-Jewish fencer Helene Mayer was invited back from the US to join the German squad with full "Aryan status." She had won Olympic gold for Germany at Amsterdam in 1928 before moving to Oakland, California in 1932 to teach German at a community college. Her participation, fueled by her Nazi salute on the podium after she captured the silver medal at Berlin, remains controversial. There were some who weren't buying any of it and international calls for a boycott before the Games intensified.

In Canada, however, the boycott efforts were confined to the radical left political fringe. Six Canadian athletes, none of whom was selected to the Olympic team, headed to Barcelona in 1936 to compete in the Olimpiada, an alternative Olympics sponsored by the Soviet and Span-ish Communist Parties. Included in that group was Eva Dawes, who had won bronze for Canada in the women's high jump at the 1932 Los Ange-les Olympics. Dawes was banned from sanctioned Canadian meets because she had competed in the Soviet Union. None of the Canadians going to Barcelona cared much about the Reds, but they gladly accepted an offer by a Toronto communist newspaper to fund their travel. The Olimpiada, however, was never held because of the sudden outbreak of the Spanish Civil War.

But misgivings or not, the real Olympics went on. The night before the Games began, many hundreds of searchlights provided a beautiful and poetic show as their beams converged above the magnificent Olympic Stadium. Those same searchlights would be used later to spot Allied planes on night raids. Tall and handsome Syl Apps — the pole vault gold medallist from the 1934 London British Empire Games and a future NHL star — carried the flag as the 160-member Canadian team entered the stadium before 105,000 spectators during the elaborately staged opening ceremonies held under a glowering and overcast sky. "Everybody wondered how the US, England, Canada and Australia teams were going to salute," says Peden. "The organizers wanted everybody to give Hitler the Nazi salute. And most countries did. We did a half salute, with our arms very low. The Americans and British simply did eyes right, which is what Canada should have done. But what was done was done." Because the Olympic salute resembles the Nazi salute (the extended arm in the former is held lower and more parallel to the ground), there was a great deal of confusion on that August day as to exactly who was giving what salute. The French team gave the Olympic salute. The German crowd, thinking it was the Nazi salute, erupted in a frenzied cheer. Despite some Canadian athletes' reservations about giving what they thought was a half-Nazi salute (there is no such thing), they were actually giving Hitler the Olympic salute. Perhaps, as Peden indicates, Canada should have simply done eyes right, as the British and Americans (the latter also placed their hats over their chests), to avoid any confusion.

The doomed airship *Hindenberg* hovered above the opening ceremonies as some sort of ominous forebear to the Goodyear Blimp. Richard Strauss composed the music for the ceremonies and a massed choir of 2000 voices and a 150-piece orchestra belted out the Olympic Hymn in the stadium (which would escape unscathed in the Allied bombing to come). The impressive marble statues that adorned the stadium were purposely anti-modern. The Nazis detested the "decadent" nature of modern art. The Berlin Games' statues were Greek in style with hard-to-miss Aryan features. Above them hung huge banners adorned by Swastikas. Spiridon Louis, winner of the first Olympic marathon in 1896 at Athens, walked up to Hitler's box and presented him with an olive branch — the symbol of peace — picked from the sacred grove at Mount Olympus. It was the last olive branch Hitler ever accepted.

The first use of television at a sporting event happened during the Berlin Olympics. The muddy and ghostly images were beamed from selected Games venues to eighteen television halls around Berlin and the Athletes' Village. A few thousand perplexed people gathered to watch and gaze into the future. Little did they know that sixty years later, this would be the medium through which 99.9 percent of the spectators would watch the 1996 Atlanta Olympics. "The TV at the Village provided a very fuzzy image," recalls Peden. "But I recognized Syl Apps warming up at the stadium. And here I was miles away from the stadium. It's hard to comprehend now what a thing this was to experience. It was very crude, but to us it was amazing. We didn't even know they were working on that stuff. I didn't even have an inkling about the concept of the thing [television]." But the lasting images of the Berlin Games were provided by film. The first Canadian shown in Riefenstahl's monumental *Olympia* is Betty Taylor of Hamilton. She twice equaled the Olympic record in reaching the final of the women's 80m hurdles. Riefenstahl's cameras (thirty cameramen hovered in zeppelins, climbed atop towers and dug themselves into the jumping pits to shoot 400km of film) show the quick-stepping Taylor getting out to a fast start in the final and appearing headed for victory before Trebisonda Valla and Claudia Testoni of Italy and Anni Steuer of Germany put on tremendous spurts to catch the Canadian at the finish. The four women crossed the line so closely bunched — each in 11.7 seconds — that officials studied the photo-finish for forty minutes before deciding on the placings. Valla was awarded gold, Steuer silver and Taylor bronze. The Italian winner and German second-place finisher gave the Nazi salute on the victory podium while Taylor watched the Red Ensign go up for third place with her arms firmly down.

Another Canadian accorded a role in *Olympia* is Phil Edwards, who is seen leading at the final turn of the men's 800m final before being overtaken by the massively-built American John Woodruff. It was actually Edwards' second lead of the final. As usual, the Canadian stormed in front to start the race. Woodruff, who was boxed in, slowed to almost a walk at 300m and let the other runners pass him. He then swerved out wide and slowly won back lost ground with his almost-scary ten-foot stride. It's estimated Woodruff was so far on the outside that he ran an additional 50m in the race. He took the lead only to feel Edwards' hand on his shorts. The Montrealer wanted to get past. And he did. But Woodruff summoned from within a powerful kick to win back the lead on the final bend and take the gold medal in 1:52.9. Mario Lanzi of Italy also passed Edwards to take silver in 1:53.3. Edwards was third in 1:53.6 for the fifth bronze medal of his Olympic career. Two days later, Edwards finished fifth in 3:50.4 in the celebrated 1500m final of the 1936 Olympics — one of the greatest foot-races of all time. The race was won in a world record 3:47.8 by another doctor-to-be, the brilliant but troubled New Zealand genius Jack Lovelock, who died under the wheels of a New

York subway train at age thirty-nine in 1949. Edwards hung tough in the stellar field but couldn't get his patented early lead to last for long. He jumped out like a rabbit to the front but silver medallist Glenn Cunningham of the US grabbed the lead away at about 400m. Edwards and the rest of the top-five finishers each bettered the old Olympic record in a race that was a classic of tactics and speed.

The biggest shock of the Games for Canada, and it was a pleasant one, was provided by the previously little-known and lightly regarded John Loaring of the University of Western Ontario. Loaring was a good athlete but had competed in the 400m hurdles only once before in his life. That one time was good enough to qualify for the Berlin Olympics. The 400m/440-yard hurdles first came to prominence at the 1928 Amsterdam Olympics and 1930 Hamilton British Empire Games, where gold was won both times by the elegant Lord Burghley. He was the personification of the gentleman athlete, and the man who ran around the Great Court at Cambridge's Trinity College in the time it took the famous clock in the tower to bong twelve times for noon (a feat falsely attributed to Harold Abrahams in the film *Chariots of Fire*).

Nobody even remotely expected Loaring to join Burghley's athletic class. But that's what the Canadian did in winning silver at the Berlin Olympics and gold two years later at the Sydney British Empire Games. On both occasions, Loaring bettered Burghley's times (52.7 seconds to 53.4 over 400m at the Olympics and 52.9 seconds to 54.4 over the 440 yards at the British Empire Games). Loaring easily survived his heat and semifinal at Berlin and seemed to be getting stronger on a muggy August fourth day. But Glenn Hardin of the US was unbeatable in the 400 hurdles. His world record of 50.6 seconds, set in 1934, would stand for close to two decades. After his second-place finish to Rob Tisdall of Ireland in the 1932 Olympic final, Hardin never lost another race. Hardin, Loaring and Miguel White of the Philippines all flashed past the leading Joe Patterson of the US down the stretch. It was Hardin first in 52.4 seconds, Loaring second for the silver medal in 52.7 and White third in 52.8. Loaring missed another medal by less than an inch. A furious anchor leg battle against Rudolf Harbig (later the world record holder in the 800m) resulted in the German star nosing in at the wire just ahead of Loaring for the bronze medal in the men's 4x400m relay. The British won gold in 3:09.0, the Americans were second in 3:11.0 and the Germans and the Canadian team of Loaring, Edwards, Bill Fritz and Marshall Limon both clocked 3:11.8.

Dropped batons cost Canada a medal but enabled it to win another in the relays. Germany set a world record of 46.4 seconds in the first heat of the women's 4x100, a mark that would last until 1952. The Canadian squad of Dorothy Brookshaw, Mildred Dolson, Hilda Cameron and Nova Scotia great Aileen Meagher also made the final. The Germans were well in the lead when they dropped the final pass. Canada would have finished fourth but the German miscue allowed them to slip in for the bronze medal in 47.8 seconds. The Americans — led by 1928 Amsterdam 100m champion Betty Robinson and Berlin 100m champion Helen Stephens — won in 46.9. Hitler summoned the four tearful German runners to his box and consoled them. The Canadian men's 4x100 relay team was swift and a real medal threat. An indication of the strength of the foursome was that three of them had made it to the semifinals of the individual 100m. Howie McPhee of Vancouver ran his 100m heat in a time that would have won at seven previous Olympics. Lee Orr, also of Vancouver, tied the Olympic record of 10.3 seconds in one of his heats. But few athletes have had to rebound from such an unforgiving moment as did McPhee, Orr, Bruce Humber of Victoria and Martin Naylor of Toronto in the 4x100. The four Canadians were tearing along and seemed headed for a silver medal in the 4x100 final behind the storied US team of Jesse Owens, Ralph Metcalfe, Frank Wykoff and Foy Draper. The Americans had entered the event under a cloud on controversy when the only two Jews on the entire US track and field team — Marty Glickman and Sam Stoller — were replaced at the last moment by Owens and Metcalfe. It was thought Owens and Metcalfe had enjoyed enough glory in Berlin and that Glickman and Stoller would race the 4x100 as originally planned. But the two Jewish runners returned home as the only members of the US track and field contingent who didn't see action in Berlin, a fact that caused the American team a great deal of embarrassment considering the political atmosphere in which the 1936 Games were held.

The Americans easily pulled ahead in the final as Owens closed out his legendary Olympics by winning his fourth gold medal. The US won in a world record 39.8 seconds, a mark that stood for twenty years. Canada, meanwhile, was on a solid silver pace. But then came the final, fatal baton exchange. Somewhere between what should have been a simple hand-off and the silver medal, came an unforgiving little slip, perhaps just a quick jerk of the wrist or something equally as simple — and deadly. McPhee attempted to give the baton to Orr. But it fell to the ground. Orr, stunned, scooped it up quickly. But the damage had been done. The silver medal vanished into thin air. Italy, Germany and Argentina all rushed ahead. Canada finished fifth in 42.7 seconds. But the four Canadians always refused to dwell on the disappointment. "All I will ever remember from my Olympic experiences is what a great, great experience of friendship it was among the athletes of the world," said Humber, when once asked about the dropped baton. Humber went on to coach the Canadian track and field teams at the 1950 Auckland British Empire Games and 1952 Helsinki Olympics. What made marching into the Helsinki stadium even more special for Humber was that agonizing moment at the 1936 Olympics when he and his mates saw the silver medal slip out of their hands as easily as a baton falls to the ground. "While he lost the medal in Berlin, he never worried about it," said Archie McKinnon of Victoria, who coached either the Canadian track or swim teams at four Olympic Games, including the tracksters at Berlin in 1936. Humber was inducted into the BC Sports Hall of Fame in 1970, the same year two Olympic medallists — skier Nancy Greene and swimmer Elaine Tanner — were also inducted. Owens, who remained a good friend of Humber's, came up to Vancouver for the occasion.

John and Margaret Naismith of Lanark County near Almonte in the Ottawa Valley were solid, Scottish farming pioneers of the mid-1800s. It would have been impossible for them to imagine that their second son, born unassumingly at the height of the Victorian era in 1861, would have such an effect on the modern sporting world — including at the 1992 Barcelona Olympics, where the publicity-generating machine known as the US Dream Team basketball squad hijacked much of the agenda. There's no way Dr. James A. Naismith himself could have known the ultimate ramifications of those now-famous peach baskets he got the janitor to nail to the balcony of the Springfield, Mass., YMCA gym in December of 1891 to keep a class of eighteen students amused and fit in the void between the football and baseball seasons. But so it was that a Canadian, in that unassuming Canadian way, bequeathed basketball to the world. Thus it was perhaps only fitting that Canadians should play a significant role when the game finally became an Olympic medal sport in 1936. The national men's club champion was to represent Canada at Berlin and the Windsor V-Fords defeated the Victoria Dominoes in the final. The Fords supplemented their squad for the Olympics with three pick-ups from the Dominoes (Doug Peden and Art and Chuck Chapman) and also Bob Osborne from Vancouver. Despite its stature today, basketball was an Olympic newcomer and treated as some sort of poor cousin at Berlin. The edifices the Nazis constructed for their Games were striking. The 20,000-seat outdoor pool was adjacent to the imposing 105,000-seat main stadium in an area of town which became the British sector of occupied Berlin during the Cold War. The outdoor 25,000-seat gymnastics venue was fitted snugly into a natural bowl in the earth in a pleasant wooded area.

Basketball, however, was held on some old outdoor clay tennis courts surrounded by about 2000 temporary bleachers. Naismith, the inventor of the game, was hardly accorded the hero's welcome one might have expected. He was invited as a guest of honour but when he got to the Olympics, there weren't even any tickets waiting for him. The American team (Naismith had been a well-respected physical education professor at the University of Kansas) arranged passes for him to attend the games and drummed up an impromptu parade and reception in his honour at the Athletes' Village, where the twenty-one teams entered in the inaugural Olympic hoops tournament were residing. Only about 200 people bothered to attend the Naismith functions. To add further insult to officialdom's apparent indifference to Naismith's presence, the oddly European-dominated International Basketball Federation wanted to tinker with his game. During the Olympics, the IBF passed a rule that banned all players taller than six-foot-three. The Americans, who had three such players in the line-up, objected and the IBF backed down. Today, the building housing Canada's amateur sports bureaucracy in suburban Ottawa sits on James Naismith Drive and Phog Allen Fieldhouse at the University of Kansas is also on a street named James Naismith Drive. Naismith may have felt snubbed at the Berlin Olympics, but the graduate of McGill was eventually inducted into the Canadian Sports Hall of Fame and the Canadian Olympic Hall of Fame. That he is a charter member of the Basketball Hall of Fame in Springfield, Mass., is a given. The old educator died in 1939, three years after watching the game he invented become an Olympic medal sport.

Canada's small but quick hoops squad ripped through the preliminary round-robin with a 4–0 record. The big game was against Uruguay, where the Canadians found themselves down by eight points with six minutes remaining. Peden, an outstanding all-around star in several sports and a member of the Canadian Sports Hall of Fame, scored eight points in the waning moments to pull it out and give Canada the win. Peden equaled the entire output of Canada's opponent in the semifinals, rifling twenty-one points as the Canadians advanced to the gold medal final with a smart 41–21 win over Poland. It rained heavily the night before and day of the final, turning the clay courts into a quagmire. The ball wouldn't bounce, making height a huge advantage. The American squad averaged 6' 6" in size to Canada's 6' and simply threw the ball up to their tall men standing near the basket. That was during the few times the horrendous conditions allowed anything resembling basketball to be played. The US led 15–4 at halftime in the bizarre game, as players slipped and slid all over the court and the sopping wet ball squirted every which way. "The Americans were so much taller than us that our only chance of beating them for the gold medal was speed," said Peden. "But with footing what it was, we couldn't make sharp cuts or dribble the ball." The teams scored just four points each in the second half as the US won the gold medal with a 19–8 victory. Chuck Chapman, whom Harlem Globetrotters' founder Abe Saperstein described as one of the two best Canadian players he had ever seen, says it is doubtful any Olympic final in any sport has been contested in such deplorable conditions. "It was as if horses had ploughed up the court before the game," he said. "You couldn't bounce the ball." Adding to the surreal quality of the game were the improvised American singlets and shorts (the US locker room was robbed during the team's final round-robin game). But that gold-medal victory over Canada represented the fourth contest in what became a sixty-two-game US winning streak in Olympic men's basketball, stretching all the way to 1972 and the controversial loss in the final at Munich. Canada's silver remains the last medal won by this country in a team sport at the Summer Olympics. The silver medals were handed to Peden, brothers Art and Chuck Chapman, Osborne, Gordon Aitchison, Jan Allison, Jimmy Stewart, Malcolm "Red" Wiseman, Edward John Dawson and Irving "Toots" Meretsky. The Windsorites wanted to take the BC players' medals to Ontario and distribute them to the players who didn't make the trip — and then have replicas cast and sent to the Chapmans, Peden and Osborne. But the British Columbians were having none of it. "Art just threw his medal in his suitcase and said 'forget it,' and we all did the same," chuckles Chuck Chapman.

The 1936 Olympics saw the addition of another sport with notable Canadian roots. Olympic canoes are direct descendants of the North American aboriginal birch-bark canoe — known to most of us through the outlandish Technicolor of 1940s and 1950s Hollywood films — while Olympic kayaks derive their lineage from the hunting vessels used by the northern Inuit. Canadian-made canoes, based on the form used by this land's natives, became one of this nation's first export success stories. Canadian canoes appeared on rivers and lakes all over Europe in the 1880s. The sport came to be dominated by Central Europeans and Canada's success in it over the years has varied. But it's fitting that Canada's only gold medal of the Berlin Olympics was provided through the 1000m Canadian singles canoeing event. It's ironic, however, that the gold was won by someone who had to pay his own way to Germany to compete in an intrinsically Canadian activity because the COA refused to fund the canoeists. There were only six competitors in the 1936 Olympic Canadian-class 1000m singles canoeing event at Grunau, thirty-seven

Francis Amyot of Ottawa gets a lift after winning gold at the 1936 Berlin Olympics.

kilometres east of the Olympic Stadium. But thirty-one-year-old Francis Amyot of Ottawa was the best of them. He wanted to be a rower but couldn't afford the money for a shell. So he built a canoe, instead. Smart move. The strapping 6' 2" and 200-pounder won the national singles title seven times and became fanatical about the sport, spending thousands of hours on bodies of water all over Ontario. Three Ottawa Rough Rider football players were glad he did. While out training one Sunday, Amyot saved the trio from drowning in June of 1933. They were being carried to their apparent deaths on the treacherous Deschenes Rapids. The three were on the brink of the rapids. But Amyot's speed enabled him to reach them before they were pulled under and his strength allowed him to stroke back upstream against the current while the three large football-ers held onto his canoe. That speed and strength held Amyot in good stead at the Olympics, where he led from the start before being over-taken by Bohuslav Karlik of Czechoslovakia at 750m. But the Ottawa paddler was relentless in his stalking of the Czech and eventually re-gained the lead with about 50m left and won the gold medal going away in 5:32.1 to Karlik's 5:36.9. Amyot, who served in the Navy during the Second World War before dying at age fifty-seven in 1962, wasn't the only canoeist to embarrass the COA at Berlin. Like Amyot, Frank Saker and Harvey Charters relied on the kindness of friends and strangers in Ottawa to raise the money to send them to Berlin. Like Amyot, they responded with medals — silver in the 10,000m doubles and bronze in the 1000m doubles. The odds were with the two — there were only five entries in each of those events.

Wrestler Joe Schleimer of Toronto was another originally left off the Canadian team but then allowed to compete after paying his own way to Berlin. He turned out to be yet another who embarrassed the COA's selection process. The wrestling and boxing were held in adjacent rings at Deutschland Hall. Fans would turn to whatever sport was providing the most exciting bout. In this rather odd arrangement, Schleimer advanced to the final stages in his freestyle class which included combatants from sixteen nations. The large American squad was made up mostly of grapplers from Oklahoma, many of whom aggressively and vociferously challenged some of the rulings made by the referees. But unless you spoke German, the refs just sort of shrugged. Schleimer was one of three to make it to the welterweight final round with Frank Lewis of Cushing, Oklahoma, winning gold, Ture Andersson of Sweden silver and the 155-pound Canadian bronze.

A spotlight highlighted each flag bearer as he walked around the track during the haunting night-time closing ceremonies. Before the ceremony was over, Peden cut off the swastika banner that was clipped to the standard above the Red Ensign. That swastika is now in the BC Sports Hall of Fame at BC Place Stadium in Vancouver. It is a reminder that beneath the grand and classical trappings of the 1936 Games lay their true, darker motives. Before Riefenstahl's *Olympia* fades out on the closing ceremonies, there are wondrous images of the Olympic divers spiraling and pirouetting in such an evocative mid-air ballet that it almost makes you want to cry. Silhouetted darkly against the sky, those divers are a celebration of the human body. No narration is needed and nationality is irrelevant in the sequence as facial features are purposely blurred. The counterpoint to that were the more than 100,000 spectators at the closing ceremonies, most with their arms raised and shrieking "Sieg Heil!" Hitler and his architect of choice, Albert Speer, envisioned for the future a glistening white stadium that would seat 400,000 and host every Olympic festival after those already awarded. "In 1940, the Olympic Games will take place in Tokyo," Hitler told Speer. "But thereafter, they will take place in Germany for all time to come in this [proposed new] stadium." Wrong on both counts.

LONDON 1948

July 29 to August 14
4099 Athletes from 59 Nations

You see its famous dome spires — invariably, it seems, against a lead-grey London sky — long before the above-ground subway train pulls into Wembley station. They are as instantaneously recognizable as the spires atop Churchill Downs, home of the Kentucky Derby. But unlike at Wembley, there has at least been a Canadian winner at the Derby. Adorning the archway walls of the main entrance to the aging but still entrancing Wembley Stadium is a large plaque listing all the winners at the 1948 Summer Olympics. Not a single Canadian name is there to be read. There have been several poor performances by Canada at the Summer Games, in terms of medals won, and London '48 is certainly near the top of that inglorious list. A single Dutch housewife easily outperformed the entire nation of Canada.

London provided a symbolic backdrop for the first Games since the Nazi Olympics of 1936. Still pockmarked and bomb-scarred from the Second World War, the city's stubbornness in refusing to fold in the face of overwhelming German air superiority was an inspiration to millions of Allied supporters around the world. So what city could have been a better choice for trying to put together a patchwork Games as the world emerged from the shadow of horror? The meticulous and organized Japanese had been well on their way to hosting the 1940 Summer Olympics, with thousands of people put to work and millions spent on sixteen sites around Tokyo. But when the nation's military leaders dragged the country into conflict against China in 1938, they told the Olympic organizers all resources would have to be directed to the war effort and work would stop immediately on Games preparations. The IOC turned to the plucky Finns, who offered to take the Games on short notice. The 1940 Games were shifted from Tokyo to Helsinki in 1938. The 1944 Games were awarded to London in 1939. But the outbreak of the Second World War knocked the entire sports world out of the ring. After the war, the IOC met in 1946 to award the 1948 Summer Games to Helsinki. But the Finns were still shell-shocked from the fighting and declined the offer. Thus the Games went to London instead. It wasn't much time to prepare, but then again, nobody was expecting much.

The 1948 Games were utilitarian but merry. London was still under rationing. Shortage of materials was a problem. Much of the bombing damage had been cleaned up but evidence of the Blitz was still there if you looked. The world, however, was once again ready for a circus. Improvisation was the order of the day, and the British, who had gone through several years of deprivation, were masters now at making do. Even more than when times are good — and when have they been good since the war for this declining world power? — the British seem to shine when in a pinch.

A temporary cinder running track was installed at Wembley and many of the buildings from the 1924 Empire Exhibition and venues from the 1934 British Empire Games were adapted for Games use. The athletes were housed in schools and military hutments at Uxbridge and Richmond Park. Berlin '36, this was not. The biggest complaint was the kitchen. The Canadians weren't used to such fatty food. Even the potatoes were soaked in fat before serving. Basics such as milk, steak and eggs were not available so a few of the more affluent teams, including the Americans and Australians, brought along their own food. The bizarrest sight was of the Aussies sharing their meals with the host British athletes. The cash-strapped Labour government of Clement Atlee came up with £600,000 to stage the Games, and the thrifty Londoners even managed to turn a profit of £15,000 on the event. Take that, Peter Ueberroth. The Canadians, Aussies, New Zealanders, South Africans and Indians — who had provided human lives and material to imperial Britain's war effort — were especially well received during the opening ceremonies. The Olympic torch was lit by Cambridge student-athlete John Mark,

*King George VI,
monarch of Britain and
the Commonwealth,
opens the 1948 London
Olympics while the
words of Baron Pierre
de Coubertin look down
from the scoreboard.*

who had been nourished during the war by food parcels sent 19,000km from the tiny town of Greymouth, New Zealand. The Americans also received a huge ovation. Germany and Japan were not invited to the Games. The Soviets were, but they declined.

If a Games city should be true to itself, London certainly was. Especially in terms of weather. The Olympic track events were held mainly under dark, sodden skies that regularly spilled large amounts of rain on the competitors. That sombre weather was, sadly, a perfect backdrop for the Canadian contingent. It was to prove a hard-luck Games for the 148 Canadian athletes and officials, who were sent by the COA at a cost of $107,000 and arrived after a six-day voyage from Halifax. Twenty-seven Canadians finished in the top six but only three medals were won.

Compare that with the performance of Fanny Blankers-Koen of the Netherlands, who accounted for four gold medals all on her own — a fact even more remarkable in that there were only nine women's track and field events contested at the London Games. As an unknown teenager competing in Berlin in 1936, Blankers-Koen was happy just to get Jesse Owens' autograph. When the war broke out and her lowland country was brutally invaded by the Germans, Koen had every reason to believe that autograph would be the highlight of her Olympic career. But after marrying track coach Jim Blankers and having two children, Fanny Blankers-Koen was back at age thirty.

Was she ever. The woman, a self-described "housewife" who left the Games before they ended to take care of her children, won gold in the women's 100m and 200m, 80m hurdles and 4x100 relay. She was given a challenge in the 100m by two Canadians. Slim and quick Viola Myers of Toronto and high schooler Pat Jones of New Westminster, BC, had breezed through a field of thirty-eight runners from twenty-one countries to make the final on a muddy Wembley track. There they came up against the incomparable Blankers-Koen, who was off like a shot and won by three yards in 11.9 seconds. The Dutchwoman was the lone non-Commonwealth runner in the final but easily dispatched silver medallist Dorothy Manley of Britain, bronze medallist Aussie-great Shirley Strickland, fourth place Myers, fifth place Jones and sixth place Cynthia Thompson of Jamaica. "It was very exciting but I wish I had done better," said Jones. "I got off to a slow start. I had run better than that in the heats." Only seventeen years old, Jones more than redeemed herself on the anchor leg of the 4x100m relay final. The Canadian foursome of Jones, Myers, Nancy MacKay of Toronto and Diane Foster of Vancouver was in fifth place when Jones received the baton from Foster on the final pass. Jones cranked it up and sped down the stretch to give Canada the bronze medal in 47.8 seconds. Blankers-Koen was even swifter. She received the baton in fourth place on the final pass but managed to pass Joyce King of Australia just inches before the wire to become the only woman to win four track and field gold medals in one Olympics. The Dutchwomen clocked 47.5 and the Aussies 47.6. "I did well to help us come through for the bronze medal but I just couldn't catch her [Blankers-Koen]," said Jones. "She was better trained. She trained and was very athletic. We didn't have those kind of full-time coaches she had in Europe." Jones' coach at the time was Charlie Mackie, a New Westminster policeman who coached track during his off hours from work. Jones started running at elementary school meets and church picnics and it was perhaps obvious to some she was destined to win an Olympic medal as a teenager. "It was just a natural thing," said Jones. "I didn't train that much, so it must have come natural. Blankers-Koen was better trained." When she returned to Amsterdam to a heroine's welcome, the grateful citizens presented Blankers-Koen with a bicycle "so she wouldn't have to run so much."

James Varaleau of Quebec finished sixth in light heavyweight weightlifting at the London Games with 112.5-kilo lifts in the press and snatch and 140 in the jerk for a 365 total. The silver medallist in the event, with a 380 total, was Harold Sakata of the United States. He became better known later to millions of moviegoers as the evil henchman Oddjob, with the lethal bowler hat flung like a frisbee, in the James Bond film *Goldfinger*. The basketball competition at London was bizarre with twenty-three teams in a mad scramble. Canada won six games and finished above .500 but found itself placed ninth overall while Chile (4–4) was given sixth place and Korea (3–5) eighth. The Canadian team launched a protest but to no avail. The hoops tournament was strange beyond just the placings. A referee was knocked out cold in a game between Chile and Iraq. The Iraqis twice lost by more than 100 points. A tiny Chinese guard scored a lay-up after scooting between the legs of seven-foot American centre Bob "Foothills" Kurland of Oklahoma A&M. In the days before the goaltending rule, Kurland would routinely knock away opponents' shots as they were about to enter his team's basket.

Czechoslovakian army officer Emil Zatopek was a magnificent winner in the 10,000m on the Wembley track. There were twenty-seven competitors from fifteen nations in that event. The odds were considerably better for Canadian Norman Lane in the gruelling Canadian singles 10,000m canoeing event, which attracted only five competitors. Lane finished exactly in the middle of the pack to capture the bronze medal in 1:04:35.3. Frantisek Capek of Prague, Czechoslovakia, used an unusually shaped canoe that allowed for better manoeuverability to win the gold medal in 1:02:05.2. American Frank Havens was second in 1:02:40.4. Douglas Bennett continued the brief tradition started by Francis Amyot at Berlin by capturing another medal for Canada in the Canadian singles 1000m canoeing event. Silver medallist Bennett was a strong second in the field of six competitors in 5:53.3, but was well off the pace set by gold medallist Josef Holecek of Czechoslovakia (5:42.0). Both men, in turn, were in another area code compared to the blistering pace of 5:32.1 Amyot set in winning gold twelve years earlier at Berlin.

Jan Vissers of Belgium lost to Gerald Dreyer, a nineteen-year-old clerk from Johannesburg, in the lightweight boxing final at the London Olympics. One of those medals could have been — some say should have been — Canada's. Eddie Haddad of Winnipeg, winner that year of the Norton Hervey Crowe Award as the outstanding amateur athlete in Canada, held the Canadian amateur lightweight title from 1948 to 1952. A supply assistant at Naden, the Canadian naval base at Esquimalt, BC, Haddad was Canada's great boxing hope at London. A quick and clever southpaw, with a lead and follow-up that appeared like flashes out of nowhere, Haddad hammered his way past three opponents into the Olympic quarterfinals. The quarterfinal bout between Vissers and Haddad was a good one with both men landing stinging blows. But it seemed to most that Haddad had easily scored the most direct punches and would be given the decision. The crowd howled its disapproval when Vissers' name was announced as the victor. Haddad sank into his corner with tears welling in his eyes. The Canadian coaches joined the crowd in hurling insults at the judges. An official protest was launched by the Canadian team. The protest was considered and then disallowed. Vissers' victory would stand. The Canadian Press news agency labeled it "a raw decision." Raw or not, it stood and Haddad was denied a semifinal berth. He recovered from the disappointment of London and continued to dominate amateur lightweight boxing in Canada. Haddad never bitched about the decision, which some fight observers still call one of the worst ever made in Games boxing (and that's saying a lot, considering Olympic boxing is about as controversy-plagued as you can get). Hard luck continued to follow Haddad in international events. He made the semifinals of the 1950 British Empire Games in Auckland, New Zealand, but was again stopped short of the title.

Because the boxing ring was located on a platform built over the Empire Games Pool at Wembley, the bouts at the London Olympics took place as soon as the swimming and diving competitions ended. The shadows of the boxers danced and played on the bluish-green water below. That was the nature of the 1948 Games, which were staged more for practicality than show. But it was still the Olympics. "The size of the whole thing was almost too much to take in," said Canadian 5000m track champion and record holder Cliff Salmond, who along with Bill Parnell and Jack Hutchins was among a strong group of BC middle-distance runners. "I was just a skinny kid and awed by the whole thing. There were 80,000 people in Wembley the day of my race. We were just a bunch of kids back then who ran on grass fields back home. There were pot holes and sometimes you ran uphill and around things. That's how poor our track facilities were at home. But we were a dedicated bunch. Yet still back then, when it came to track, all Canadians believed that the Swedes and Finns were supermen. We were, in effect, intimidated."

HELSINKI 1952

July 19 to August 3
4925 Athletes from 69 Nations

As unrelenting rain pelted the Olympic Stadium during the opening ceremonies of the 1952 Summer Games and the Soviets stepped in military precision through pools of muddy water on the cinder track like officers marching off to war, neither they nor the Americans dipped their flags when passing the reviewing stand. The old world order was dead. The mantle had been passed from the spent Britain, France and Germany. In the new neighbourhood, the Americans and Soviets were the bullies of the block and they lowered their colours for no one. And certainly not for each other. This was 1952 and the Cold War was thriving in all its icy fury. "The Soviets sought not a place in the sun, but the sun itself," said cold warrior John Foster Dulles, US Secretary of State from 1952 to 1959. "They would not tolerate compromise on goals, only on tactics." And one of those tactics clearly was to seek moral victory on the battlefield of sport. But there appeared a twenty-three-year-old woman, dreamlike in flowing white night gown against the slate grey day of the 1952 opening ceremonies. Believing herself to be an ancient Greek goddess, she entered through the main gate to the track and did a half circle of it and mounted the official podium as 70,000 looked on — many believing she was part of the official ceremony. She reached the microphone and began to utter the word "Peace" before being dragged away by police. Barbara Rotraut Pleyer was later described as a "half-deranged" West German student who had come to address "Humanity." And so it was that the Angel of Peace appeared in the first-ever Olympic meeting between the post-war blocs of East and West.

Maybe somebody was listening to her. This first meeting between the communist and capitalist athletes was almost a love-in. So fascinated were they by each other, that not even the separate Athletes' Village the Soviets demanded for their performers — and those from the satellite countries of Poland, Bulgaria, Romania, Hungary and Czechoslovakia — could keep the two sides apart. Less than half the 1075 Eastern Bloc athletes in Helsinki attended the Soviet flag raising, "peace" speeches and unveiling of a twelve-foot portrait of Stalin in their Village, which was quickly dubbed the Otaniemi Sportsgrad. Most were too busy getting chummy with their capitalist counterparts in the Western athletes' Village in the northern district of Kapyla.

Canada's rowing shells had been smashed and severely damaged in a ship's storeroom during a North Atlantic gale and the Soviets offered assistance. "They said they were very sorry to hear about it and will do anything to help," said Canadian team boatbuilder Gordon Jennens of Kelowna. The Soviets offered Canada some of their shells but the Canadians, not knowing how to respond to the surprise gesture, turned them down with a polite no thanks. Jennens worked around the clock to fix the Canadian boats, but to no avail. The rowers had to borrow pre-war shells from the Swedes in order to compete. Not surprisingly, the Canadian oarsmen bombed in the '52 Olympics and perhaps shouldn't have said no to the Red gift-horse offer of modern shells. The Americans, for their part, extended the hand of friendship to the Soviet athletes. When the Soviet boxers wandered in to watch the Americans train, instead of getting the heave, they received a warm invitation from coach Pete Mello to stay and watch. After noticing the Soviets taking notes on crumpled scraps of yellowing paper, US boxing team manager Dr. Barondale gave them sheets of white stationary and told them to write away to their heart's content. By comparison, the Canadian boxers got booted out by South American coaches when they dropped in to watch the Argentinians train. You go figure. So the Canadians went over to the Philippines camp, where they were invited to stay and spar. "That's okay, they're little guys," said featherweight puncher Len Walters of Vancouver, father of 1984 L.A. Olympics boxing bronze medallist Dale Walters, who himself made it to the quarterfinals of the 1952 Games with a broken hand before losing in a decision to Leonard Leisching of South Africa.

But the Soviet hierarchy was less concerned about goodwill than gold medals. Sports, and the Olympics in particular, were clearly targeted as propaganda instruments to show the superiority of the communist system. The differences between Canada and the Soviet Union at Helsinki were jarring, even taking into consideration the vast population difference between the two countries — then at 14.4 million to 200 million. The Canadian Olympic Association fell short of its Helsinki budgetary goal of $150,000 and had to cut the size of the team. Only $103,972 had been raised, and with a $10,000 carry-over from 1948, the total was $113,972. In the days before Sport Canada and federal funding, it was catch as catch can. Money was not raised by public donations, as in most other countries at the time, but by approaching large corporations in Canada. The Ontario government chipped in $7,500 and the city of Toronto $2,500 to bump Ontario's overall private and public total to $26,835. The BC government promised $3,000 to help bump up that province's paltry private donations of $5,000 but never delivered. Petty jealousies arose. Ontario track and field officials were irate when two of their athletes were left off the Olympic team to make room for BC athletes. BC had seven swimmers on the team while Ontario's lone aquatic performer had to be dropped, again eliciting howls of complaint that BC had raised less than one-fifth the money Ontario did for the trip to Helsinki. Hamilton business people raised $3,900, only to have hometown diver Irene MacDonald (who rebounded to win bronze in 1956) and thrower Jo Brennan left off the team for lack of funds; they were also bitter that Nova Scotia and Newfoundland governments flatly refused to give any money despite having one athlete each on the Canadian team. Meanwhile, it was estimated in 1952 that the Soviet Union was spending one billion rubles (about $250 million) annually to promote their athletic programs and that twice that amount was being spent by Soviet industry to produce sports equipment. Aside from the elite component, Soviet trade unions supported a wide range of sports clubs to which citizens could belong for the price of a pair of socks. It was no surprise this sporting juggernaut washed over Helsinki like a red wave and challenged the US for supremacy.

Canada's athletes remained short of cash once they got to the Games. Three Canadian boxers were so desperate for extra funds at Helsinki that they went into the washing and pressing business in the Athletes' Village. They printed up cards which read: "Canadian Olympic Cleaning and Pressing." The venture went well until one of them went to answer the door but left the hot iron sitting on a pair of pants owned by a very large Japanese wrestler. The hole was hard to hide and profits went into purchasing a replacement pair of trousers for one angry wrestler. The Canadian basketball players were embarrassed when they had no gifts to give their opponents in the traditional exchange before the game. They received minted club medals from the Italians, books from the Hungarians and crested money clips from the Israelis, but could offer nothing in return. Canadian athletes in Helsinki weren't even provided with extra team pins to trade and so the Canadian pins became a collector's item in the Village.

A team of seventy Canadian athletes and officials arrived in Helsinki July 7 by plane from Montreal. Waiting for them there was twenty-four-year-old Jack Burney of Vancouver, who had paid $100 of his own money to come from Germany where he was serving with the US army. He believed he was on the Canadian team but was in for a huge shock and broke into tears when informed the opposite. Burney had bettered the Canadian qualifying standard of 54.5 seconds in the 400m hurdles a total of eight times in 1952 and was led to believe by some administrators that would be enough. But COA president Sidney Dawes of Montreal said only those who made the standard at the Olympic trials in Hamilton were eligible. Burney was shattered. "I've been training for the last six months," he lamented. "I've sent my times to Canada and it looks as if somebody's pulled a fast one. The US army gave me a thirty-day furlough to come here. I turned down a chance to go to the US Olympic trials — the army volunteered to pay my expenses — because I wanted to compete for my own country. And now I get this." Canada, which performed so poorly at Helsinki save for three medal performances and a couple of fourths, could ill afford to lose somebody like Burney. But when have amateur sports bodies in this country ever done the logical thing? "Burney was Canada's potential point-getter in track at the '52 Olympics," said Fred Rowell, the BC rep to the national Olympic track and field committee. "How many men have we got who can beat an American Olympic runner?" Not many, as it turned out. Henry Roxborough of Toronto, a long-time observer of the Canadian Olympic scene, was more biting than Rowell when discussing the 1952 team. "I have observed some athletes wearing the Maple Leaf who would have conferred a favour upon their native land if they had stayed home and gone for a walk with the family dog," he said. Ouch!

The first five days of the 1952 Olympics went miserably for Canada. "Everybody likes the Canadians at Helsinki," wrote *Toronto Star* sports editor Milt Dunnell. "Since we're not beating too many folks, there's no reason why they should be sore at us, excepting of course, our boys who are in the pants-pressing business." The July 24, 1952, edition of the *Star* shows pictures of New Zealander Yvette Williams' winning leap in the women's long jump and American Cy Young's winning throw in the javelin with the caption: "Everything and everybody seems jet-propelled at Helsinki — except Canadians." A total of thirty-three countries had points after the first five days of the Games (in those days, tables were kept and points awarded for finishes in the top six). But Canada wasn't even on the board yet. "While the Americans and athletes from some Commonwealth countries are stalking records and collecting scoring points, Canada is faced with the humiliating prospect of finishing the Olympic track and field program without a point for the first time in history," lamented the usually unemotional Canadian Press. "Canada's athletes can't keep up in the sizzling pace that kept the stadium in a constant uproar."

Athletes outside North America live for the Olympics. The Games are the pinnacle of sporting conquest, so the sports contested in the Olympics become a part of the national consciousness. But that's outside North America. "They say of the Olympics, the importance is not that you win but that you compete, and that is right as rain," Dunnell noted. "But there is nothing in the rules that says you have to lose all the time. We will continue to lose as long as track and field is something in which there is a flurry twice every four years when there's a junket to the Olympics and the Empire [Commonwealth] Games in the offing. In a way, it's a matter of national emphasis. If Canadians prefer to throw a football instead of a javelin, or run ninety feet to first base instead of 400m, that is their privilege. But as long as track and field is a poor relative at home, you cannot blame the kids who are doing their best here at Helsinki."

But then came Day Six. And lightning struck out of nowhere — not at the track, but the shooting ranges. Meet George Genereux, a lean and crew-cut seventeen-year-old high school student from Nutana Collegiate in Saskatoon, who used to tag along with his dad hunting prairie chickens. The younger Genereux clearly learned well during those excursions. The unflappable teenager was set to star in one of the most nerve-wracking finals of the entire Helsinki Games as he aimed for gold in the trap shooting event. The field of forty competitors from twenty-two countries quickly narrowed: after the first day Genereux stood in second place behind Galliano Rossini, a twenty-five-year-old army lieutenant from Ancona, Italy. Genereux stormed to the lead on the second and final day and finished the competition with 192 points out of a possible 200, an achievement made even more noteworthy considering he had been shooting seriously in competition for only four years. Rossini had faded to seventh place and the only shooter with a chance to catch Genereux was Knut Holmqvist of Sweden, a thirty-four-year-old furniture merchant from Malmo who was in only his first year of competitive shooting.

Holmqvist and Genereux had tied for second place at the world championships a week before in Oslo. But this was the Olympics, where medals carry a great deal more currency in emotion and prestige. As the tension mounted, the Swede needed a perfect twenty-five in his final round to tie the Canadian. He was flawless through twenty-three shots, but missed the second-to-last clay pigeon. Thanks to a nerve-wracking final score of 191 to 192, Canada had finally struck gold at Helsinki. The medal winner was a previously unknown high schooler who was quickly dubbed "huelimatta taysmestari" by the host Finns, which loosely translates to "a grand shooter despite his youth." Genereux was unknown no more, going on to win the Lou Marsh Award as Canada's top athlete of 1952 — the youngest person ever to do so.

How close can you come to an Olympic medal without actually winning one? Ask Gilmour Boa, a civil engineer from Toronto who likened shooting to a religion and shot an almost heavenly 399 out of 400 in the small-bore prone rifle event at Helsinki. But there wasn't room for a single error in this competition as Josif Sarbu of Romania and Boris Andreyev of the Soviet Union shot perfect 400s. To make matters even tighter, Arthur Jackson of the US and Erich Sporer of Germany tied with Boa at 399 points in the field of fifty-eight competitors from thirty-two countries. Boa would go on to win the King's Prize at Bisley, bronze at the 1956 Olympics and gold at world championships and Commonwealth Games. But it was heartbreak in Helsinki as he was awarded fourth place on countback. After the competition, Boa offered some of his Canadian shells to winner Andreyev in exchange for some keepsake Soviet shells. The Russian perhaps got the feeling somebody was looking over his shoulder and nervously returned Boa's shells the next day and said he didn't want to trade.

Another tough fourth-place finish came in the men's 4x400 track relay. Nobody expected Canada to challenge the superstar Jamaican gold medallist team of Arthur Wint, Herb McKenley, George Rhoden and Les Laing, which won in a world record 3:03.9. But Canadians Doug Clement, John Hutchins, John Carroll and James Lavery were only one second off the old world record in finishing fourth in 3:09.3.

Weightlifter George Gratton of Montreal, a 1950 and 1954 Commonwealth Games gold medallist, had better luck. He pressed 122.5kg, snatched 112.5 kilos and jerked 155 kilos for a 390 total and the silver medal in middleweight weightlifting behind three-time Olympic medallist American Peter George's total of 400 kilos. Gratton died tragically in an automobile accident just after the Helsinki Olympics. The Gratton Trophy, named in his honour, is still presented to the best lifter at the Canadian championships.

The magnificence of Emil Zatopek, who ran with such a pained grimace he appeared to be dying with each step, defined the Helsinki Olympics in individual terms. After winning the 5000 and 10,000m, the Czech was a late entry in the marathon — a race he had never before contested. "Am I going too fast or too slow?" he asked the stunned favourite, Jim Peters of England, as the two ran at the head of the pack in the marathon. Peters — who two years later would capture the horrified imagination of millions with his agonizing marathon ordeal in the Commonwealth Games at Vancouver — became unnerved and collapsed by the curb as Zatopek sped by to win his third gold medal of the 1952 Olympics. Zatopek's wife, Dana, who was born on the same day as her husband in 1922, won the women's javelin to bring the Zatopek family total to four gold medals at Helsinki.

The biggest female stars of the Helsinki Olympics may have been the Aussie runners, led by a young stenographer from Melbourne named Marjorie Jackson who recorded a gold medal sweep in the 100 and 200m. But the crusty, veteran coach of the Australian men's track team wasn't impressed by female athletes being in the Olympics. "I wouldn't give you a bob for a bagful," said Percy Cerutty, fifty-seven. Sometimes the women themselves seemed to agree. Shockingly by today's standards, Jackson quit her sprinting career at age twenty-one after two Olympic and seven Commonwealth Games gold medals. "I got married [to Aussie cyclist Peter Nelson, whom she met on the plane to the Helsinki Olympics] and a woman couldn't be married and be a world-class athlete back then and do both justice," said Jackson, who would likely have won numerous more gold medals.

The Russians were accused of intimidating the Finnish officials in the boxing ring at the Messuhall quonset hut. "The Finnish refs are simply scared to death of the Soviets," complained US coach Pete Mello. The Soviets were quite adept at the Good Cop, Bad Cop routine. While they may have leaned on referees and judges, the approach was quite different in their hospitality lounge where the Soviets threw big parties for Westerners. "Russian grog gave a lot of scribblers red eyes, even if it didn't give them Red ideas," said the *Toronto Star*'s Milt Dunnell, about the bashes the Soviets threw for Western journalists at Helsinki. But the second place Americans stormed back on the final day with some key victories, including future world professional heavyweight boxing champion Floyd Patterson's gold in the middleweight class, to eclipse the Soviets in the unofficial Olympic points standings 557 to 529 (Canada finished tied for twenty-fourth). The Soviets, however, were watching and learning. It was like something out of a spy movie at the basketball hall as Russian officials skulked around the sidelines making diagrams and taking notes and pictures of the American tactics on the court.

Yet even as the sports race would soon come to mimic the arms race between Western and Eastern blocs, the 1952 Games were still quaint by today's standards. "I guess we were all very pedestrian journeymen compared to the contemporary world," said Bob Hutchison, now a BC supreme court judge, who sprinted for Canada at the Helsinki Olympics. "We had none of the jazzy training methods that they have today," added Hutchison, whose father Bruce was an icon of Canadian journalism. "We had to run on grass in Victoria, where we didn't get our first cinder track until 1951.

"It was a different world back then and sport had a different place in it," recalled Hutchison. "They were still sweeping up bombed-out cities. Seven years after the war, there was still rubble and craters everywhere. I suppose it still holds true that much of the world goes to sleep hungry each night. But now, sport — much more than could ever have been imagined at the 1952 Olympics — has taken on such an all-consuming glitter that even supposedly amateur track stars are millionaires," he mused. "I guess we were the last of the true amateurs. The tradition was that sport was for fun. I guess the world has gone past that stage now."

In many ways, the Helsinki Games were the departure point. From then until Seoul in 1988, the Olympics carried the weight of the Cold War on its shoulders as both sides used gold medals as the ammunition to prove their system was superior. And not even an appearance by a deranged Angel of Peace was about to change that.

MELBOURNE 1956

November 22 to December 8
Equestrian held June 10 to June 17 at Stockholm
3342 Athletes from 67 Nations

He had eyes that looked right through you. And he let nothing stand in his way. He was a self-made multimillionaire and owned three Vancouver hotels. But what coach Frank Read's business world lacked in excitement and challenges, he made up for in other ways. He bought a big new Oldsmobile every year and wore Gucci shoes. He had a gardener, cook and pool and lived in a palatial mansion overlooking Horseshoe Bay. He was very yang about everything. But his rowers were generally quiet and large, raw boys who came from the Okanagan, Vancouver Island or the lower mainland of British Columbia. Mix this young, malleable and respectful brute strength with Read's electric and driven personality and something was bound to happen. It did in the form of one of the greatest rowing juggernauts in the world from the 1954 Vancouver Commonwealth Games to the 1964 Tokyo Olympics. The highwater mark was the 1956 Summer Olympics in Melbourne, where Read's UBC crews proved more than medal-worthy.

The UBC program was hardly large. Once Read's reputation for gut-wrenching training became known, only a few people were crazy enough to turn out for it. The entire 1956 program had only enough oarsmen to make up the two boats that won the Canadian titles and qualified for Melbourne. Those twelve strokers and one coxswain were it. And the gold medal fours hadn't even seen a rowing shell until about a year before when Read had approached the strapping young men on campus and asked if they wanted to become rowers. "I guess I look back on the gold medal now and shrug it off as taking advantage of an opportunity that was presented to us really out of the blue," said Lorne Loomer. "I hadn't even seen a racing shell the year before. How extraordinarily lucky we were to get into this. My dad was a schoolteacher and sports was totally alien to me. But then along came Frank Read and we soon found out what he was all about. He was making a philosophic statement, not a sporting one. He told us if we had the dedication and courage to come back two times a day for gruesome training, we couldn't help but win on the racing course and could later only be successful in life at large. That such a small group should reach international domination during this period is really remarkable. It was this man's personality and absolute refusal to take second best that pushed those boys to find themselves and their inner beings."

Read was hardly a master of rowing technique. If you wanted the finer points of how to keep your craft straight as you rowed down a pond in Stanley Park, look elsewhere. Read's coaching philosophy was quite simple. If you are more physically fit than anybody else and willing to endure endless pain to reach that fitness level, then nobody can beat you regardless of their technique. The UBC oarsmen stayed at ramshackle Crew House at 1888 West Georgia (which was furnished with old dressers and tables from Read's hotels) so they would be just one block away from the Vancouver Rowing Club boathouse in Stanley Park. Wake up call was 4:30 A.M. and the rowers were on the water at Coal Harbour by 5:00 A.M. doing six to eight miles in the morning plus a time trial. In the evenings from 5:00 P.M. to 8:00 P.M., it was ten miles to the Second Narrows Bridge and back, plus a time trial. The rowers were consuming 7000 calories a day and still losing weight. "People can't believe this," winced Loomer. "If you weren't ready by 5:00 A.M., he used language like my mother and father never knew. We were scared of him. When the fours beat the eights one day, he made us all do it over again — another ten miles to the Second Narrows. Both crews won the Canadian trials on the Welland Canal that year with no style, only desire. But when we saw the other crews way back behind on on the horizon, we thought this intangible might even be enough at the Olympics. Frank's philosophy was that if you dared to dream and if you worked toward that dream, it's going to come true."

But the fours almost didn't get there to take their shot at Olympic gold. The Canadian Olympic Association had only enough money to send the eights crew, and the fours seemed out of luck. But Read went to work and got BC Lieutenant Governor Frank Ross, Colonel Vic Spencer and Walter Owen to pitch in their own money to send the fours. "Frank had always promised us — all you have to do is pay attention to rowing and I'll make the rest happen for you," said Loomer. He came through. Once in Australia, Read refused to let his rowers march in the Olympic opening ceremonies at the Melbourne Cricket Grounds because he didn't want their strength sapped in the heat. They were there for one purpose only.

And that began in earnest for the fours a few days later against crews representing eleven other nations on Lake Wendouree, about ninety kilometres from Melbourne. The first heat and semifinal were no contest, with the UBC fours winning easily by six and ten lengths, respectively. But the Olympic final started out like a horror show when all four nervous young men missed the water with their first stroke. They were in last place at 500m. Loomer remembers thinking: "Have we done all this to come to such a dismal end?" But stroke Don Arnold called for a "ten," which means go all out. The Canadians pulled even with the leading French, Italians and Americans at the halfway point at 1000m and then won going away by more than five lengths in 7:08.8. The United States took silver far behind in 7:18.4 and France bronze in 7:20.9. And Read was right in every way. All four gold medallists had successful professional lives. Loomer hailed from Nelson and became a pharmacist and accomplished painter in Victoria. Later in life, rowing on Elk Lake would help in his rehabilatation from a near-devastating stroke. It was during that time he received a letter from an aged Read, which read: "I like to keep up with the welfare of my boys — I still think of you as my boys. The spirit within is a powerful force and with faith and confidence it can work for you." Arnold was also from the interior of BC and became a professor at UBC. Archie McKinnon was from Cranbrook and became a millionaire Calgary businessman. Walter D'Hondt of Vancouver became a high-level Boeing executive in Everett, Washingon. None of them talk much about their gold medals. "In our day, if you talked about it, you were bragging and not being humble," said Loomer. "The world has changed but I guess we're still the same. We feel the real champions are the people like Jean Beliveau. The quiet ones."

The United States had won seven consecutive Olympic gold medals in the men's eights, but that streak looked all but over when the Yale crew finished behind the Aussies and Read's Canadian boys in the first heat. Read's crew went on to easily defeat Sweden, Italy and Czechoslovakia in their semifinal race. The Americans, however, also qualifed for the semifinals through repêchage. They won their semifinal but advanced to the final against the fit Canadians and exuberant Aussies knowing that no eights crew had ever won the gold medal in the Olympics after losing its opening heat. Read's boys looked nervously across at the Americans. Could the Yalies break this longstanding tradition or would the Canadian stamina prove triumphant? The Canadians were all bright and highly motiviated young men who came from all over the province to end up under Read's spell at UBC. He recruited most of them for rowing after noticing their size as they walked to and from classes. Some had not even been athletes in high school. Phil Kueber of Duncan, a future Calgary lawyer, and Richard McClure of Tsolum, a future engineer for Scott Paper in Vancouver, came from small-town Vancouver Island. The interior boys, Bob Wilson of Kamloops and Wayne Pretty of Winfield, both went into engineering. Bill McKerlich, later superintendent of schools in Salmon Arm, grew up in tough East Vancouver. His father was a cop who had been killed while on duty and his mother raised three sons by herself. Lawrence West was also from Vancouver. David Helliwell died in 1993 after a career as a Vancouver chartered accountant. Doug McDonald from Saltspring Island became a successful developer. Carlton Ogawa, from Salmon Arm and of Japanese descent, was the coxswain and eventually got into forestry. But on November 27, 1956, these nine young men from British Columbia had no care about the future beyond the barely more than six minutes that would decide Olympic gold.

About 30,000 fans lined the pleasant, tree-shaded shoreline of the lake to cheer for the Australian crew in what would turn out to be a tense and tight final. Canada and Australia fought for the lead at the halfway point but the Americans were soon on them and forged to the front. But not by much. The Yale men raised their stroke rate to thirty-eight, which was enough to shake off the Aussies but not Read's crew. Finally the Americans laid it all out and cranked the pace to a muscle-popping forty strokes. But Read's crew hung in there and it was a raging battle all the way, with the Americans outlasting the Canadians to win by less than half a length. The Yale crew took gold for the US in 6:35.2 and UBC silver for Canada in 6:37.1. The Aussies hung in gamely but settled for bronze in 6:39.2. "We're the toughest crew ever put together and we beat the best," said an emotional and tearful Yale captain Tom Charlton. The medals were presented to all the rowers by the crusty IOC presi-

Gerry Ouellette shows off his Olympic gold medal.

dent Avery Brundage. If the thirteen Canadian rowing medallists from that blazing November day Down Under were protective of theirs over the years, they came by it honestly after witnessing one of the bizarrest moments in Olympic history on the dock. After being presented with the single sculls gold medal, Vyacheslav Ivanov of the Soviet Union was so happy that he leaped off the podium with such force he dropped his medal and it rolled off the dock and into the lake. He dove in after it but to no avail. The IOC provided him with a replacement. He didn't really need it since he won gold again at 1960 in Rome and 1964 in Tokyo. Decades later, a diver found the lost gold medal sitting at the bottom of Lake Wendouree.

There aren't too many Canadians whose likeness is depicted on the stamp of a foreign country. You pretty well have to be a Norman Bethune or Alexander Graham Bell to get that type of treatment. Or a Gerald R. Ouellette. Gerald R. Who? A Windsor sharpshooter, that's who. An Olympic gold medallalist, that's who. After he won the smallbore prone shooting title at the Melbourne Games, the Dominican Republic issued a one-centavo stamp in 1957 showing Ouellette staring down the barrel of a rifle. Canada didn't honour him in the same fashion. It's nice to know there are other countries who appreciate the value of an Olympic gold medal. Ouellette always had steady hands. He was a thirteen-year-old student at Lowe Vocational High School in Windsor when he also went into cadets. Major Wyn Jennings noticed in cadets that Ouellette had sharp eyes and steady nerves and coaxed him into taking up shooting as a sport. It became obvious the youngster was a natural as he swept up cadet and junior titles with ease, before progressing on to win provincial and national crowns. He had been to Bisley three times since taking up smallbore in 1952. But still, Ouellette was not considered much of a threat against the world's best at the Melbourne Olympics. In fact, teammate Gilmour Boa came in with a much heftier reputation and held the world record for smallbore prone at 598 (600 is a perfect score). A day before the prone event, Boa had seemed unbeatable in the three-position smallbore competition, firing a perfect opening prone round of 400 to set the forty-shot world record. But his forty attempts in the kneeling and standing positions weren't as successful and Boa faded to a sixth place finish. Ouellette, meanwhile, bombed out and finished well back in the field of forty-four competitors from twenty-eight countries.

Things were hardly looking bright when Ouellette and Boa made their way back to the shooting venue the next day, December 5, for the prone event. Ouellette had been very disheartened the previous night after his failure in the three-position event and the veteran Boa looked for ways to lift his friend's spirits. Since Boa's rifle had proved perfect the day before in the prone portion of the three-position event, the two Canadians decided to share it for the prone final, where shooters are allowed two hours to take sixty shots with a .22 rimfire rifle at fifty metres. But by using the same rifle, Boa and Ouellette had to complete both their rounds in the same two-hour period. Boa went first and coolly tied his own world record of 598. With less than an hour left to fire, Ouellette took the rifle. After hitting twenty straight bull's-eyes, Ouellette was advised by Boa to take a three-minute rest to calm the nerves. After Ouellette reeled off another twenty perfect shots, Boa told him to take another breather and relax.

There was less than fifteen minutes left when the cherub-faced Ouellette readied himself for his final twenty pulls at the trigger. After another fifteen straight bull's-eyes, most of the shooters assembled to Ouellette's area. The pressure now was immense as the borrowed rifle crackled for the fifty-sixth time. Another bull's-eye. Then another retort and another perfect shot. Only three remained. Bang, bang. Shots fifty-eight and fifty-nine were perfect, too. Ouellette's mouth was dry and his palms sweaty but his hands and arms failed to betray even the hint of a shake. He pressed the trigger for the last time. Ouellette remembers knowing deep inside that he wouldn't miss that last shot. Boa grabbed him by the shoulders as the other shooters crowded around to slap his back. The twenty-one-year-old Windsor teacher and tool designer had recorded a perfect score of 600 to set the world record. Or had he? It was learned later the Australian organizers, used to imperial and not metric measurements, had actually set the range at 48.5m in distance. So Ouellette's world mark was disallowed. But the Olympic gold medal was still his. Boa settled for the bronze medal behind Ouellette and silver medallist Vassily Borissov of the Soviet Union (599). But the real star of the piece may have been Boa's rifle. Frank Read and that rifle helped account for two gold, a silver and bronze in an era when Summer Olympic medals were as rare for Canada as a palm tree in Kenora. Ouellette and Boa went on to win titles at Bisley and medals at the Commonwealth and Pan-American games. Ouellette made it back to the Olympics twelve years after Melbourne, placing sixth in the three-position smallbore competition at Mexico City in 1968.

Few Canadian athletes or teams had put the time and money into their sport in the 1950s that the equestrian set had. The 1952 experience had been a major blow. There had been a great deal invested in training on the grounds of Badminton House in England prior to the Helsinki Olympics, and when they were subsequently shut out of the medals because of injury and illness to both man and beast, it was a disappointment. But the riders, under the tutelage of Major Gordon Gayford, were back for another shot in 1956. Because of strict Australian quarantine laws, the 1956 Olympic equestrian events were held June 10–17 in Stockholm. Jim Elder, Brian Herbinson and John Rumble, all youthful and skilled, were entered in the three-day team event. And they had the right connections in this upscale sport. Their mounts for the Olympics had been loaned to them by friends. You know — the kind that can afford to buy and keep horses. Rumble's mount Kilroy was a Canadian-bred hunter that had never before taken part in a jumping event. The Irish-bred Tara, ridden by Herbinson, was a veteran of Helsinki. Elder's mount Colleen was another Irish-bred with experience. At first, things didn't look any more promising than during the Helsinki rout. Canada was seventh out of nineteen nations after the first-day dressage and faced an uphill battle. The cross-country course two days later was so brutal that animal rights groups protested its severity. An overnight downpour didn't help matters as the riders took to a muddy and treacherously slippery course. More than sixty horses fell, twenty-two riders were tossed, eleven had four or more faults and six teams were forced to withdraw. During one stretch of the course, four horses were stuck in the same ditch. In one of the great rides in Olympic history, Rumble on Kilroy finished the course with a clean round. Herbinson almost had a clean round except for one fault when Tara erred in clearing a water jump. Elder coaxed an often reluctant Colleen through with only two faults. In the most adverse conditions, Canada had only three faults and vaulted from seventh to third place with the show jumping to come. The Canadians held firm and didn't slide from third on the final day. The British, who live for this sort of thing, were too tough and well ahead at -355.48 for the gold medal. Germany took the silver at -475.91 and Canada the bronze at -572.72.

Pat McCormick of Long Beach, winner of four gold medals, was probably the greatest of the American females who dominated Olympic springboard diving. Americans had won twenty of the first twenty-one medals presented in the event from 1920 at Antwerp to 1952 at Helsinki. Irene McDonald of Hamilton became only the second diver ever to crash the Stars and Stripes party in women's springboard. The gifted McCormick, springboard and platform champion at Helsinki in 1952 and Melbourne in 1956, was pregnant in the lead-up to the latter. She had continued training while pregnant and gave birth to a son seven months before the Melbourne Games. She put a lock on the gold medal with an untoppable score of 142.36. Teammate Jeanne Stunyo recorded a 125.89 total to capture the silver medal while the third American diver, Barbara Gilders, was moving in for bronze and yet another US sweep. But McDonald (121.40) came through with a strong performance in the field of seventeen competitors to edge Gilders (120.76) for the bronze. McDonald later became known to millions of Canadians during CBC telecasts of the Olympics and Commonwealth Games for her expert diving commentary. And twenty-eight years later, a Canadian would finally have the last laugh on a McCormick in Olympic women's springboard diving. Sylvie Bernier of Ste. Foy, Quebec, won the gold medal at the 1984 Los Angeles Games and shunted Pat McCormick's daughter, Kelly McCormick, to the silver medal placing. McDonald was in the booth at USC calling the diving for CBC that day.

Canada is probably the only Commonwealth country to which the Melbourne Cricket Grounds, that sport's holiest site after Lord's in London, means nothing. So it was perhaps only fitting the MCG proved such a wasteland for Canada at the 1956 Olympics. The Canadians were beaming under the beating sun when the youthful future Aussie running great Ron Clarke lit the torch, Miracle Miler John Landy took the athletes' oath and Prince Phillip declared opened the Games on November 22. But it was all downhill after that for the Canadian track and field team. Some great stories were written on that cinder track. The world

*Graceful Irene McDonald
flies through the Aussie
air en route to a diving
bronze medal at the 1956
Melbourne Olympics.*

got its first glimpse of Soviet man-as-machine when Vladimir Kuts, betraying little emotion and running like a programmed robot, virtually ground his opposition into the red cinder in scoring a double victory in the 5000m and 10,000m races. "The American lead has been liquidated," crowed the Soviet youth newspaper, *Komsomolskaya Pravda*, on the day the Russians overtook the US atop the Melbourne Games medals table. The Soviets finished with thirty-seven gold, twenty-nine silver and thirty-two bronze to the Americans' thirty-two gold, twenty-five silver and seventeen bronze. Bobby Joe Morrow, the deeply fundamentalist footballer-turned-sprinter known as the Texas Tornado, churned his way to three gold medals in the men's 100 and 200m and 4x100 relay to aid the US cause in this sporting Cold War. His alter ego was Aussie flash Betty Cuthbert of Merrylands, New South Wales, who scored the same three gold medals on the women's side. Cuthbert wasn't sure she would even make the host nation's team and so bought tickets for the track and field competition the first day they went on sale.

The Aussies were impressive at home, finishing third in the medals table behind the Soviets and Americans with thirteen gold, eight silver and fourteen bronze. That's not bad for a country that had a population of ten million at the time, and it's quite a contrast to Canada's sorry showing (five silver, six bronze) as host at Montreal twenty years later. The Aussies were especially impressive in the pool at Melbourne, with superstar Dawn Fraser and the supporting cast of Murray Rose, David Theile, Gary Chapman, John Devitt, Lorraine Crapp and Jon Henricks providing almost complete domination.

The Iron Curtain lifted, but ever so briefly, with the power of love. The gold medallist hammer thrower, burly Hal Connolly of the US, fell in love watching women's discus gold medallist Olga Fikotova of Czechoslovakia during her practice throws. There was, of course, a mountain of brutish red tape to cut through. But after an appeal directly to the president of Czechoslovakia, the two were married in Prague the following year and moved to California. They competed together in three more Olympics but couldn't duplicate the success of 1956 when both were inspired by the first blush of blooming love. The union produced four children. Canada could have used a good East-West love story among its ranks because there was precious little else to cheer about at the MCG. The best Canadian performance in field was turned in by intense Ontario high jumper Ken Money, whose admirable leap of 6' 8" (2.03m) was two inches better than that achieved by Canadian Duncan McNaughton in winning gold at the 1932 Los Angeles Olympics. The hard-working Money took fifth place at Melbourne. The gold medal at 2.12m was won by Money's polar opposite — the gifted but not-so-hard-working Charlie Dumas of the US — who was famous for his lackadaisical attitude to training. Canada's top track athletes were Laird Sloan, Murray Cockburn, Doug Clement and Terry Tobacco, who ran fifth in the 4x400m final in 3:10.2 behind the winning Americans (3:04.8).

The leader of the Canadian foursome, however, was Tobacco from the tiny Vancouver Island coal mining community of Cumberland. As a wisp of a seventeen-year-old grade eleven student, he won bronze in the 440 yards and silver in the 4x440 relay two years earlier at the 1954 Vancouver Commonwealth Games. An unfortunate tactical error cost him a good shot at an Olympic medal in the individual 400m at Melbourne. In the semifinals, Tobacco was told to stay close to American Lou Jones, the world record holder at 45.2 seconds. That way the Canadian was sure to get through to the final. But Jones had a bad leg that day and Tobacco stayed with him when he should have gone ahead. There was a photo finish for third place and Tobacco was the odd man out. The sad fact is that Tobacco's searing anchor leg of 45.3 seconds in the 4x400 Olympic relay would have won him the gold medal in the

400m individual final. Tobacco's 45.3 was the fastest the 400m was run at the 1956 Olympics and faster than any Olympic gold medal-winning time up to that point. American Charles Jenkins of Cambridge, Massachusetts, won the 1956 gold medal in 46.7 seconds, far slower than Tobacco's relay time. But that's life.

The Melbourne Olympics at times looked to be going south more figuratively than literally. The slowly paced and stately city astride the Yarra River at Port Phillip Bay, which grew because of the Victoria gold rush in the 1850s, took its sweet time in getting ready. There was a point when it appeared as if Melbourne might have to give up the Games, which it won over Buenos Aires, Argentina, because of the Commonwealth bloc vote. It finally took a visit from Avery Brundage himself and some headline-grabbing verbal kicks in the backside to get the Aussies moving on preparations for the first Olympics ever held in the Southern Hemisphere.

When the Games opened, they did so under the two huge political clouds of 1956 — the Suez crisis and the Soviet supression of the Hungarian revolt. Some suggested the Games should be cancelled, but Brundage scoffed at the idea. "The Olympics belong to the people and are contests between individuals and not nations," he thundered. Despite some nasty incidents, including a bloody Soviet-Hungary water polo match, the tension eventually melted under the blazing Australian sun. At the closing ceremonies on December 8, thanks to a suggestion in a letter to the IOC by a young Australian schoolboy of Chinese descent, the athletes marched in mixed for the first time in the history of the Games.

The Australian concept of mateness — where "you're no bloody better than anybody else" — seemed to rub off on others as this fortnight progressed. No longer would protocol dictate that each athlete stay with his or her own team during the closing. The athletes mingled freely, and happily, in a giant mass of humanity on the infield of the MCG as the first Games in the Southern Hemisphere officially came to an end. Even the crusty Frank Read, who barred the Canadian rowers from marching in the opening ceremonies to conserve energy, allowed his heavily medalled boys to go for a run in the infield. The time for training and war games was over. American gold medal basketball stars from the University of San Francisco, Bill Russell and K.C. Jones, locked arms with two large Soviet shot putters. Lovebirds Connolly and Fikotova walked together holding hands. Afterward, the laid-back Aussie fans left the stadium and went home to throw another shrimp on the barbie to celebrate a job well done.

ROME 1960

August 25 to September 11
5348 Athletes from 83 Nations

In all the elaborate pomp and ceremony of the Olympic Games, the one thing steadfastly steered clear of is any form of religious display. The Roman emperor Theodosius I, a Christian, shut down the ancient Olympic Games in 393 (for all time, he thought) on the grounds they were a pagan festival. The modern Olympics, still pagan in nature, gained their revenge by coming to Rome 1566 years later. Theodosius I presumably rolled over in his grave. But the modern Romans didn't care about him. The Olympics were a big hit. The 1960 Summer Games were a rare blend of antiquity and modernism held in the Eternal City and flowed over the senses gently. The ivy-covered Maxentius Basilica public hall, built in about the year 300, was the fitting site for the ancient sport of wrestling. Fencing was held at the ancient Palace of Congresses. The Terme di Caracalla, where Roman senators and merchants took baths and massages at about the time of Theodosius I, hosted the gymnastics competition. The marathon was trod partly on the Appian Way, the ancient road upon which marched Caesar's great armies, and ended near the Colosseum and Roman Forum under the Arch of Constantine. The new facilities, funded by a lucrative Italian national soccer lottery, included the 100,000-seat Olympic Stadium, Olympic Velodrome, seven-pool Swim Stadium, mock-ancient Marble Stadium for field hockey and the Little and Big Sports Palaces, the latter of which hosted basketball and boxing and featured an appealing geodesic design. The rowing venue, twenty kilometres south of Rome and the site of Canada's only medal at the 1960 Summer Olympics, was also ancient. But it was built by nature, not man. The circular Lake Albano was formed by the fusion of two ancient volcanic craters and is nourished by underground springs. In about 490 A.D., the Romans created a spillway to give the lake an outlet. Looking down on all this, atop the emerald hills which surround the lake, is the Pope's summer palace, Castel Gandolfo.

It's not known if the Pope was in residence there September 3, 1960, when the six finalists from the field of fourteen crews lined up for the Olympic final of the men's rowing eights. The US had won this event for eight straight Olympics going back to Antwerp in 1920. The UBC crew representing Canada had finished second to the US, represented by Yale, at the 1956 Melbourne Olympics and again second to the Americans, represented by Penn, at the 1959 Chicago Pan-American Games. In between was a gold medal for the UBC boys in the eights at the 1958 Cardiff Commonwealth Games. Lake Albano was certainly more accessible than Northern Wales' remote Lake Padarn, site of the '58 Commonwealth Games regatta, and definitely more pleasant than the sewage-strewn Chicago Sanitary and Ship Canal, site of the '59 Pan-Am Games regatta.

But regardless of venue, Vancouver coach Frank Read's hard-driven rowers were always there; always vying for gold. The crews eyed each other nervously at the start line for the Olympic eights final. The American team, represented by the US Naval Academy at Annapolis, was under intense pressure. Not only had US crews owned this event since 1920, but the American Mediterranean fleet was stationed nearby at Naples. So Lake Albano was rife with admirals and other US navy brass who came expecting their cadets from Annapolis to win gold. It was that kind of pressure that earlier destroyed the Oxford crew, who had been oversold by the English press before bombing out in the heats. Germany, with rowers from the strong Ratzeburg and Ditmarsia Kiel clubs, came into the final with thirty-nine consecutive wins behind them. The 1960 Canadian eights, meanwhile, had rowed together just five times before the Olympics as Read juggled his men right up to the national trials looking for the right combination. He sometimes liked to toy with his rowers by creating an air of uncertainty. But the Canadian boat was anything but uncertain as it sliced through the Olympic heats with a strong and veteran crew from British Columbia. Don Arnold and Archie McKinnon from the BC interior and Walter D'Hondt of Vancouver had won gold in the fours at the 1956 Olympics, while Bill McKerlich was a member of the 1956 Olympic silver medal eights. The newcomers included Nelson Kuhn and stroke Glen Mervyn, two more strapping boys from the interior/Okanagan whom Read nabbed when they got to Vancouver. Lanky David Anderson, later the national Revenue Minister in Prime Minister Jean Chretien's cabinet, was from Victoria. "I fitted the dimensions and I was determined to row," recalled Anderson. "And obviously, UBC was THE place to do it then. So I left Victoria College. I learned quickly enough that once accepted into the UBC rowing group, you put your faith in Frank. We just did what he said. We didn't question Frank. Sometimes all you have to do is believe. And we believed that anything Frank did or said would help us win. You couldn't get away with that kind of coaching today. But back then, it worked." John Lecky was another member of the Olympic eights with a Vancouver Island pedigree, having gone to school and rowed at tony Shawnigan Lake School. Lecky was the first grandchild of H.R. MacMillan, the lumber tycoon who helped shape the economic face of British Columbia. The coxswain was Sohen Biln, who didn't become a big hitter in national politics or business like some of his crew mates but settled down to a contented small town life as a pharmacist in Castlegar, British Columbia.

Germany cranked it out right from the start in the Olympic final. It was clear the Germans weren't going to be headed as they stroked for the gold medal in 5:57.18. Canada put up a stiff fight, keeping the Germans within shouting distance throughout much of the final before settling for the silver medal in 6:01.52. Czechoslovakia was well back to take the bronze in 6:04.84. The Americans settled for fifth place in 6:08.06 as their Olympic streak in the men's eights came to a shattering end.

There was no formal federal amateur-sport funding infrastructure back when Anderson was a rower and not a politician. Instead, there was the humiliation of the rowers having to go to Empire Stadium with tin cups during BC Lions football games to beg for money to get to the Olympics. And if that didn't work, there were always Read's business connections. He would take a few BC movers and shakers he knew up to a corner office on the top floor of the Marine Building, then one of the tallest structures in Vancouver. An expensive bottle of Scotch was opened as the lords of finance looked down at the rowers stroking in Coal Harbor. And then it was time for Read to say something like: "Yep, I think we've got a good group for the Olympics again this time." "Frank would go out and shake the money tree and somehow we got there," recalls Anderson.

With such a cap-in-hand approach to sport funding, it's hardly surprising Canada won only one medal at the Rome Olympics. The closest the nation came to a second medal was in the men's 4x100 medley swim relay where Bob Wheaton, Steve Rabinovitch, Cameron Grout and Dick Pound finished fourth in 4:16.8, but a solar system away from the world record the gold medallist Americans established in 4:05.4. Wheaton, who won two silvers and a bronze at the Cardiff Commonwealth and Chicago Pan-Am games and hadn't lost a backstroke race in Canada in three years, quit after the Rome Olympics at the age of eighteen. "There were never any funds available back then for national-team athletes and we were always scrounging around for money," said Wheaton, later the owner of a successful family construction company in British Columbia. "And the battles going on as to who would be chosen for the Canadian team were just atrocious. There were heated arguments — all based on regionalism. There were shouting matches on how many athletes from Western Canada were chosen for the last Games and how many the East had. The athletes were just pawns in a political chess match. It was a loathsome experience and I had my fill of it." As far as scrounging for money, it's ironic that Wheaton's 4x100 medley teammate at Rome — Dick Pound of Ocean Falls, BC — later became vice-president of the International Olympic Committee responsible for negotiating television rights. The Montreal lawyer, sixth in the individual 100m freestyle at Rome and the gold medallist two years later at the 1962 Perth Commonwealth Games, managed to finagle a deal worth $1.25 billion with NBC for the combined US rights to the 2000 Sydney Summer Olympics ($705 million) and the 2002 Salt Lake City Winter Olympics ($545 million).

Mary Stewart of Vancouver made the final and finished eighth in the women's 100m freestyle at Rome in 1:05.5. The brilliant but difficult Dawn Fraser of Australia, who hadn't lost a 100m freestyle race since the last Olympics, became the first woman ever to defend an Olympic swim title by capturing the gold medal in 1:01.2. She then got into a tiff with her Aussie swim teammates, who refused to speak to her for the rest of the Games. Irene MacDonald, bronze medallist at the 1956 Olympics, gave Canada sixth place in women's spingboard diving at Rome with 134.69 points. Ingrid Kramer of Dresden, Germany, won both the springboard and platform events, marking the fourth consecutive time that happened in Olympic competition.

Canada's rather pathetic overall performance at Rome (ninety-seven athletes competed in thirteen sports) left some to openly wonder just how committed Canadians and Canadian society were to success at the Summer Olympics. " … The swimmers and BC oarsmen saved Canada's national face," said long-time Canadian Olympic observer Henry Roxborough, in summing up Rome in his *Canada at the Olympics*. "In the main, however, Canadian athletes lacked the dedication of athletes from other countries. The training program of New Zealand's Peter Snell included running eight miles each morning before breakfast, working at his job during the day, and practising again before dinner. In Canada I have been a judge at some important meets where the number of athletes exceeded that of spectators and there is little college support for any form of competition leading to Olympic representation. It takes considerable desire in impressionable youths to overcome the handicaps of a lethargic public and uninterested educationists."

There were some classic moments at the Rome Olympics — provided, of course, by other nations. Running barefoot and in just his third marathon, a member of Emperor Haile Selassie's Imperial Bodyguard captured the gold medal in a night race illuminated by thousands of flaming torches held by Italian soldiers. About fifteen years before, the Italian army had been plundering and laying waste to Ethiopia. Just down the road from the Arch of Constantine, where the marathon ended, was the historic Ethiopian obelisk from Axum which the Italians stole from Bikila's homeland and transplanted in Rome. Now it was Abebe Bikila's turn to conquer Rome as the first black African to win the Olympic marathon. This great runner from the hills of East Africa would also win the marathon at the 1964 Tokyo Olympics before ending his days in a wheelchair after an automobile accident in 1969.

The stern and hawk-like Herb Elliott of Australia was unbeatable in the mile and 1500m between 1958 and 1961 and won forty-four consecutive races. He ran the opposition into the cinder with his brilliant 1500m gold medal victory at the Rome Games in a world record 3:35.6. A year later and in his prime at age twenty-three, he quit running. "Once that hunger [for winning Olympic gold] had been satisfied, I lost interest altogether," he said. "And there was a family to educate and a home to build and pay off. The first fifteen or twenty years of married life must be a selfish sort of existence where job and family come first."

New Zealanders Peter Snell and Murray Halberg struck for gold within an hour of each other at the Olympic Stadium in the men's 800 and 5000m, respectively. Kiwis back home in the tightly knit little country could hardly believe it as neighbour phoned neighbour in giddy delight. Halberg had fought back with incredible determination after his shoulder and arm were severely damaged in a rugby game in 1950. At age seventeen, he had to re-learn how to write, grab simple objects and dress and feed himself. Left with a withered and useless left arm,

Halberg turned to running as the lone sport available to him after his injury. His gold medal speaks volumes about the capacity of the human spirit to bounce back from almost any calamity. UCLA teammates and training partners Rafer Johnson of the US and C.K. Yang of Taiwan took the decathlon down to the final event in the late hours of a memorable Rome night before the American ultimately prevailed. Johnson was accompanying Robert Kennedy eight years later through the kitchen of the Ambassador Hotel in Los Angeles when the leading 1968 candidate for US president was gunned down. Johnson lit the torch during the opening ceremonies of the 1984 Los Angeles Olympics. Cassius Clay, a brash young man with lightning quick hands and feet, captured the light heavyweight boxing title at Rome and later threw his gold medal off a bridge into the Ohio River after being refused service at a whites-only restaurant in his hometown of Louisville, Kentucky. As Muhammad Ali, he became one of the best-known human beings on the planet. The late Wilma Rudolph, the twentieth of twenty-two brothers and sisters in Clarkesville, Tennessee, was told as a child she would probably not walk after contracting double pneumonia and scarlet fever and being diagnosed with polio. "Wilma will walk, I'll see to that," asserted her mother, Blanche Rudolph. Her family took turns massaging Wilma's shrunken legs. At the 1960 Rome Olympics, Wilma Rudolph won gold medals in the women's 100 and 200m and 4x100 relay.

But for Canada, there was pain and a huge national misunderstanding in the men's 100m. Armin Hary, a troublesome and self-taught runner from Frankfurt, Germany, became the first man to run the 100m in ten seconds flat during a race in Zurich on June 21, 1960. Less than a month later, the nineteen-year-old rising flash from British Columbia, Harry Jerome, struck with a 10.0 clocking of his own to tie the world record during the Canadian Olympic trials July 15 in Saskatoon. Throw in the fancied American Ray Norton and the stage was set for the explosive 100m event of the Rome Olympics. But Jerome never got to the final. Leading in his semifinal race, the Canadian suddenly pulled up and was passed by the entire field. Jerome had pulled a hamstring, but initial confusion as to why he stopped running led to an unfair label as a quitter — as if anybody in their right mind would actually give up in the middle of an Olympic semifinal while holding the lead. It was Hary who won the gold medal at Rome in 10.2 seconds.

Jerome's haughty air of indifference toward the media didn't help as he brushed off writers and broadcasters. The injury was explained by Canadian track officials an hour or so after it happened. But Jerome's career never quite recovered from the blow of those confused initial bulletins on Canadian radio and television. With yet no medals at Rome (the rowing silver came two days after the 100m final) and few prospects for any, the Canadian media were especially high-strung during the glamorous 100m competition because there was a genuine Canadian gold medal hope. Jerome's injury in the semifinals was a bitter enough pill for a Canadian media that saw its best potential story evaporate into the Rome air. And Jerome's aloofness and seeming indifference only exacerbated the situation. Yet his great but rocky track career was far from over, as we would learn at the 1964 Tokyo Olympics.

TOKYO 1964

October 10 to October 24
5140 Athletes from 93 Nations

Yoshinori Sakai was not an emperor, prime minister or famous athlete. But his being selected to light the torch to begin the 1964 Tokyo Olympics was more eloquent and moving than could be imagined. Sakai was born on the outskirts of Hiroshima on August 6, 1945, the day the atomic bomb devastated his city. From the ashes of a ruinous defeat nineteen years before, emerged the most efficient, modern and costly Olympics ever staged to that time. Sakai, and the immensely succesful Games which followed his lighting of the torch, were statements. This was Japan's coming-out party and a chance to prove that "Made in Japan" — synonymous at the time with cheaply made trinkets — now meant something else entirely. It meant the economic future belonged to them. And in 1964 they proved it. The first Olympics held in Asia were the most sleek and modern ever. Estimates on the cost of the Games, and their related public infrastructure improvements, range from $560 million to $2 billion US, as the Olympics were the catalyst for a vast urban renewal campaign. If Rome proudly presented a backdrop of antiquity for the 1960 Games, Tokyo's face was of technology and freshly laid concrete. Not even unrelenting rain could deter the enthusiasm of the Japanese as huge and impressive throngs sat beneath umbrellas to watch events. But more important, these were the first of the mass-television Games as images from Tokyo were beamed to households around the world in the way we understand today. For the first time, the live crowd became insignificant and unimportant compared to the REAL crowd — the hundreds of millions, later billions, of people watching on worldwide television. In Japan alone, NHK (that country's equivalent to the CBC) reported that 99 percent of Tokyo's citizens watched at least part of the opening ceremonies on television. That's what you call penetration.

There were many times that Canadian rowers Roger Jackson and George Hungerford wondered if they would ever be part of the show. Jackson had moved west from the University of Western Ontario because the UBC rowing program, which had won gold at the 1962 Perth Commonwealth and 1963 Sao Paulo Pan-American games and Canada's only medal at the 1960 Rome Olympics, was light-years ahead of any other program in the country. Jackson was placed into the fours, the second-strongest boat behind the elite UBC eights. Disaster struck at the 1964 Canadian trials in St. Catharines when his crew drifted all over the course and finished second. "It was a huge disappointment," he recalled, thinking that his Olympic dream was over. "I thought too bad — fate had dealt us a blow." But Jackson and Wayne Pretty from BC's Okanagan region, who had won a silver medal with the UBC eights at the 1956 Melbourne Olympics, got to hold on by a thread. They were picked as the spares for the national champion UBC eights heading to represent Canada at the Tokyo Olympics. But when George Hungerford of the eights crew came down with mononucleosis, Pretty was selected to replace him. Hungerford was dropped down to spare with Jackson.

It was evident by mid-September that Hungerford had to get better soon or he wouldn't be fit for even that. It was decided to enter the two spares in the coxless pair-oars at the Tokyo Games, an event not even contested at the Canadian championships. It was almost an afterthought — something to keep Jackson and Hungerford in shape in case they were needed for the eights crew, which was receiving all the attention. In an effort to aid his recovery, Hungerford stayed in bed after the morning workouts. In a move that was unheard of, Hungerford and Jackson, both about 6' 5" and 184 pounds, trained without a rudder because they needed to have bowman Hungerford concentrate solely on his power and stamina (the bowman steers a coxless shell by use of a foot-controlled rudder). That they could keep their rudderless shell in a straight line was truly a testmament to the skill of these so-called spares. Each morning in Tokyo, the pairs would race the eights in training. Hungerford was getting stronger by the day and that was encouraging. "It was absolute murder out on the course training every day," said Jackson, who was used to it by now because of the equally brutal UBC training regimen back home on Coal Harbour. "We were dry heaving and wretching every bloody morning," recalled Jackson.

Then came show time at the new, man-made Toda Olympic rowing course. "There was a lot of black humour between me and George — like saying 'let's at least beat Bulgaria,' which was considered the weakest pairs crew," said Jackson. But the two Canadians did better than that. They found themselves with the fastest time after the four heats and so advanced straight to the final, which was a real break for Hungerford who was still ailing and not quite to full form. "Over the first 500m, we were like scared kids," recalled Jackson, about their heat victory. "But then we started passing the other boats one by one. George was getting tired and we were afraid we couldn't maintain our pace. No matter how many times you train, an actual race is worse than the worst workout you've ever had. During our heat, we knew excruciating pain. It was a very uncomfortable feeling. It didn't seem like sport."

Not a single Canadian journalist turned up to watch the final because Jackson and Hungerford were still considered such longshots and superstars Harry Jerome and Bill Crothers were performing that day in track at the main stadium. Jackson and Hungerford held a slim lead over Germany and Finland at the 1000m mark in the pairs final. "I was worried about George and sensed that was the time to break away," said Jackson. "I shouted 'Ten!' — which means go all out. And we just churned and pulled away from everybody." But at 1700m and with the finish line just 300m away, Hungerford began to tire and his oar went in the adjacent lane and began skimming the styrofoam lane markers (which is legal). Concerned the oar would catch on the markers and all would be lost, the Canadians had a sense of panic. "I remember thinking to myself: 'What do we do?'" said Jackson. "There was 200m left now and we were both really hurting. I wished they would just call the race off then and there and declare us the winners. I remember the Germans in the crowd were chanting 'Deutschland, Deutschland' and me thinking 'No bloody way.'" But it was the Dutch rowers Steven Blaisse and Ernst Venemans who passed the fast-closing Germans and came onto the Canadian stern with just ten strokes remaining. "I just panicked," admitted Jackson, who shortened his stroke. The mistiming caused the shell to shudder but the Canadians readjusted and finished in a dead heat with the Dutch. The mono had taken so much out of Hungerford that he was in a state of collapse. Jackson, sucking for a breath of air, turned to a photographer at

Exhausted but happy upstarts Roger Jackson (front) and George Hungerford on the Tokyo Olympic rowing course with their gold medals.

the finish line and asked "Did we win?" The photographer just shrugged. Jackson remembers thinking about himself: "You idiot. You blew it, you blew it." But Hungerford collected just enough air in his lungs to look to his partner and gasp: "I managed to hold it, George. I held the boat." He sure did. But Hungerford couldn't get out of the shell and Jackson had to pull him up. "I still marvel at what George was able to do," says Jackson. The two were led down a red carpet to the podium where IOC president Avery Brundage was waiting to present them with their gold medals. And that's when it hit home. "It overwhelmed me for the first time at that moment," said Jackson. "This wasn't just another college race. Up until then, it felt like every other gut-wrenching race on Coal Harbour or Lake Washington. All of a sudden I thought, 'My God, this is the Olympics. And we won.'"

The flag and anthem debates were raging in Canada at that time. "O Canada" had just been introduced to replace "God Save the Queen" while the nation and Parliament were agonizing over the proposal to replace the historic Red Ensign with the simple but poignantly stylized red Maple Leaf. Since this was Canada's first, and as it turned out, only gold medal of the Tokyo Olympics, the ceremonies would prove interesting. They still raised the old Red Ensign for Jackson and Hungerford but played "O Canada." The fact no Canadian journalists were there to witness it still rankles Jackson. "Nobody wanted to go out to Toda that day," he said. "But the idiots should have looked at the rowing tradition of Canada at Melbourne in 1956 and the fact it provided our country with its only medal at Rome in 1960." Still in a state of shock, Jackson and Hungerford wandered back to the Athletes' Village wearing their gold medals *under* their sweat tops. Lynn Davies, the great Welsh long jumper who had just edged Ralph Boston of the US at the stadium, walked past Hungerford and Jackson with his gold medal dangling proudly over his sweat top. The two Canadians looked at each and began to laugh at their own modesty. They then went for a quiet walk around the Village to savour the moment — with their medals still hidden from view. By then word had spread like wildfire among the Canadian media at the stadium that Canada had won gold in rowing. Writers and broadcasters rushed to the Village to try and locate Hungerford and Jackson, who were in the middle of their long walk. With deadlines upon them, the reporters were desperate for stories on who exactly these two rowers were, how they won and what they were doing to celebrate. "They couldn't find us so they created these incredible stories that we were out on the Ginza getting our bodies rubbed in hot tubs by geishas," laughed Jackson, who went on to a distinguished career at the University of Calgary and the Canadian Olympic Association as one of Canada's premier administrators in the field of amateur sport. "Some of the stories were just a riot. Actually, all we did was go for a walk and then crash out in our rooms." Instead of a night of wild partying in the fleshpots of Tokyo, the two Canadians celebrated by guzzling seven Cokes each.

On a cloudy and muggy October 16 in the main stadium, the day after Jackson's and Hungerford's rowing gold, the eight survivors from the field of forty-seven entrants from thirty-two nations gathered for the start of the men's 800m final. Clad in the famous black singlet of his country, the world record holder and defending Olympic champion from 1960 awaited the gun without a twitch or nervous glance. So supreme was Peter Snell's ability that the rest of the runners seemed in awe of it, as well they should have been. George Kerr of Jamaica, who couldn't overtake Snell in the 880 yards final two years earlier at the Perth Commonwealth Games despite a valiant attempt, glanced anxiously over at the Kiwi. Also warming up was a thin and crew-cut twenty-three year old from Markham, Ontario, whose eye glasses were something right out of Buddy Holly. Bill Crothers, who began in track at Agincourt High School before graduating from the University of Toronto's school of pharmacy in 1963, had finished out of the medals in the 880 yards at Perth. But Snell admitted later to being more worried about Crothers in the Olympic final (because of his speed of forty-six seconds over 400m) and the emerging and stylish Wilson Kiprugut of Kenya than about Kerr.

Crothers was an intense young man who ran with a great deal of passion and perhaps even anger. With Harry Jerome and Bruce Kidd, he represented one third of Canada's world-class track triumverate of the 1960s. Crothers was extremely upset over what he perceived as a lack of commitment by the national track authorities in the 1960s to use the trio's success to promote the sport in a meat-and-potatoes North America where hockey and football ruled. "There was just a belief that an athlete was supposed to stay out there and compete and not have any opinions about how to better his sport," said Crothers. "They didn't take advantage of Jerome, Kidd and myself to build up the level of support for track and field in Canada. It was always my belief that we should build up Canadian track and field but there was very little opportunity for Canadians to compete in events in Canada or to go to a good Canadian university track program." (Crothers and Kidd were the only Canadian track and field stars of note in the 1960s who did not compete for a US university.)

The man whose quest for Canadian track acceptance led to run-ins with the sport's unbending and pathetic national bureaucracy of the 1960s ran into the Canadian record books at the Tokyo Olympics. His performance at Tokyo, and that of Jerome, probably did more to elevate track in Canada than a hundred meets held across the country could ever hope to do. The knock against Crothers was his tendency to get boxed in. After winning his heat and semifinal in the Olympics, Crothers stayed on the outside and managed to keep in touch with the leading group. It was Snell who allowed himself to be boxed in as Kiprugut and Kerr stormed to the front, where they remained until about the 600m mark. Snell fought his way out of the box and pulled wide, then blasted past Kerr and Kiprugut. He was gone. Crothers, meanwhile, was also still out wide. He saw his chance and cranked it up a notch to slip past Kerr and Kiprugut down the stretch for the silver medal. Snell won in an Olympic record 1:45.1 (his world record was 1:44.3). Crothers' time of 1:45.6 was the fastest ever for somebody not named Peter Snell and it stood as the Canadian record for an incredible twenty-nine years until finally broken by Freddie Williams in the semifinals of the 1993 world track and field championships in Stuttgart, Germany. Kiprugut was through in 1:45.9 for the bronze medal. It was the first-ever Olympic medal for a Kenyan and ushered in the era of their astonishing world domination of men's middle- and long-distance running. Kerr settled for fourth place in 1:45.9 while Americans Tom Farrell and Jerome Siebert were fifth and sixth, Dieter Bogatzki of Germany seventh and Jacques Pennewaert of Belgium eighth.

Snell, who also won the Olympic 1500m at Tokyo, only decided to enter the 800m just days before the event — which would have left Crothers a golden boy. But being second to the world's best was not too shabby. "Snell's ability and determination were immense," said the Canadian, who eventually owned two Crothers Pharmacy stores from 1965 to 1989 in Markham and Unionville on Ontario Highway Seven. Crothers had also made it to the 400m semifinals at Tokyo and won silver medals at the 1966 Kingston, Jamaica, Commonwealth and 1967 Winnipeg Pan-American games. But his greatest moment after the 1964 Olympic silver medal came on June 10, 1965, at Varsity Stadium in Toronto. Canada may not be a track and field country on the level of some others, but you didn't need a hammer to drill into Canadian heads the allure of an 880 yards showdown between Crothers and Snell on Canadian soil. About 20,000 fans showed up at Varsity Stadium that afternoon: and they got to voice their throaty approval as Crothers defeated Snell by two yards. Crothers followed that with another win over Snell in Oslo. In six meetings between Crothers and the man who is probably the greatest middle-distance runner in history, it was four to two for Snell. Crothers stayed close to home in Markham, eventually becoming the chairman of the York Regional School Board. But Snell left New Zealand, which may be too small for heroes. Like Olympic and Commonwealth great Jack Lovelock before him, Snell feared he could not live anything approaching a normal life in his home country after his successes. His celebrity almost overwhelmed the place. So he left for a largely anonymous life in the United States as a professor/researcher at the University of Texas, where his name aroused far less attention. Snell was invited back to New Zealand and carried in the Queen's Baton — the equivalent of the Olympic torch — to start the 1990 Auckland Commonwealth Games. His Canadian rival Crothers also stayed clear of track after the 1960s, and in the 1990s confines his sporting energies to old-timers hockey.

Harry Jerome was magnificent but aloof. Unwilling to defend himself against largely unwarranted criticism, he played the pouting prince who many saw as unfit to ascend to the throne. Part of the trouble was that Canada had hardly been a powerhouse at the Summer Olympics in the post-Second World War era. Then along comes a man who is a bona fide gold medal threat in one of the true glamour events — the 100m. The expectations of the Canadian public and media, starved for a marquee performance at the Summer Games, were immense. The few medals since 1948 in sports like rowing, canoeing and shooting were fine but they hardly carried the currency of track gold, especially that of the 100m. Jerome was too good in too big an event. Mixed with huge national expectations, it was an alchemist's combination that would prove explosive. Jerome came to the Tokyo Olympics followed by two black clouds from previous Games. The world record holder had cased up at seventy-five yards and finished last in the final of the 100-yard sprint at the 1962 Perth Commonwealth Games. This came after a similar incident in the 100m semifinals at the 1960 Rome Olympics. The Canadian press and public went into an uproar over what they perceived as Jerome's poor attitude — as if he actually went out to purposely lose those two races. He had pulled a hamstring in the Rome race and torn the big muscle in the front of his left thigh at Perth. Both were bad injuries at the most inopportune of times. What was worse was Jerome's inability to explain himself and those situations. In his arrogant brushing off of the media in Rome, he did immense damage to his reputation. Unable to get his side of events, the Canadian media quickly labelled him a quitter. When the truth of the injury came out, the damage in the public eye had already been done. Most people acknowledged his speed and brilliance. He co-held both the world records in the 100m (10.0 seconds) and 100-yard sprints (9.1 seconds) for four years in the 1960s. But many doubted his ability to perform under pressure. "There is no doubt that Jerome is worthy of the world records he holds, but he is one of those sprinters who prefer a clinical atmosphere to the pressure of a major competition like this," wrote the *London Times* at the 1962 Commonwealth Games.

The injury in the Perth final was so severe that Jerome left the Games early and was under the scalpel of surgeon Hector Gillespie in Vancouver before they ended. The muscle had shredded so badly at Perth that Gillespie was able to place his entire fist within the resulting indentation. Jerome was out of racing for a year and the injury was so serious that people were ready to write him off as an almost-genius whose career hallmark was underachievment. Many thought he should be happy to walk without a painful limp, never mind get back into world-class sprinting. But Gillespie persuaded Jerome to take up running again, if only as a means of rehabilatation. He told the frightened Jerome that he need not worry about losing the use of the leg. So Jerome fought back to make a remarkable recovery and qualify for Tokyo: his detractors watched in disbelief. Bill Bowerman, Jerome's coach at the University of Oregon where the Canadian went to school on athletic scholarship, labelled Canadians "just plain greedy [for medals]" because of the pressure he felt had been put on Jerome in the past.

Jerome was a complex character — a black man in a white country who carried the hopes of a nation on his shoulders and who had already twice bowed under the weight. He was very sensitive about race and, being feisty, often got into scraps in the schoolyards of lily-white North Vancouver, where his broken family moved when he was twelve. He was born in Prince Albert, Saskatchewan. His father was a Pullman porter for the Canadian National Railway. The younger Jerome's speed was noticed by P.E. teachers at North Vancouver High School and he was encouraged to join the local track and field club, the Optimist Striders. It was pretty clear from the outset that Jerome was something of a prodigy. His first race for the Striders included an opponent who used to taunt him because of his skin colour. When he won that race with ease, leaving his former tormentor in the cinder dust, Jerome knew he had found a way to answer back at the world.

He was only eighteen when he smashed Percy Williams' thirty-one-year-old national record in the 220 yards and nineteen in 1960 when he clocked 10.0 seconds in the 100m at the Olympic trials in Saskatoon to share the world record with the volatile and self-taught 1960 Olympic champion-to-be Armin Hary of Frankfurt, Germany. The Jerome/Hary world record (later matched by Bob Hayes and Horacio Estevez) stood for eight years until American Jim Hines became the first man to run under ten seconds by clocking 9.9 in the semifinals of the 1968 AAU Championships in Sacramento en route to his Olympic gold medal in 9.95 later that year in Mexico City. Perhaps it was because Jerome had beaten the odds just to get to the Tokyo Olympics that the pressure now seemed off him. Nobody was expecting much this time around. And it was just like Jerome to confound everybody once again. But he was the same old Jerome in some ways, winning the Olympic trials in St. Lambert, Quebec, while wearing sweatpants and dark sunglasses and with a casual disregard for the competition that hardly endeared him to his fellow runners.

At Tokyo he advanced with ease through the field of seventy-three entrants from forty-nine countries. In one of the Olympic semifinals, the leading runner let up after tearing a rib muscle. But this time it was wasn't Jerome, but Melvin Pender of the United States. Jerome sped by the stricken Pender to win the semifinal ahead of other fancied runners Gaoussou Kone of the Ivory Coast and Enrique Figuerola of Cuba. All four advanced to the final, including Pender, who insisted on running despite intense pain. Bob Hayes was the winner of the other semifinal. The powerfully built but pigeon-toed runner from Florida had forty-eight straight victories going into the Olympic final on October 15 and was the clear favourite. Hayes, Jerome and Figuerola were off like cannonballs. As soon as they passed the ten-metre mark, it became obvious these three would battle for the medals. It was Hayes who unleashed a powerful kick to pull away from the Canadian and Cuban to win by about eight yards in 10.0 seconds, thus tying the world mark co-held by Jerome. Both Jerome and Figuerola, the first Cuban ever to win an Olympic medal in track and field, flashed across in 10.2 seconds, but the edge given to the Cuban.

Jerome expressed satisfaction with winning the bronze. He could be accused of being a quitter no more. Even though Olympic gold ultimately eluded Jerome, his bronze medal at Tokyo in 1964 was as good as gold when you consider there was a good chance two years earlier he would never again walk properly, let alone run like the wind. Hayes went on to a starry football career as a wide receiver with the Dallas Cowboys. Jerome went on to take a fourth in the Olympic 200m at Tokyo and continued to redeem his reputation by winning the 100 yards gold medal at the 1966 Commonwealth Games in Kingston, Jamaica, and the 100m gold at the 1967 Pan-American Games in Winnipeg. He made it to the final of the 1968 Olympics in Mexico City but a seventh place finish, despite a clocking of 10.1 seconds, convinced him his time was up at age twenty-eight. By then Jerome was much more mellow and at ease. He faded from the competitive scene with a sense of grace. He stated he would like to stay involved in amateur sport by working with Canadian children. Jerome earned a Masters Degree in Education at the University of Oregon and had an easy rapport with kids and was a well-liked P.E. teacher at Templeton High School in Vancouver. He remained true to his words and promoted and taught track to youngsters across Canada. Funded by the feds, he ran sports clinics from St. John's to Victoria. Dubbed the "Jerome Road Company," the former sprint great and about half a dozen other national team athletes travelled the country putting on training and coaching clinics. Jerome, at last, seemed content and at peace. But one week after Percy Williams killed himself in Vancouver in 1982, Jerome was crossing the Lions Gate Bridge to North Vancouver as a passenger in a car when he suffered a brain aneurysm. He died on the way to hospital at age forty-two.

Judo is one of the activities at the heart of the Japanese sporting/cultural tradition and so the organizers were keen to include it on the Olympic agenda for the first time in 1964. There was really no other place then to learn this ancient art, so Alfred Douglas Rogers of Vancouver moved to Japan in 1959 to master its intricacies. To help pay the bills, Rogers took on the role of a badass in more than fifty Japanese films, including *Godzilla*. At 260 pounds, Rogers was hard to miss on the mat or the silver screen. Go to your places of worship; the Canadian will not harm you. Rogers never could explain how it was possible in those movies to warn all of Tokyo with a single megaphone. But he did recall one western in which he played Wyatt Earp next to a raft of Japanese actors who played the parts of cowboys — and Indians! But acting was just a means to an end for Rogers. He studied and practised the craft of judo intensely for five years in Japan and when the Olympics rolled around, he was ready. Rogers mowed over the heavyweight class to reach the gold medal final against his Japanese friend Isao Inokuma. For Canada, with no tradition in Asian martial arts, any medal would be a bonus: the fluky result of one lone Canadian's quixotic quest to be the best in what was then an exotic and little-known sport.

Rogers and Inokuma were practice partners and used to sparring against each other. Each knew the other's moves too well and so the final was a slow-moving affair with each man looking for a moment of weakness in the other. The pressure was clearly on Inokuma, who was performing in front of his own countrymen who followed the sport passionately and expected him to win. The 1964 Olympic preliminary matches lasted ten minutes, while the final stretched to fifteen minutes. That's an eternity in judo, where things can lumber along and then suddenly end in a snap throw. Olympic matches now are all five minutes. Rogers and Inokuma guarded their vulnerablities well and neither could end the bout with a throw, pin or choke. The final went the full fifteen minutes, with Inokuma winning on a *kinsa* or close decision. Judo was not included in the 1968 Mexico City Olympics so Rogers had to be content with his silver medal from Tokyo. He followed that up with a bronze medal at the 1965 world championships and gold at the 1967 Winnipeg Pan-American Games. He returned to Canada in 1966 to take up a career, not as an actor but an airline pilot.

MEXICO CITY 1968

October 12 to October 27
5530 Athletes from 112 Nations

And so it was that the steaming, sweltering summer of discontent ended in the shadow of the timeless rock and stone of Popocatepetl and Ixtacihuatl. Bobby Kennedy and Martin Luther King were cut down and American city ghettos went up in blazes. For the first time, Americans in large numbers balked at fighting a war and took to the streets while student and labour protests sent shock waves through France. The Mexico City Olympics would not escape unscathed from the tumultuous and watershed year 1968. Faced by boycott threats from thirty-two African nations, black American athletes and the Soviets, panicked Mexican organizers asked the IOC to rethink its position on allowing South Africa back into the Games (it had been banned from the 1964 Tokyo Olympics because of apartheid). Under intense pressure, the IOC overruled its earlier decision to allow the South Africans to participate at Mexico City and again barred them, over the objections of Avery Brundage. Mexican student activists, seeing no point in spending millions on a circus in a country beset by crushing poverty, protested on the eve of the Games. Hundreds of protesters were brutally gunned down on October 2 in the Plaza of Three Cultures, just ten days before President Gustavo Diaz Ordaz declared the XIX Summer Olympics open during a brightly festive opening as hurdler Enriqueta Basilio climbed ninety steps to the cauldron to become the first female ever to light the Olympic torch.

It seems that nothing must be allowed to stand in the way of the Games. The government admitted to thirty-five dead but more reliable sources put the figure at 267 killed and more than 1200 wounded. And then there were those gloved black fists on the Olympic podium that, to this very day, are the most enduring symbol of that angry year. But political heat comes and goes and the ancient Aztec capital of Tenochtitlan, conquered by the Spanish and now known as Mexico City, has seen a lot of it over the centuries. Perched on a plateau valley at 2240m, the city sits on a dry and shaky pie-crust of earth that many thousands of years ago boasted lakes and rivers that made the Aztec capital a sort of Venice of the New World.

Perhaps it was written among the Aztec legends that a Northern Princess would one day come to do battle, as the loyal subjects back home in her kingdom cheered her on. That budding young Canadian princess had stormed the ramparts of her kingdom's former overlords and laid waste to them with four gold medals, three silvers and two world records in the outdoor pool at the 1966 Commonwealth Games in Kingston, Jamaica. Then it was time to conquer the lands around her fiefdom, which the sixteen-year-old princess did with two gold medals, three silvers and two more world records at the 1967 Pan-American Games in Winnipeg. So it came to be that her entire kingdom was watching, and expecting a golden show, from the princess at the Olympic Games of 1968 under the ancient volcanic gaze of Popocatepetl and Ixtacihuatl.

Bringing that kind of pressure to bear on a seventeen year old was highly uncharacteristic for the kingdom of Canada, which had experienced only limited success at the Summer Olympics since the end of the Second World War. Nothing was ever really expected of it at the Summer Games and Canada usually delivered just that. But that's exactly why the build-up was so great for this princess, who for all the world looked to be a queen in waiting. A kingdom which had seen too few world beaters at the Summer Games appeared to finally have one. And the loyal subjects of the kingdom could almost feel golden victory coming their way. How sweetly it would uplift a defeatist national psyche. Ah, yes — that elusive taste of Olympic victory. The young princess was sent off to the ancient Aztec capital with great fanfare and tremendous expectations riding on her slender shoulders. Victory was assured, the media trumpeted. Our little princess was to rule the waves and be crowned

An anxious Elaine Tanner looks back at the score-board after the women's 100m backstroke final to find a silver medal placing at the 1968 Mexico City Olympics.

a queen. But all was not right in the mind of the princess, who was just a high school girl with the weight of an entire kingdom on her shoulders. "Usually before a race, you're concentrating on strategy, the other swimmers, the race," said the princess, a.k.a. Elaine Tanner. "But at Mexico City, all I could think about was the twenty million people who were expecting me to win."

Only 5' 2", Tanner was a pocket princess. It was during a club meet that a swim coach from Prince George, BC, shouted "Way to go, Mighty Mouse," and the nickname stuck. Mighty Mouse went on to become a heroine in a country starved for Olympic success in a glamour sport. Although born in Vancouver, Tanner actually learned to swim when her family moved to California for six months when she was eight. Initially she didn't even want to take swim lessons, but was soon winning first-prize ribbons in children's meets. When the family returned to Vancouver, Tanner joined the Dolphins Swim Club and came under the tutelage of 1964 Canadian Olympic team swim coach Howard Firby, who described her as a "water-borne creature." He put her on a relentless training schedule that was as grueling as it was successful. And so it was that Tanner stood on the starting blocks for the women's 100m backstroke final at the boldly designed Olympic pool on October 23, 1968, waiting to snatch the greatest sports prize in the world. With world record holder Karen Muir (1:06.4) out of the Games because of the ban on South Africa, Tanner was the overwhelming favourite. The West Vancouver schoolgirl had set Olympic records of 1:07.6 and 1:07.4 in the heats and semifinals. The gun for the final sounded, and an entire kingdom rose in front of its television sets to watch their tiny princess slay the dragons of the world.

At the half-way point, Tanner was dead even with Kaye Hall, who was the same age as Tanner and had grown up in nearby Tacoma, Washington. There seemed no cause for worry: Tanner had easily beaten Hall several times in meets all over the continent and had also bested her the previous day in the Olympic semifinals. But something stirred in Hall that day of the final as both girls hit the wall for the turn. She could probably never have done it again, but she did it the one time it counted the most. Hall baffled the experts and was off like a motor boat over the final fifty metres. Tanner turned in a tremendous final fifty, too, but it wasn't enough. An inspired Hall finished in 1:06.2 to break the world record while Tanner clocked 1:06.7 for the silver medal. Tanner had two days to shake off the "defeat" and focus on the 200m backstroke.

Again, the world record holder Muir (2:24.8) was not present and again Tanner was the prohibitive favourite. Again, she breezed through the heats and semis to the final. Again, she was upset by an inspired American who was given little chance against her. Lillian "Pokey" Watson destroyed the field with an Olympic record 2:24.8 in the final. Tanner again won silver (2:27.4).

The young Canadian princess would never become a queen. And it hurt. Devastated and distraught, Tanner put up a brave front with a smile as she stood on the podium for her second silver medal. But her heart was breaking. She was in tears as she burst through her dorm door in the Village and crashed to the bed defeated and broken at just seventeen. She felt some paper below her. It was several dozen telegrams from back home congratulating her on her medals and saying how proud people were. She remembers her tears staining the telegrams as she read them. That moment has always stayed with Tanner as her Olympic highlight. But mostly, what has stuck is the overwhelming sense of "failure" at Mexico City and a Canadian public that greeted her return to Vancouver not with parades and presents — as it had for Percy Williams in 1928 — but with a small smattering of friends and supporters at the airport. It is remarkable that a nation which up to that time had only very modest success at the Summer Olympics, should consider two silver medals to be a disappointment. But that is the nature of build-up and hype. And it cost Tanner. It cost her more than could ever be imagined. It affected the rest of her life.

"Emotionally, I died," she said. She fought feelings of failure and profound insecurity and struggled through two failed marriages and numerous careers punctuated by periods of unemployment. Being awarded the Order of Canada didn't help. Everywhere she went, she saw those two days in Mexico City, where her fairytale came to an end.

The princess would not go on and live happily ever after. "It shattered me," she admitted. "Because I didn't feel loved, I denied myself food and went to ninety-four pounds." She went to job interviews, application in hand, only to be told the boss couldn't believe the great Elaine Tanner would need a job to make ends meet. It took Tanner more than two decades to finally put the past behind her. Those two Olympic "losses" had made her almost an emotional cripple. She finally began to turn it around with a successful third marriage and an alternative approach to mental and physical health as a certified holistic counsellor. "That's the whole intrigue behind the mind-body connection," she said, in an interview with the *Victoria Times-Colonist*. "That [the Olympics] was a great learning experience for me, even though it took me years to figure it out. Sometimes I get up at three in the morning and just sit and look at the stars. I know what a fine line it is to make it or not. It's been a struggle, but you learn to appreciate simple things. A lot of the really hard times we go through can really be gifts in disguise. I've learned a lot from my losses and may be a richer person for it. Maybe losing the gold medals helped me more than winning."

What happened to Tanner "really was a tragic thing," says Ralph Hutton, who won silver for Canada at the Mexico City Olympics in the men's 400m freestyle. "To this very day I still can't understand why I won silver and was considered a success and she did the same thing and was not considered a success. She really struggled after that and has been through a lot emotionally. She was constantly hounded by the media and became the darling of the Canadian press. She was naive and didn't know how to deal with all that attention. And the media was not very helpful. I remember reporters telling her point blank: 'The country is really going to be let down if you don't win gold.'"

Hutton, later a Vancouver policeman, also had his own pressure to worry about. He went into the Olympic men's 400m as the world record holder at 4:06.5 and as a swimmer known as the Iron Man after winning medals in all fourteen events he entered throughout the 1966 Kingston, Jamaica, Commonwealth and 1967 Winnipeg Pan-American games. Throw in the fact Canada hadn't won a medal in an individual Olympic swimming event since George Hodgson at Stockholm in 1912. Hutton was from the tiny, mist-shrouded mill town of Ocean Falls, BC, which boasted 1800 people. But out of this remarkable little place, which was 350 miles north of Vancouver and accessible only by ship or float plane, came a swimmer for every Canadian team at the Olympics from London in 1948 to Montreal in 1976. From this isolated town, hemmed in by and perched on the side of mountains hard by the Pacific Ocean and with only a

Ralph Hutton (in lane six) at the start of the 1968 Olympic men's 400m freestyle final in which he won the silver medal.

stinky pulp mill and plank streets, emerged kids who went on to swim in the great capitals of the world — London, Rome, Tokyo, Mexico City. Unlike almost every other Canadian community, Ocean Falls didn't have a hockey rink. But it did have a pool, built by the Crown Zellerbach Pulp and Paper Company in the 1920s. And it had an English-born swim coach named George Gate who came to town in 1948. Out of that pool, carved in the heart of the Pacific rainforest, came Olympians Jim and Leo Portlance (London 1948), Alan Gilchrist (London '48 and Helsinki 1952), Lenore Fisher (Helsinki '52 and Melbourne 1956), Ron Gilchrist (Melbourne '56), Richard Pound (Rome 1960 and later an influential International Olympic Committee vice-president), John "Sandy" Gilchrist (Tokyo 1964 and Mexico City 1968), Hutton (Tokyo '64, Mexico City '68 and Munich 1972) and Ian Mackenzie (Munich '72 and Montreal 1976). "It was like growing up in a Boy Scout camp," says Hutton. "You were either climbing the mountain or boating. And in the winter, if you didn't swim in the pool you did nothing. So we all swam in the pool. There was nothing else to do." The Ocean Falls Swim Club won the national team championship five out of six years between 1960 and 1965 despite having only two competitors — Hutton and John Gilchrist. But Gates moved to Montreal in 1965 and Crown Zellarbach harvested what riches it could and then left, too. An attempt by the BC government to keep the town alive failed in the 1970s and now only about thirty people remain.

But the echoes of countless hours spent in that old Ocean Falls pool were ringing in Hutton's ears as the world record holder, attempting to become the first individual Canadian swim medallist in fifty-six years, stepped onto the starting blocks for the final of the 400m freestyle. Hutton had topped American Mike Burton by a tenth of a second earlier that year in Lincoln, Nebraska, to set the world record and the two men knew the Olympic final was going to be close. Burton was feeling ill leading up to the qualifying races and fainted in an elevator at the Athletes' Village the day before the heats were to begin. He conserved energy through the heats but still reached the final. "I hadn't beaten him by much when I set the world record so although I was the favourite, it wasn't by an over-whelming margin," says Hutton. And, indeed, October 23 was going to be Burton's golden day and not the Canadian's. The American took the lead at the halfway point and kept increasing it until he touched the wall in an Olympic record 4:09.0 but well off Hutton's world mark. The boy from Ocean Falls churned furiously and was home in 4:11.7 for the silver medal. Bronze medallist Alain Mosconi of France (4:13.3) wasn't a threat to either of the first two men. Hutton's silver medal was greeted with cheers in Canada. Later that day, Tanner won the first of her two silvers and the nation frowned. Hutton, too, experienced frustration later at Mexico City despite being the only swimmer at the Games to qualify for three individual freestyle finals. He placed fifth in the 1500m freestyle in 17:15.6 while Burton took gold in 16:38.9.

There is no more disheartening finish at an Olympics than fourth place, the first placing after the medallists get their glory. The men's 200m freestyle — which featured Hutton, the brilliant Michael Wenden of Australia and the world record holder and five-time Olympic gold medallist Don Schollander of the US — was the killer swimming event of Mexico City. If there is one race Hutton would love to have back, it's the 200m freestyle final at Mexico City. Wenden added his second gold medal of the Games by denying Schollander a sixth career Olympic gold. The Aussie was first in an Olympic record 1:55.2 and Schollander sec-ond in 1:55.8. There was a furious battle for the bronze medal with John Nelson of the US (1:58.1) outreaching Hutton (1:58.6) at the wall. "I really felt I could have done better," said Hutton. Underachievement, real or perceived, is not something the competitive and talented Hutton took too kindly. "The attitude of Canadian people in general is that they are not willing to pay the price to be successful," he said. "It's just not in our nature." It was, however, in Hutton's. But further disappointment awaited in the 4x200 freestyle relay, if fourth place in the Olympics can really be described as disappointing. While the Schollander — and Mark Spitz — led Americans (7:52.33) and Wenden-fueled Aussies (7:53.77) battled almost stroke for stroke for the gold, the Canadians were locked in a struggle for bronze with the Soviets. The Canuck squad consisted of Ocean Falls products Hutton and John Gilchrist, Ron Jacks of Vancouver via the Indiana University Hoosiers, and George Smith of Edmonton. The Soviets prevailed in 8:01.66, leaving fourth place to the Canadians in 8:03.22. Swimming the first leg for the Soviet squad was Vladimir Bure, father of Vancouver Canucks hockey sensation Pavel Bure. The Canadian team also boasted a famous future family connection. Ron Jacks' brother, singer Terry Jacks, headed the popular band the Poppy Family and then went solo with the monster 1974 worldwide hit "Seasons in the Sun." When the elder Bure moved to Vancouver to be with his NHL star son in the 1990s, he came across both Jacks and Hutton at an old-timers swim function at UBC.

The Canadian women's 4x100 freestyle relay team of Tanner, Angela Coughlan, Marilyn Corson and Marion Lay captured a bronze medal. Pushed hard by Lynette Bell of Australia on the anchor leg, Lay responded by outduelling her Down Under rival as the Canadians took third in 4:07.2. The Aussies, to whom swim success at the Olympics and Commonwealth Games seems second nature, had to settle for fourth place this time in 4:08.7. The American team, led by Jan Henne and Linda Gustavson from the powerful Santa Clara Swim Club, won gold with an Olympic record 4:02.5. East Germany was second in 4:05.7. The great Dawn Fraser, suffering the effects of a ridiculous four-year Australian Swim Federation ban for stealing the Japanese flag at Emperor Hirohito's palace on a lark during the 1964 Tokyo Games, wasn't in Mexico City to defend the women's 100m freestyle title she won at the 1956, 1960 and 1964 Olympics. The 1968 final was a blanket finish with three Americans and Canada's Lay within a whisker of each other. Henne touched first for gold in 1:00.0, Susan Pedersen and Gustavson second and third, respectively, in 1:00.3 and Lay in 1:00.5 for fourth. Bev Boys of Pickering, Ontario, also had a close call in women's platform diving, placing fourth with 97.97 points. The bronze medallist, Ann Peterson of the US, had 101.11 points. "I don't think you ever come to terms with coming so close in the Olympics," says Boys, who won eleven Commonwealth and Pan-Am games medals and finished fifth in the 1972 Munich Olympics. "Fourth is tough. In many ways, you might as well be forty-fourth. Close only counts in horseshoes. Sometimes I think of just how close I was to an Olympic medal. When you miss the Olympic podium by such a small margin twice, it's something you always think about." You can probably guess that Boys was a fairly intense competitor. She dedicated her entire early life to diving. But she was taught how to dive but not how to live. She was thirty years old and had never filled out a job application, something that would come back to haunt her when she was finally thrown into the so-called real world. She had a rocky work and business career until she finally landed on her feet as the sport coordinator for Dive BC. Boys was so dedicated as an athlete that the lack of facilities didn't stop her. She once trained by jumping off a windmill and into a leech- and water-snake-infested canal at Picton, Ontario. She also wedged the boards from an old bowling alley between a couple of rocks and spent a summer diving into a river off that. It is people like Boys, who have more than paid their dues, who deserve to win Olympic medals. But deserving and getting are two different things.

Debate still rages over the controversial "black power" salute delivered by Tommie Smith and John Carlos as they stood on the podium after winning gold and bronze, respectively, in the men's track 200m. Reflecting at once both anger and sadness, it remains one of the most significant and emotive athletic images of all time. You sense their frustration at feeling like warriors for an American nation that shunned and discriminated against them at home because of their skin colour. "Winning gold medals for a country where I don't have my freedom is irrelevant," said Smith. "I'm a fast nigger, but still just a nigger at my school [San Jose State]. Nobody sees that I'm a serious student. That's not my role to the white folks." But what if everybody who had a beef against somebody showcased it at the Olympics? It would be chaos and the Games could not function. What if Czech medallists had made some sort of protest against the Soviets for invading their country that year or if Arab medallists made protests against the Israelis or the Pakistanis against the Indians? There is some sympathy and understanding behind the IOC's pressuring of the US Olympic Committee to boot Smith and Carlos out of the Olympics — even though it was purely a symbolic move since the two had already left. But that is not to deny the furious tenor of those times.

Led by charismatic and forceful San Jose State sociology and anthropology professor Harry Edwards, a black boycott of the US Olympic team had been under active consideration. "I will use whatever tools necessary to bring unity to the black race," said Edwards. "If it means an Olympic boycott, so be it." Many prominent black American athletes of the time supported Edwards' cause, including former Cleveland Browns superstar Jim Brown and 1956 Melbourne Olympian and Boston Celtics legend Bill Russell. Kareem Abdul-Jabbar, then known as Lew Alcindor of UCLA, refused to join the gold-medallist 1968 US Olympic basketball team which included Spencer Haywood and Jo-Jo White. The boycott movement briefly gained momentum after the IOC's decision to readmit South Africa, but then faded after the IOC reversed its decision. But Edwards promised some show of protest at the Games and Smith and Carlos, who were both San Jose State runners, delivered with a black lightning bolt that jolted the entire Olympics. Smith raised his black-gloved right fist and refused to raise his head to acknowledge the American flag while the national anthem played. Carlos raised his black-gloved left fist and shut his eyes and hung his head to the right. Aussie silver medallist Peter Norman was in front of them on the second of the podium's three tiers and oblivious to what was transpiring behind him.

The medals presenter, British blueblood and 1928 Olympic 400m hurdles champion Lord Burghley, stared straight ahead at attention and later expressed anger at what he said was political intrusion upon the sacred nature of the victory ceremonies. Smith called the action a victory for black people everywhere. "White people seem to think we're animals," said his defiant mate Carlos, who later had a brief and unsuccessful stint as a wide receiver in the Canadian Football League for the Montreal Alouettes. "They think we're some kind of a show horse. They think we can perform and they can throw us some peanuts and say, 'Good boy, good boy.'" It's not known how many horses eat peanuts. But while Carlos may have proved himself a poor candidate for veterinary school, or the CFL, he made his point. When his actions received the support of the all-white Harvard men's eights who were representing the US in the 1968 Games, Carlos snapped back: "We don't need whitey."

But the US black camp was clearly split at Mexico City. Nothing symbolized this more than the actions of George Foreman, a high school dropout who grew up on the hard streets on the wrong side of Houston. He called Smith's and Carlos' actions "stuff for college kids who live in a different world." Foreman instead waved a small American flag after winning the heavyweight gold medal. As with Smith and Carlos, reaction was swift and mixed. Foreman was labeled everything from a true patriot to an Oreo — black on the outside but white inside. Foreman went on to greater fame by winning the world professional heavyweight crown in 1973 and then losing it to Muhammad Ali in Zaire before remarkably regaining it twenty years later in 1994, while looking like a jovial butterball. He said he wasn't making a political statement at the Olympics in Mexico City. He was just proud to be an American.

The rarefied air at 2240m proved a double-edged sword. Fears of competing at that altitude became almost hysterical in the years before the Mexico City Games and some even predicted possible deaths. That never happened but those who said those fears were unjustified were also not completely right. The altitude did some weird things to the 1968 Games. The longer distance events were adversely affected, with the times being generally poor. Not surprisingly, runners from high-altitude countries such as Kenya and Ethiopia acclimatized the best. That was dramatically demonstrated in the first track event, the 10,000m. The great Ron Clarke of Australia, holder of more world records than any man alive, stumbled across the line in sixth place looking like one of the zombies from *Night of the Living Dead*. Doctors rushed to his side with oxygen tanks while winner Naftali Temu of Kenya and silver medallist Mamo Wolde of Ethiopia (who later won the marathon, an event in which Canadian Andy Boychuck was tenth) pranced around the track for their victory laps. Rumours that Clarke had almost died were greatly exaggerated. He was fine after a day's rest. But in the "explosive" events such as the sprints and jumps, it was quite another matter. The usual constrictions of wind resistance didn't seem to apply during that Mexican fortnight. Jim Hines, a bulky Texas Southern rocket who openly opposed the attempts at a black boycott of the US team, set the world record in taking the men's 100m in 9.95 seconds. After so many highs and lows, Vancouver's Harry Jerome bowed out of his stormy but admirable racing career by making the final in a field of sixty-four sprinters from forty-two countries and finishing seventh in 10.1 seconds. That 100m final was the first all-black final of any track and field event in Olympic history. Abby Hoffman matched Jerome's finish by placing seventh among twenty-four competitors from sixteen nations in the women's 800m in 2:06.8. The American winner, Madeline Manning (2:00.9), was said to have been spurred on by the garlic-smelling sweat emanating from the European women in the final. It was world records-o-rama in all men's track events from the 800m on down to the 100.

World or Olympic records were also set by the great Kip Keino of Kenya in the 1500m, Willie Davenport of the US in the 110m hurdles, American Dick Fosbury in the high jump, Victor Saneyev of the Soviet Union in the triple jump, Randy Matson of the US in the shot put, Al Oerter of the US in discus, Gyula Zsivotsky of Hungary in hammer,

Janis Lusis of the Soviet Union in javelin and Bill Toomey of the US in decathlon. The air was even thinner at 2245m than it was at 2240. No pole vaulter had ever cleared 5.20m (17') in the history of Olympic competition. At Mexico City, nine men did it despite having trouble concentrating because the Smith-Carlos victory podium furor erupted right in the middle of the vault competition. The winner was Bob Seagren of the US at 5.40m.

But nothing could quite prepare the world for what happened on an overcast October 18 in the long jump pit. Bob Beamon almost jumped into the year 2000. It was the first twenty-first century performance of the twentieth century. Well, it actually fell seven years short as Mike Powell finally broke Beamon's mark at the 1993 world track and field championships in Stuttgart. But what Beamon did on that day at the Mexico City Olympics can't be overestimated. It was maybe the single most astonishing achievement in sports history, eclipsing even Roger Bannister's historic breaching of the four minute mile on May 6, 1954, at Iffley Road, Oxford. With the 1960 champion Ralph Boston of the US, 1964 titleist Lynn Davies of Britain and world co-record holder Igor Ter-Ovanesyan of the Soviet Union entered, Beamon was just another good outsider with a shot at cracking the medal circle. Beamon was the fourth of the seventeen finalists to jump after the first three had fouled on their first attempts. Prone to fouling himself, he was nervous as he raced down the runway. Witnesses insist that there was something unusual about that day. It was raining sporadically and the air seemed electric and prickly with the threat of lightning. There was lightning, all right. But it came in the form of an unfancied American who became Superman. Beamon hit the board and threw himself in the air. He seemed to have entered a vacuum in space because for one twinkling moment the normal laws of gravity didn't seem to apply. As if lifted by the unseen hands of the ancient Greek gods, Beamon practically sailed through the air until he was about six feet off the ground. Observers say it almost looked as if the whole thing was happening in slow motion. He came down and hit the sand so hard that he bounced right out of the pit. Beamon had outjumped the optical measuring device being used to measure the leaps. Startled track officials had to rummage around for a good old-fashioned steel tape to measure his jump. They looked at each other in disbelief and then relayed the finding to the scoreboard keeper, who flashed the numbers 8.90m.

But the metric system just doesn't do poetic justice to what Beamon had accomplished. Unfamiliar with metric, he asked Boston what 8.90 meant. Boston was almost ashen-faced when he turned to his friend and the man he had been helping with coaching tips. "Bob, you jumped over twenty-nine feet," said Boston, who co-held the world record of 8.35m — just a few inches over 27'. No human in recorded competition had ever reached the 28' barrier and now Beamon had *surpassed* that seemingly unreachable mark completely on his way to 29'. It was almost too much to believe. The official measurement was 29' 2½". In the thirty-three years previous, the world record had advanced only 8½". But in a few miraculous seconds, in an event in which records are broken incrementally by fractions of inches, Beamon had atom-bombed the world mark by almost two feet. Overcome with the immensity of his achievement, Beamon's legs buckled and he collapsed to the ground in tears. The silver medal went to Klaus Beer of East Germany at 8.19m or 26' 10½" and the bronze to Boston at 8.16m or 26' 9¼". They were still on earth; Beamon was on another planet. It wasn't until the 1980s that Lutz Dombrowski of East Germany at Moscow in 1980 and Carl Lewis at Los Angeles in 1984 both managed to claw a quarter inch past 28' — still 14" short of where Beamon landed during his freakish leap into history.

Mexico City's Olympic Stadium is a humble place, not a humbling place. While the mighty Azteca Stadium of soccer juts like a steel bowl out of the ground amid the noise and grime near central Mexico City, the Olympic Stadium is nestled gently — almost softly — in the cool and quiet foothills on the outskirts of town. Made from local stone and with a low profile that makes an understated visual impact, it is at one with the earth around it. Built in 1952 and refurbished for the Games, it boasts a lovely Diego Rivera mural that runs the length of its main-entrance side. It seems an oasis perched above the dusty hurly burly of Mexico City life in the valley plateau below. Here, American gold medallist Dick Fosbury revolutionized high jumping with his Fosbury Flop, the method used by virtually every jumper now. And the great American Al Oerter took his fourth straight Olympic discus title at age thirty-two. But this stadium was also the fitting place for an unassuming country like Canada to strike its greatest blow at the 1968 Summer Olympics, which it did just before the closing ceremonies on the final day. Equestrian events may not rival the NHL or major league baseball for fan appeal but the Prix Des Nations jumping teams had a built-in audience assembling in the Olympic Stadium for the closing ceremonies on October 27. "It's pretty tough in front of a crowd like that because if you ever lift your eyes and see that many faces, it breaks your concentration," says Tom Gayford, who along with fellow Toronto riders Jim Elder and Jim Day arrived unfancied and unheralded at the stadium for the final event of the XIX Summer Olympic Games. The teams from the US, Germany and Britain were favoured for the medals, with the Soviets, French, Italians, Brazilians and Australians touted as the main challengers in the field of fifteen teams. "We felt we could get a piece of it but never figured we would win it," admits Gayford. The three Canadian riders and their wives, not wanting to rely on anybody else, got up at 4:00 A.M. that day and packed and shipped their horses to the stadium themselves. At the halfway point, Canada was in third place and Gayford quipped: "Let's quit now and take the bronze." Very Canadian humour. But stockbroker Gayford, refrigeration installer Elder and horse trainer Day rose above that and elevated themselves to Olympus. Equestrian, as with rowing, shooting and canoeing, had kept Canada in the medals during some of its leaner Olympic years. As with those other three sports, it wasn't because of a wide base of support in the country but instead the tenacity and will of a small band of people in certain clubs who stubbornly produced Olympian results. And these people never seemed to give up. Elder had won a bronze medal with John Rumble and Brian Herbinson in the three-day event of the 1956 Olympics, while Gayford first competed at the Games in 1952 at Helsinki.

It was a brilliant, clear day and off in the distance the usually cloud-shrouded peaks of Popocatepetl and Ixtacihuatl were visible as the three Canadians glided smoothly over the hurdles on the lush green stadium turf as if guided by the hand of Zeus. Elder, on The Immigrant, had scored 27.25 fault points. Day, riding Canadian Club, got through with 36.00 and Gayford, atop Big Dee, 39.50. Canada had 102.75 points. The longshots had pulled off a gold-medal upset. France took silver with 110.50 points on the reverse-scoring system and Germany bronze with 117.25. "I couldn't believe it," says Gayford, who managed the Canadian equestrian team for more than a quarter century and who remained good friends with Day and Elder through the years. "But we were focused. We had been doing this for so many years." The final national anthem played for victory at the 1968 Summer Olympics was "O Canada."

An hour later, thousands of white sombreros rustled in the stands during the simple but heartfelt closing of these Games that were held in a poor Latin American country which surprised its critics by delivering a warm and memorable event in a heated and angry year. The chants of *"Mayheeco ... Mayheeco"* rumbled down from the terraces as national pride became almost too much to bear. Many athletes had gone home but those left in the stands broke through the barriers and joined those who had been selected to march. That is exactly the kind of spontaneity and joy the stern and sour men of the IOC under Brundage liked to suppress. But it was impossible to stop this time. Among the carefree and happy throng was gymnast Vera Caslavska, whose training was interrupted when Soviet tanks rolled into Prague but who still managed four golds and two silvers in Mexico City. She wasn't strolling around the infield alone. She had married Czech teammate Josef Odlozil, the 1964 Tokyo 1500m silver medallist, in a civil ceremony during the Mexico Games. A less popular couple (the Soviets, and indeed Americans, were coolly received by the Mexicans) was Mikhail and Sinaida Voronin, who struck a blow for communism by winning eleven medals between them in gymnastics. Much more popular was 1500m champion Kip Keino, although the Kenyan tactic of using his teammate Ben Jipcho as a rabbit to destroy the timing of world-record holder Jim Ryun of the US, was frowned upon by track purists. When he was barely ten and Kenya still under British rule in 1950, Keino stumbled upon a leopard feasting on a goat. A year later, he was mugged by highway robbers along the dirt backroads of his country but managed to escape. Both times, little Kip turned and ran as fast as he could. And he never stopped running. He ran so great, so long and so hard that he became one of the all-time great Olympians. Strolling next to him during the closing ceremonies were three middle-aged men. Canada was unable to crown its Olympic queen but at least it had three kings in Day, Gayford and Elder.

But there were others who wrestled with personal demons courtesy of the competitions at Mexico City. It took Elaine Tanner — who is beautiful and charming and deserved to have everything going for her win or "lose" — more than two decades to shed the trauma of not winning gold and to turn her life's downward spiral into forward momentum. And for John Carlos, a peculiar thing happened at his son's graduation ceremony from an inner city Los Angeles high school in 1992. Knowing Carlos was present, one student lifted a clenched fist in tribute. Slowly and without vocal comment, all the graduating seniors — none of whom were even born in 1968 — followed suit. The moment was both eerie and moving as jagged memories of Mexico City washed over the gym. But not much had really changed. Colour, race and ethnicity still counted for an awful lot in most places and stood in the way of people really understanding each other; and probably always will. Carlos stood and acknowledged the graduates' gesture. Then he sat down and quietly wept.

MUNICH 1972

August 26 to September 10
7156 Athletes from 122 Nations

Olympic innocence died a hard death in Munich. Many of those who were there or saw it unfold on television seem frozen by the moment, even these many years later. The images are impossible to shake. The sight of a somber Jim McKay, his garish yellow ABC Sports blazer at odds with his pale face, coming on screen to say that something had gone terribly wrong in the Athletes' Village, will always stay with those millions who saw it. It would turn out to be McKay's finest moment of reporting in a career built on covering the Olympics for American television. Vietnam may have brought the brutality of war into North American living rooms on a nightly basis, but the Munich massacre was the first single major international news event television covered live wall to wall as the story was actually breaking. Much of what was transpiring in the Israeli team compound was fed to the world by two Canadians. The Canadian team of 239 athletes and eighty-three officials was housed in apartment blocks 25 and 29 of Connollystrasse, the Village street named after the American field athlete James Connolly who won the hop, step and jump gold medal at the first modern Olympics in 1896 at Athens. The Israelis were nearby the Canadians, in apartment block 31. Many of the Canadians had gathered in the television rooms of their blocks to watch Game Two of the historic Canada-Russia hockey series from Maple Leaf Gardens in Toronto. The Soviets had stunned all of Canada with their illusion-shattering 7–3 first-game win at the Forum in Montreal. So it was with a great deal of interest the Canadians at the Summer Olympics gathered for West German television network ARD's satellite transmission of the second encounter. Inspired by Pete Mahovlich's truly marvelous short-handed goal, Canada beat the Soviets 4–1 and there was much cheering and hollering in the two Canadian blocks.

The final buzzer at Maple Leaf Gardens sounded about an hour and fifteen minutes before six shadowy figures, thousands of miles away in Munich, effortlessly scaled the hardly imposing two-metre-high wire fence that circled the Munich Olympic Athletes' Village. It was 4:00 A.M. in the Bavarian capital and dawn was about to break. The six were joined by two others already in the Village with passes, one as a cook in the Village restaurant and the other as a Village groundskeeper. At 4:25 A.M., the eight rang the doorbell of Apartment #1 at 31 Connollystrasse. It was Death calling. During the terrifying madness that ensued, Israeli wrestling coach Moshe Weinberg and weightlifter David Marc Berger grabbed knives and inflicted cuts on the Palestinian terrorists before they were fatally gunned down. In the harrowing first few moments of the siege the neighbouring Malawi, Korean, Trinidadian, Ceylonese and Cambodian athletes slept soundly when the shots rang out; about six Canadians, sleeping restlessly after the excitement of the hocky game, awakened easily when the shots fired. Seeing nothing from their windows, they went back to bed. But while the Village slept, the first acts of the most notorious terrorist incident in sporting history were being played out. Several of the Israeli athletes, alerted by gunfire, managed to shimmy out windows of Apartments #2 and #5. But nine weren't as lucky. By 5:00 A.M., the world was slowly learning what was transpiring.

CBC journalists Bob Moir and Don Wittman stumbled right into the heart of it. "Don [Wittman] and I had been watching the Canada-Russia hockey game the night before," recalled Moir, in an interview with the *Victoria Times-Colonist*. "The next morning, we got up and all hell had broken loose. There were German police surrounding the Athletes' Village and people were lining the hills around it as we walked up." As they wandered nearer, wondering what the commotion was about, the two Canadians noticed a large unguarded bush at one point along the perimeter fence. "You want to go in?" Wittman asked. "Why not," Moir replied. "We were young and stupid, I guess," he says now. "But Don and I have always done things like that. We always went after the story." Lifting the fence for each other, they scooted into the Village and ran to the Canadian apartment at 25 Connollystrasse, right across from the hostage drama. A few members of Canada's medical team were still in the Canadian compound when Moir and Wittman snuck in. They were about fifty metres away and could see the Israeli hostages sitting cross-legged in a circle while armed Palestinian guards, from the Black September faction, hovered over them.

The two Canadians fed reports all day to CBC Radio. Twelve hours after the drama began, German police were thinking of ending it. Moir and Wittman realized they could be in the middle of a war zone and began to worry. The cops were positioning themselves in the most advantageous adjacent points, including at the Canadian compound. By 4:00 P.M., Moir and Wittman were helping the police put on their bullet-proof vests. An hour later, the command came to take aim in preparation for shooting. It was then it really hit home to the Canadian journalists exactly where they were and what the outcome of this whole affair would be. The police confided in the two Canadians that the terrorists were not going to leave West Germany alive. "Don and I looked at each other," Moir says, "and said what the fuck are we doing here?"

In the give and take of negotiations and time buying, the nine hostages were boarded on a bus and taken to two helicopters in the Village, which in turn transported them and their captors to Furstenfeldbruck airport. Knowing that a desperate confrontation was in the offing, Wittman and Moir watched the Israeli athletes being loaded onto the Volkswagen bus. "It was a sad scene," said Moir. Black September demanded the release of 234 Palestinians in Israeli jails and also of Ulrike Meinhof and Andreas Baader, the leaders of the notorious Baader-Meinhof Gang, terrorists who were imprisoned in West Germany.

As four of the Black September men inspected the Lufthansa Boeing 727 jet at Furstenfeldbruck airport, police opened fire. It was an ill-conceived and poorly plotted strategy, with only five sharpshooters aiming in night conditions at great distance with no infrared sights. The terrorists had time to answer the fire and retrench. The Israelis were sitting ducks, tied and blindfolded in the helicopters. The German police were stymied. When they launched an attack with six armored cars, the terrorists exploded a grenade that ripped apart one helicopter and then shot the hostages in the other. All nine Israeli hostages, five Black September terrorists and a German policeman were killed at the airport (the families of the hostages filed suit in 1994 against Germany and Bavaria for $55 million in compensation). This was the most cruelly ironic turn of events for a sporting spectacle that the West Germans had hoped would erase memories of their Nazi past and which they dubbed The Games of Peace and Joy. The remains of the Dachau concentration camp and an apartment house once used by Adolf Hitler and Eva Braun were down the way from Munich's main hotel district where Olympic guests stayed. But that was all in the horrifying past. This was the new West Germany that was supposed to be celebrated.

After the airport fiasco, Moir and Wittman coolly did what they were paid to do. "It's kind of an odd reaction, but there was no reaction from us" says Moir. "The only reaction was to get the story." On September 6, the Olympic Stadium of sport was jammed for a memorial service for the slain Israelis. Athletes and officials from Arab nations and the Soviet Union did not attend. The eighty-four-year-old IOC president Avery Brundage, whose "the Olympics comes first" reaction during the day of crisis has been much criticized, was adamant the Munich Games should continue and not be suspended. "The Games must go on and we must continue our effort to keep them clean, pure and honest," he said, during the stadium memorial ceremonies. That was one of his decisions most observers, including Israeli Prime Minister Golda Meir, agreed with. Cancellation would have meant capitulation to terrorism. Others did not take as kindly with the decision to continue the Games. Red Smith of the *New York Times*, probably the greatest American sportswriter, was unimpressed. He said the memorial service was more like a "pep rally" for the Olympic movement. Canadian high jumping great Debbie Brill was also unmoved by Brundage's words. "[Brundage] said the Games were all about the overcoming of hurdles and that the fallen Israelis would have wanted us to continue to compete," she relates in her book *Jump*. "[Brundage said] We couldn't let them down. God, we're talking about a bunch of dead people ... people who have just been killed. Don't let them down? They're fucking dead!" After a day of mourning, the Olympics continued. But they weren't the same for many, including the man responsible for bringing them into millions of Canadian households. "The Games were very mechanical after that," said Don Brown, the executive producer of CBC's television coverage of the Munich Olympics. "There was no sense of elation. It tainted the medals after that. The athletes were very reserved and guarded about feeling happy about winning. The massacre made sport seem irrelevant. The Games, though, had to keep going. But what I'll always remember is the tragedy of the German people, who went to great lengths to put their nation's past behind them for the Games and who had done a lavish job in preparing for them. Now there were people crying because the whole memory of the Holocaust was brought back to them during what should have been a happy celebration. I'm a bawler, anyway, and I started crying when I saw this huge German man in tears. The Games will be remembered for the massacre. They won't be remembered for much else. When I think back on them, the sporting events are out of focus for me. I couldn't even tell you the Canadian highlights of the Games. You think back on the Munich Olympics and all you remember is the image of death."

Some athletes, like Brill, were openly torn. She was horrified that most of the competitors were trying to put the massacre out of their minds by concentrating on their sporting events. "For me, competing in the Olympics now seemed at the very least incongruous, perhaps tasteless, and certainly irrelevant," she writes in *Jump*. "The original idea of a bunch of athletes from around the world gathering together to celebrate their talent and their spirit seemed to have been utterly lost. I saw the Olympics as a great wheel, churning relentlessly. Horrible things could happen, but the wheel would keep turning."

Munich changed forever how Games are staged. Gun-toting Canadian soldiers in berets and undercover plainclothes security agents were everywhere in Montreal four years later. Nobody articulated the cold-shower shock of Munich better than American long jumper Willye B. White, who was competing in her fifth Olympics. "It was the most devastating experience of my entire life," she told reporters. "The Olympic Village was a special place to me. When I left Mississippi in segregated times [her first Olympics were as a sixteen-year-old in 1956 at Melbourne], the Olympic Village educated me. The Olympic Village was a family, unity. Blacks and whites lived side by side as one family. The massacre split the family. It was the beginning of the end of a good thing. It is difficult for me to explain what it feels like to witness and be part of a memorial service held in the Olympic Stadium and watching the Olympic flag of peace flying at half mast. You see, in the Olympic Village all the athletes from all nations are family." Until Munich. And Mark Spitz wasn't about to stick around the Village. The handsome American superstar had won seven gold medals, all in world record times, in the pool at Munich before the massacre. But he was Jewish. And he was spooked. He was quickly taken out of Munich under security protection. Something that will always stay with Spitz is being chosen to light the flame for the 1985 Maccabiah Games in Tel Aviv. The stadium was dark, with only Spitz's flame lighting the way. Running beside him were three girls whose fathers had been killed in the Munich Olympics massacre. "It was weird," noted Spitz. "It was pitch black in the stadium and I kind of became their surrogate father, like a link with something from the past. It was an eerie feeling, like I was putting life back into these people inside the stadium. I'll never forget that."

In terms of competition, the Munich Games will forever be associated with Spitz and his incredible run of gold-medal victories. At the start of the 100m butterfly, Spitz was expecting to break his own world record. Amongst his competitors was Vancouver's Bruce Robertson. "I wasn't even thinking about Spitz," said Robertson, who became a chartered accountant. Robertson had qualified fourth for the final and set his sights on the bronze medal. He was in lane six while Spitz was in four and East German great Roland Matthes in two. Robertson's main aim was to beat Jerry Heidenreich of the US in lane five and slip in for the bronze. Spitz won in 54.27 seconds to break his own world record. And taking silver was Robertson in 55.56 (with teammate Byron MacDonald, later a television analyst for swimming, coming sixth in 57.27). "Beating both Matthes and Heidenreich for the silver was a bonus," he said.

Robertson was again in Spitz's wake in the 4x100 medley relay. East Germany's robotic backstroke machine Matthes had spotted his team the lead with a world record on the opening leg of the final. Robertson and Spitz battled on the third leg, the butterfly portion of the relay. Spitz hit the pool with a good lead but Robertson churned furiously and managed not to lose much distance. He gave Canadian anchor freestyle swimmer Robert Kasting of Lethbridge a strong third-place position to hold against the fourth-place Soviets and their anchor-leg swimmer Vladimir Bure, the father of current Vancouver Canucks hockey sensation Pavel Bure. The elder Bure was a Russian Rocket himself but Kasting not only held him at bay but almost managed to catch East German Lutz Unger. The Canadian team of Kasting, Robertson, Eric Fish and Vancouver's Bill Mahoney won the bronze medal in 3:52.26, exactly one second ahead of the Soviets. All four of the Canadians posted personal best times in the final. Spitz won his seventh gold medal as the Americans set a world record of 3:48.16. The East Germans were second in 3:52.12. "We got what we wanted," said Robertson. "We were shooting for the bronze. We knew it was a foregone conclusion the Americans would win the gold. But nobody expected us to overtake the East Germans, which we almost did."

As the rowers did in 1956 at Melbourne, 1960 at Rome and 1964 in Tokyo, the swimmers saved the Mexico City and Munich games from being almost complete washouts for Canada. Of the ten medals Canada won at the 1968 and 1972 Summer Olympics, swimmers accounted for eight of them. Four of this nation's five medals at Munich were won in the pool (the fifth was due to David Miller, John Ekels and Paul Cote

Canadian silver medallist Bruce Robertson (right) and American gold-medal sensation Mark Spitz (middle) smile at the crowd after the 100m butterfly final.

capturing bronze in soling class yachting). Three of the Munich swimming medallists started out splashing together in pre-kindergarten summer classes at Crescent Beach, near White Rock in British Columbia. Robertson, Mahoney and Leslie Cliff grew up together in summer club programs. "There was a lot of swimming talent, kids with great skills, coming out of small-town Canada like Crescent Beach and Ocean Falls," says Robertson. "I think it was a kind of freakish coincidence." And then there was the fortunate accident of having a man like Deryk Snelling to give these kids some focus. Snelling put together the most extensive and demanding training program young Canadian swimmers had ever seen. And from his Vancouver Dolphins Club emerged Olympic medallists like Robertson and Cliff. In fact, in a complete reversal from almost every other event on the Olympic sporting program, Canada practically owned the women's 400m individual medley swimming event over the span of the 1972 and 1976 Olympics — winning three of the six medals. Snelling was part of the revolution in world swimming that saw records tumble like tenpins. An example is the women's 400 individual medley. So greatly had times improved in this event that Montreal Games silver medallist Cheryl Gibson (4:48.10) and bronze medallist Becky Smith (4:50.48) of Canada would have won gold with those times at Munich while none of the Munich medallists would even have made the

Montreal final with their clockings. Gail Neall of Australia broke the four-year-old world record in capturing gold in 5:02.97 at Munich while Cliff of Vancouver won the silver medal in 5:03.57. Again, none of the Munich medallists in the women's 200m backstroke would have made the final in Montreal with their times. Melissa Belote of the US broke her own world record in winning at Munich in 2:19.19, her third gold medal in three days at the Games. Compatriot Susie Atwood won the silver in 2:20.38 while Donna Marie Gurr of Vancouver took the bronze medal in 2:23.22.

The translucent spider's web awning that hung above both the pool and $45 million Munich Olympic Stadium, gave the central Olympic venue area a futuristic look. Canadians, however, had trouble turning in futuristic performances on the track or infield. Abby Hoffman, who later did so much to further the cause of amateur sport in Canada by becoming one its more respected administrators in the COA and Sport Canada, was the only Canadian to reach a track final at Munich. Her time of 2:00.17 in the women's 800m final would have been good enough for the gold medal at Mexico City four years earlier. That's how remarkably fast the times were being eaten away during this period in athletic history. Hoffman took more than six seconds off her time from Mexico City, where she finished seventh, but still came in eighth at Munich in a field of thirty-eight competitors from twenty-six countries. The final was very close, almost a blanket finish. Hildegard Falck of West Germany lifted the home crowd by winning in 1:58.55. There were five Eastern Bloc runners in the eight-woman final (and now we know they were probably on steroids) while Hoffman was the lone non-European to make it. "People [Canadians] look at eighth place and say 'only' eighth place without realizing how hard that was to accomplish at the Olympic level," said Hoffman, an articulate person with a great deal of integrity and inner strength. "I'm not ashamed to say I'm proud of what I accomplished in Munich."

Bruce Simpson gave Canada a fifth place finish in the pole vault with a height of 5.20m. The US had won gold in this event at every Games since the first modern Olympics at Athens in 1896. That streak came to a controversial end when 1968 Mexico City champion Rob Seagren, who like many of the leading vaulters was hurt by the sudden eve-of-competition ban on the new Cata-Poles, went down to defeat. Wolfgang Nordwig of East Germany, who had never switched to the new poles and preferred the old ones, took advantage of the situation to win gold at 5.50m. Seagren settled for silver at 5.40m and was so incensed that before he left the stadium he shoved his pole onto the lap of the track official who had ordered the ban. Canadian John Beers was fifth in the men's high jump at 2.15m in a field of forty competitors from twenty-nine nations. Winner Yuri Tarmak of the Soviet Union leaped 2.23m. The bronze medallist was a brash American teenager named Dwight Stones, who would one day hold the world record. Stones and Canadians Beers and John Hawkins were the lone non-Europeans in the top-ten, which included six athletes from the Eastern Bloc. Brill, the only non-European in the women's high jump final, was eighth with a personal best 1.82m in a field of forty competitors from twenty-two countries. Sixteen-year-old Ulrike Meyfarth of West Germany, only third in her national trials, came out of nowhere to win the gold medal at 1.92m and become the youngest individual track and field winner in Olympic history. This group of jumpers had staying power. Three of the Munich finalists placed in the top-five twelve years later at the 1984 Los Angeles Olympics: Meyfarth, Brill and Italy's Sara Simeoni. Meyfarth fittingly bookended her youngest-ever record at Munich by becoming at L.A. the oldest-ever winner of an Olympic high jump competition. Brill was fifth in 1984.

Archery, a sport requiring icy nerves and unwavering hands, made its Olympic debut in 1972. Donald Jackson appeared to be on his way to give Canada a medal but then fell off the pace and finished a still-commendable sixth among the fifty-five archers from twenty-four countries in the men's individual event.

Munich was a strange and unhappy experience for many of the Americans, not the least being the unfortunate sprinters Eddie Hart and Rey Robinson, who were serious threats in the men's 100m. Told by their coach Stan Wright that the quarterfinals were just after 6:00 P.M. on August 31, Hart, Robinson and Bob Taylor slowly sauntered to the stadium shuttle bus. It was about 4:00 P.M. and they were in no hurry so they stopped along the way at the ABC studios in the International Broadcasting Centre. There on the monitors they saw runners warming up for the 100m and Robinson asked if it was a replay of the earlier heats. No, they were informed. It was a live feed. Wright had apparently read 16:15 as 6:15 P.M. The quarterfinals were scheduled to begin in less than five minutes! Panic stricken, the three sprinters jumped in an ABC car and were driven at screeching speed to the stadium which was less than a mile away. But it was too late for Hart and Robinson. The first two quarterfinal heats, in which they were to run, had just ended. Taylor got to the line just in time to take his sweat pants off and get in the blocks for the third quarterfinal heat. As can be imagined, Hart and Robinson were practically inconsolable that day. Taylor went on to win the silver medal behind Valery Borzov of the Soviet Union. Hart received some consolation when he ran the anchor leg as the US won the 4x100 relay.

If Seagren, Hart and Robinson thought they were jinxed, nothing matches what their compatriots went through in the men's gold medal basketball final at Munich: it is a game every basketball fan, regardless of nationality, carries in his or her heart. The Americans, who had never lost a game in Olympic basketball, thought they had won a thrilling come-from-behind victory when Doug Collins sank two free throws with three seconds left, giving the US a 50–49 lead. The Americans mobbed themselves on the floor after the buzzer sounded. But the Soviets had called time out a moment before. So the clock was reset. The buzzer again sounded to end the game after the Soviets in-bounded the ball but were unable to score. The Americans again went crazy in celebration. But William Jones of Britain, the autocratic chietain of FIBA, the basketball world governing body, came out of the stands to the scorer's table and ruled the Soviets hadn't been given enough time. The clock was reset to three seconds. What happened next almost defies description as Ivan Yedeshko launched a desperate court-length in-bounds lob from his baseline. Incredibly, it was caught by Sasha Belov under the US basket as two American defenders fell away in confusion. Belov turned and dropped in the lay-up. The game ended for the third time, but now with the Soviets the gold medal victors at 51–50. While the Soviets wildly dogpiled on the floor, team manager Herbert Mols and US coach Hank Iba protested vehemently and lodged an official complaint. One of the referees and the timekeeper refused to sign the game sheet because they said what had happened was wrong. Next day Jones appointed a five-member FIBA panel to rule on the matter: its members included a Soviet and two other Eastern Bloc officials. Surprise. The vote went three-to-two to uphold the Soviets as the gold medallists.

Few people remember this travesty with more emotion than Victoria high school basketball coach Gary Mols, whose father was the manager of the 1972 US Olympic hoops team. "It was a complete scam and my dad was really disappointed," says Mols. "But I told him: 'Look at it this way — people will remember this [US] team long after all the other teams are forgotten because no one will ever forget this game.'" The Americans refused to accept their silvers and boycotted the medals ceremony. Those medals still sit in a vault at IOC headquarters in Lausanne and there is a sworn pledge among the Americans that no member of that team nor any of his descendants will ever claim them. "That's an iron-clad pact and no team or family member will ever break it," says Mols.

The Games of Peace and Joy had turned into the Games of Politics and Death. It was all too much for some people. Brill was smoking a joint with two Canadian teammates atop the roof of their dorm in the Athletes' Village before heading to the closing ceremonies. Canada's greatest female high jumper looked across to the stadium and saw spectacular and colourful props being readied for the finale. It just didn't feel right. She describes it as nothing short of "disgusting." Something snapped in her. The three Canadians left the roof, threw their track suits in a pile in their rooms and headed out of Munich to Italy rather than go to the closing ceremonies. As night fell on the ceremonies, the crusty Brundage declared closed the Munich Olympics of 1972 and invited the youth of the world to gather in four years at Montreal to celebrate the XXI Games of the modern era. He ended it with one word, a curt "äuf wiedersehen," and then stepped down from the dais for the last time in his twenty-year reign as IOC president. The crowd roared and flash bulbs popped all around the bowl. The words and numbers Montreal 1976 burned on the scoreboard. But even Brundage wasn't so sure about that. The blinkered old man refused to acknowledge that the link between the Olympics and politics was now indissoluble, but that a co-existence — no matter how uneasy — was possible. His successor Lord Killanin noted that Brundage, when handing over the IOC reins of power, said he believed the Munich Games would be the final Olympics. For eleven Israeli athletes, they were. But a sense of closure on this chapter came twenty years later at the 1992 Barcelona Games when judo athlete Yael Arad won Israel's first-ever Olympic medal. She dedicated the silver medal to the families of those Israeli athletes who died at Munich, with the hope that "this will close the circle."

MONTREAL 1976

July 17 to August 1
6085 Athletes from 92 Nations

If you thought the biggest balls in the Montreal Olympics were the ones in the basketball competition, think again. The biggest belonged to Jean Drapeau. He alone had the balls to dream the vision. He alone had them to go into the bidding for the 1976 Olympics without any financial guarantees from the federal government. He alone had the balls to subvert the competition by using the Cold War to Montreal's advantage. He alone had the balls to dream up wildly imaginative — but hugely impractical — edifices. He alone had the balls to go out of the country and hire a French — as in France — architect to bring his vision to the world. He alone had the balls to make it to the Opening Ceremonies of the Olympics with an unfinished stadium. He alone had them to let the Queen — in Quebec, no less — open the Games in a shameless snub to those in the federal and provincial governments who dared take control of the event away from him in the latter stages. He alone had the balls to state that the Olympics could no more incur a deficit than a man could have a baby, and then presided over a project that ballooned from $310 million to, at last estimate, more than $3 billion. He alone had the balls to burden taxpayers with that legacy for years to come.

The turtleback velodrome is now the Museum of Natural History. At the impersonal, concrete Big Owe across the way, it took years after the Olympics to finally complete the tower/kevlar roof section of the stadium. During the Games, the exposed steel rods of the unfinished 160m tower stood as sentinels reminding everybody of just how close to the brink this great enterprise had been driven. And some of the concrete blocks still don't fit any better than they did on the opening day of the Games when the world was met with temporary ramps, stairs and wooden walkways with gaps that revealed the ground many metres below. The smell of the bonding paste used to hold together the large concrete blocks was heavy in the air and filled one's nostrils immediately on entering the stadium for the opening ceremonies — sort of like walking into a new "spec" home.

The Olympic Stadium remains a foreboding, sterile and cavernous place to play Expos baseball, despite being specifically built for that post-Games use. It sits there as a striking piece of work, in its own way, when viewed from the outside. But it is absolutely soulless inside. And that's the prevailing memory many Canadians have of the 1976 Games, the only Summer Olympics ever held in this country.

What went wrong with Canada's Games — our Olympics? Nothing actually during the Games. That is, of course, unless you like your Canadians and Africans golden. Despite not a single gold medal for Canada — the only time that has ever happened to the host country in the history of the Summer Olympics — and a twenty-nation Third World (mostly African) boycott of the Games over a New Zealand rugby tour of South Africa that unfortunately struck at the very heart of the track competition, it was an almost flawless sixteen days of competition that produced a string of memorable performances from Nadia Comaneci, Kornelia Ender, Bruce Jenner, John Walker, Alberto Juantorena, Lasse Viren, Teofilo Stevenson, Sugar Ray Leonard, Leon Spinks, Vasilyi Alexeev and Greg Joy.

It's just those six years before that fortnight — and the two-decade debt hangover since — that have been why many Canadians don't look back on the Games with the same degree of satisfaction they do with the 1988 Calgary Winter Olympics or the five Commonwealth and Pan-American games this nation has hosted. Most people remember the profoundly moving moment when twelve-year-old Robyn Perry, a Calgary schoolgirl representing all the children of Canada, nervously yet steadfastly climbed the stairs with her little legs to reach the cauldron to light the flame to begin the '88 Winter Games; or even hometown hero Diane Jones-Konihowski running into the Edmonton stadium in

1978, and 1994 Lillehammer biathlon double-gold medallist Myriam Bedard rollerblading into the Victoria stadium with the Queen's Baton in 1994 to start the last two Canada-based Commonwealth Games. But less well remembered in the national public imagination are two fifteen-year-olds from 1976 named Sandra Henderson and Stephane Prefontaine — one symbolically of English descent and the other of French. Their story is really very touching. They were selected to represent the two founding cultures of Canada and jointly run the torch into the stadium at Montreal and light the flame in the infield to start the XXI Summer Games of the modern Olympic era. Wearing simple white T-shirts and shorts, they did just that in front of the watching eyes of the world. Years later, they were married. This poignant little story is unknown by most Canadians, virtually none of whom could today name the final torch bearers in Canada's only hosting of the Summer Games.

That's because Canadians outside of Quebec, and more than a few inside, feel no warm glow and little sense of pride for having hosted the Summer Olympics, the greatest multi-sport spectacle on the face of the earth. The reason is that most Canadians never felt a sense of ownership of the Games. Such dreams often start as one person's singular obsession. Then that must be transferred to the community. But the Canadian public never really bought into Jean Drapeau's vision. It remained his, almost exclusively. And that is one of the greatest shames in Canadian sporting history. Montreal should have stood as our proudest moment in sport — our chance to finally stand atop Olympus. It is grindingly sad that most Canadians rate it not anywhere near the top of their personal pantheon of shining Canadian moments — falling somewhere far short of Paul Henderson's goal and Joe Carter's home run.

The 1976 Olympics were not so much won by Montreal as lost by Los Angeles and Moscow during those almost surreal days surrounding the vote in May of 1970. The US wanted the Games in 1976 to add a spectacular exclamation mark to its bicentennial year. Henry Kissinger's State Department was working behind the scenes, trying to massage and cajole the princes, princesses, dukes and millionaires that compose the IOC. The State Department went so far as to send American coaches to Africa to help enhance the sporting structures there. It was all part of a calculated effort. President Richard Nixon sent a personally signed letter to every IOC member, guaranteeing the full backing of the US government to the L.A. Olympic bid. Moscow, meanwhile, had the entire Soviet communist governmental machine working into overdrive. "The Russian tactics were incredible," recalled John Kilroy, a millionaire businessman and leader of the Los Angeles bid committee, in an interview with *Sports Illustrated* writer William O. Johnson Jr. "At one party given by Queen Juliana in Amsterdam, there were these two burly Communist bastards, and they had a member of the IOC in a corner, and every time the poor fellow tried to get away, they'd slam him back in the corner. The Russians had a few of those big burly guys who never smiled standing at all four corners of the balcony over the lobby. They were making notes on who was talking to whom. I thought I was in some kind of a weird foreign spy movie."

But no spy movie was ever like this. While the Soviet and US governments were promising full support, Drapeau had no such guarantee. Far from it. With his artistically successful but financially disastrous Expo 67 in Montreal (which cost more than double the original estimate of $60 million) still fresh in mind, a proposal to fund the Olympics in Montreal failed to make it through Parliament. Drapeau looked to be hung out to dry. But nothing fazed this little character who, fittingly enough in a way, wanted to become a missionary during his youth. Armed with no money, and none promised, he went on the attack. He was the vice-busting chief magistrate in Montreal during the 1950s and if the mob couldn't stop him, the Reds and Tinseltown certainly weren't about to, either. Crimson in the face and on the verge of tears, he exclaimed to the IOC: "The whole history of Montreal is our guarantee. It is a history of challenges met and defeated. That is the guarantee I bring to you."

And it didn't hurt to drop a reminder here and there about the Soviet tanks that rolled into Prague two years earlier and the US planes bombing Cambodia and the students who had been shot just a week earlier by the Ohio National Guard at Kent State. A crafty little devil, this Drapeau. Faced with a financially well armed but politically explosive Cold War showdown between L.A. and Moscow, the IOC took the coward's way out on May 12, 1970. Buoyed by full Commonwealth support and a few more votes from the Americas region, Montreal survived the first ballot. It got twenty-five votes to twenty-eight for Moscow and seventeen for Los Angeles. The dumbfounded Americans were out of it early. The final ballot read: Montreal forty-one votes, Moscow twenty-nine. The Russians, faces red and veins bulging in their necks, walked out of the room in disgust. Soviet reporters from *Tass* and *Pravda* angrily began pounding out stories of a capitalist conspiracy while Los Angeles mayor Sam Yorty, no liberal to begin with, said he was at least glad the Games stayed in the "free world." As the decision was announced, Drapeau raised his hands to his face and began to weep like a baby. He cried openly for fifteen minutes, just sitting in his seat with a disbelieving look on his face. The man who had taken an astounding 95 percent of the votes in the last Montreal mayoralty election, had again accomplished the impossible. He brought the Games to Canada, a nation whose government had refused to put up any sort of financial guarantee to underwrite the massive enterprise.

And fittingly, money or the talk of it, would become the hallmark of the 1976 Montreal Olympics in the years preceding and following the Games. There was money to be made from the Games, but the organizers couldn't find a way to tap into it and the taxpayers were stuck in a big way. ABC paid $25 million for the US television rights to the Montreal Games and then proceeded to make a $77 million profit by selling ads for up to $72,000 per minute. The Montreal organizers budgeted $50 million from non-US broadcasters but realized less than $10 million. A year after the Montreal Olympics, NBC paid $87 million for the US rights alone to the 1980 Moscow Games. Business and the Montreal Games were fated never to mesh. Montreal netted less than $9 million from non-television commercial sponsorships, a paltry sum compared to the bills that were mounting. Part of the problem was timing. Montreal slipped in just before the era of major sponsorship money that is routinely thrown at Games now. The US television rights alone for the 2000 Sydney Summer Olympics went for $705 million. Summer Olympic host cities are now almost guaranteed an outside hit of up to nearly $1 billion. Montreal sure could have used that kind of money.

How did the costs go up so wildly? "Inflation!" Drapeau loved to bellow when questioned as to why the bills were skyrocketing. That had something to do with it. Montreal was preparing for the Games during a time of sharp inflation. And there is also a lot to the reports of rampant corruption in the Quebec construction industry that drove up prices. And the unions ransomed the organizers with strikes at the most inopportune times when construction deadlines were tight. More than thirty-five weeks were lost to either strikes or construction slowdowns. And so then overtime, and its premium wages, was needed to make up for that and bring the projects in on time. But more than anything it was a grand vision running wild without anybody or any institution able to keep it in check. A temporary outdoor track was built for the 1975 world cycling championships in Montreal for less than $1 million. Why couldn't the same track, which was good enough for the worlds, not suffice for the Olympics? There was no need to spend in excess of $70 million on an indoor velodrome of dubious post-Games value. Atlanta, by comparison, is spending only $6 million US on a temporary velodrome at Stone Mountain Park for the 1996 Olympics. Not just any garden variety architects would do, either. Drapeau had been struck by the impressively designed Parc des Princes soccer stadium in Paris and he went after its French architect, Roger Taillibert, with a passion so arduous you half expected him to propose marriage. Then there was the small matter of Taillibert's fee, which some estimated was as high as $50 million. When some people complained Taillibert was making more money than all the architects in Quebec combined made in 1974, they were dismissed as parochial whiners who couldn't recognize world-class talent if it hit them in the face. The feds answered with a national Olympic lottery and coin program to raise money and the province of Quebec reluctantly knew it was on the hook for millions.

Premier Robert Bourassa offered to pay four-fifths the provincial share with Montreal picking up the rest, meaning about a $200 million deficit for the city. Drapeau scoffed that as far as he was concerned, the Olympics were self-financing and thoughts of a deficit were only delusions in Bourassa's mind. But it didn't seem to matter, one way or the other. Drapeau's vision was mesmerizing, not only to himself but to hundreds of thousands of others in Montreal. Grand edifices in a soon-to-be grander city. Why a tower on an Olympic stadium? It was not needed. But it was spectacular and it was big and Drapeau had to have it as a lasting monument to his megalomania. The promise and the dream were seductive. Drapeau's opposition seemed to be paralyzed by fear of his power and popularity and the fact the approaching Olympics were blinding much of the public with glittering visions of a city bursting onto the world stage with dramatic flourish. The Games critics, mostly a motley anti-establishment bunch of "granola" types in the Montreal Citizens Movement, seemed hamstrung by the prevailing public acceptance.

By the time the Games organization was finally wrenched away from Drapeau and handed over to the Quebec government's Olympic Installations Board, headed by Dr. Victor Goldbloom, the Mad Hatter's crazy money party had taken its toll. Goldbloom's job was to make sure the basic, minimum facilities and services would be ready by the time the world arrived on July 17, 1976. Montreal was being whacked by bills at every turn. Organizers had to come up with an unexpected $90 million for the Athletes' Village after the feds failed to deliver on their promised funding. And after the terrorism at Munich, a multimillion-dollar bill for security would be unavoidable. Montreal had no option but to respond with 16,000 police and soldiers, and the Games that were supposed to represent peace and joy took place in a city that at times resembled an armed camp. At last estimate in 1995, Drapeau's little baby had cost Quebeckers more than $3 billion. The province still owes about $300 million on a debt that won't be retired until after 2005. The city of Montreal finally paid off its $150 million debt in 1994. The Olympic Stadium, once budgeted for an unbelievably optimistic $30 million, has become an economic sinkhole that has gobbled up in excess of $800 million in labour costs, overruns and problems with its retractable roof.

In the final days leading up to the Games, however, politics overshadowed economics by a wide margin. First there was the ironically named New Zealand All-Blacks, the famous national rugby side which toured the white-power apartheid pariah South Africa earlier that year to play the Springboks. At the eleventh hour, IOC president Lord Killanin was presented with a letter in his suite at the Queen Elizabeth Hotel in downtown Montreal. Many of the African nations demanded New Zealand be barred from the Montreal Olympics. The exasperated IOC said rugby wasn't even an Olympic sport and it had no grounds on which to expel the Kiwis. Suddenly there came knocks on the dorm doors of black athletes from twenty nations in the Games Village. They were told to pack. They were going home. Many were in tears as they headed for the airport, staggering from the emotional blow of suddenly realizing their one moment to shine, or at least participate, on the biggest world stage was gone before the opening ceremony. Sprinter and medal hopeful James Gilkes of Guyana, a Commonwealth country in South America that joined the boycott, stood his ground and had to be almost forcibly thrown out of the Village. The biggest loss occurred on the track and in boxing. The boycott deprived the world of a 1500m rematch between John Walker of New Zealand and Filbert Bayi of Tanzania, who had locked horns two years earlier in a classic world-record race at the 1974 Christchurch Commonwealth Games won by Bayi. Without Bayi in the field to challenge him, the great Walker won the rather lackluster Olympic 1500m in an uninspired time.

In 1970, Canada's Liberal government dropped its recognition of Taiwan in favour of recognizing the People's Republic of China. Trade was at the heart of the decision. One billion people in mainland China eat a lot more Canadian wheat than seventeen million Taiwanese. In 1975, boxers and cyclists from Taiwan were denied entry into Canada for Olympic test events in Montreal because their island entity insisted on describing itself as the Republic of China. The IOC must not be big on foreshadowing because they did nothing in 1975, hoping the problem would just go away and doubting Canada would do anything quite so rash during the Olympics. Wrong. Mitchell Sharp, acting secretary of state for external affairs, informed the IOC on May 28, 1976, that Taiwan would not be allowed into Canada for the Games if it insisted on calling itself the Republic of China. Killanin waited until the week before the Olympics to protest to the Canadian government but to no avail. He then asked the Taiwanese to participate on Canadian terms. What's in a name? Apparently a lot. Taiwan refused and its athletes, coaches and managers were sent home from the Games. The communist People's Republic of China was not even a member of the IOC at this point and wouldn't have participated in Montreal regardless of Taiwan being there or not. But this matter had little to do with sport and everything to do with Canada's trading market in China. Canada was indulging its own selfish motives. The reaction in the world press was hostile to the Canadian action, which was seen as a transparent and obvious move to enhance its trade relations with mainland China. But the Liberals were willing to accept the media's wrath in order not to offend the Communist Party in the People's Republic. Canada had clearly transgressed one of the most important points in the Olympic Charter: "Free entry must be accorded to teams from all National Olympic Committees recognized by the International Olympic Committee." What if every host nation began cherry picking countries it didn't like, for whatever reasons, and sending them home at will just before the Games? But whoever said the Olympics were purely about sport? They are about everything but sport and Canada proved that by barring Taiwan in 1976.

East Germany also knew what the Olympics were about — a chance to showcase the socialist system as superior to the decadent West. With a population of merely sixteen million — about eight million *less* than Canada at the time — East Germany won six more gold medals than the US at the Montreal Olympics (forty to thirty-four) and finished second only to the Soviet Union's forty-seven. The husky but attractive Kornelia Ender was typical of how the East German sporting machine worked. Its net was everywhere at youth and child meets. Ender was noticed as a six year old, swimming for a factory sports club in Bitterfeld. She was taken from her parents and placed in a specialized training school at Halle. She was a full-time child swimmer, not a full-time child. She exploded for four gold medals and a silver as a seventeen year old at the Montreal Olympics. Sport officials in the former East Germany admitted in 1991 that their swimmers and many other athletes had been given steroids since childhood. Ender became a physiotherapist and many years later sloughed off the revelations. "Medical men are the real guilty people," she told the media. "They know what they have done. When they gave us things to help us 'regenerate,' we were never asked if we wanted it. It was just given to us. We had no say."

At the Montreal Forum, another Eastern Bloc performer was weaving her own special brand of magic that was to entrance the world. If the

Montreal Olympics are remembered for one thing beyond its financial woes, it is fourteen-year-old Nadia Comaneci. Every once in a while comes an athlete who so captures the public imagination that he or she overshadows the rest of the event. Nadia was that person. Prior to 1976, no gymnast had ever received a perfect mark of 10.00 at the Olympics. Comaneci scored one on the first day of the gymnastics competition and then stunned the world with a total of seven maximum scores of 10.00 to become one of the most celebrated heroines in Olympic history. While it's difficult to objectify Comaneci's performance in a subjectively judged sport, few would argue against the assessment that she was virtually seamless at the Forum. But perfect and flawless? Seven times? Is that humanly possible? There is little doubt the whole Comaneci phenomenon began to build on itself at the Montreal Games. With much of the world tuning in each night to watch this wonder woman-child, the pressure was on the judges to reward her brilliance with the perfect scores the world wanted to see. And after all, didn't Nelli Kim of the Soviet Union also record two perfect scores at Montreal? One thing is for sure, Comaneci's perfection — real or imagined — didn't hurt the sport or the Games. Only a few gymnastics purists were arguing that it is perhaps beyond human reach to be perfect for an entire routine and that a 10.00 may be a technical impossibility. But that's semantics. The Olympics are marketing. And the world was eating this up like candy. How many men fell in love with this girl-woman through their televisions? Pixieish and cute, her persona was magnetic, captivating and almost impossible to resist. She was the Olympic sweetheart to end all Olympic sweethearts — the kind that inspired a chart-topping pop music instrumental hit "Nadia's Theme."

But little fairy princesses grow up. It's odd, these many years later, to see a plumper and generally less-appealing Comaneci in her new American life. But she went through a lot after she appeared as a slim teenager at the Forum. Back in Romania after the Montreal Olympics, she was kept on a tight leash by the sports authorities. "After I got back to Romania, I had no clue of the impact my performance had on the world," she told the media, after fleeing to the US in a daring and dangerous bid for freedom in 1989. "All that information was kept from me." She didn't have an inkling that "Nadia's Theme" was selling millions of records in the West. She was finally informed but didn't even know what a gold record was. She asked her mother if it was real gold and if it could be melted down. After defecting, Comaneci appeared to be used by the man who helped her escape from Romania. He seemed to be keeping her a virtual slave and trading off her name. Comaneci began looking

A leap for joy: Greg Joy after clearing the bar for the high jump silver medal at the 1976 Montreal Olympics.

like a chunky matron with garish make-up. Strange rumours began circulating about her, including one in 1994 that she had died. Comaneci was far from dead and began putting her life back together with Bart Conner, a 1984 US Olympic gymnastics gold medallist, to whom she became engaged in 1995. Her five medals (three of them gold) from Montreal sit undisplayed in a box underneath the television stand of her home in Norman, Oklahoma. Those famous medals are nicked and badly scuffed from their hair-raising flight across the Romanian border one cold and tense night. The ribbons have fallen off. "Some people sleep with their Olympic medals under their pillows," Comaneci has said. "I don't live in the past. Everybody knows I won them. What am I going to do? Wear them around my neck every time I go out?"

Canadian Greg Joy doesn't wear his medal from the Montreal Olympics around his neck, either. But that doesn't mean it's out of mind. How could it be? Featured for many years on a television sign-off clip, Joy's leap for joy after clearing the bar to win a medal in the men's high jump was one of the last things thousands of Canadians saw late each night before going to sleep. Badly in need of a lift on the second-to-last day of the Games, the country got one in the most unexpected of fashions. All eyes were on Dwight Stones, the American world record holder for the high jump. But just days before he was due to compete, Stones began to unravel. He attacked the Montreal organizers as being "rude" to their invited guests from around the world for failing to finish the stadium on time. Of greatest concern to him was that the retractable roof was unfinished and so unable to keep out the elements. Stones took a very sharp angle in his approach, which meant that good footing on a dry surface was important to him. Somebody should have clued him in. Even if the retractable roof had been ready, it couldn't have been used because all Olympic track and field competitions must take place outdoors, regardless of the weather. His comments were distorted in the media as all Quebeckers being rude. He was roundly booed by the locals in the stadium during the first day of the high jump competition. The boisterous Americans in the stands retaliated by booing Canadian high jumpers' Claude Ferragne and Robert Forget of Quebec. Stones walked into the high jump area the next day wearing a T-shirt which on the back read: "I love French Canadians." Not only were the Quebeckers in the stands unimpressed, but officials made him take off the shirt. The day was dark and overcast. Stones' worst fears were about to be realized. It started with a drizzle as the high jump final progressed and then opened up into a cascading downpour. Massive puddles began forming in the high jump area and an irate Stones demanded track officials do something. He wasn't happy with their efforts so he grabbed a mop himself and tried to clear some of the puddles. Several other jumpers, including Joy, also mopped in a futile effort to keep the area dry. Stones was in a panic. He could see the gold medal slipping away.

But then there was the unheralded Canadian wearing 158 and with his spiked running shoe on his left foot held together at the toe by just some white tape. Joy, who crept into the medal hunt completely by surprise, kept his cool and looked unflappable. He matched the other finalists — six of the eight were from Europe — jump for jump. Stones topped out at 2.21m or 7' 3" and angrily grabbed his kit and stormed into the dressing room. (A week later, under brilliant sunshine in Philadelphia, he would break his own world record. But he had to settle for the bronze medal at the Olympics.) While Stones was fuming, one of the most dramatic moments in Canadian Olympic history was unfolding. Joy approached the bar as it stood at 2.23m. The stadium went silent. The rain was pounding down as he planted and lifted. He seemed to defy the dank conditions and cut through the air like a razor. He was up and over.

The stadium erupted, shedding all the pent up frustration that lay within. After two weeks of hearing the American fans, who took control of the stadium, this was a catharsis. So *this* is what it feels like. It was also, finally, something to cheer about at home in front of their television sets for millions of Canadians who saw, for the most part, all the medals go to others. "It was perfect drama ... the second-to-last day of the Olympics, the rain, the fans cheering," says Joy. "I couldn't have written a more perfect script." It really didn't seem to matter after that that the slim and willowy Pole, Wszola, cleared 2.25m for the gold and Joy was unable to match it. The jump for the silver medal was good enough for a host country that had seen its athletes deliver precious few moments of true glory at its own Games. That was the jump replayed for years each night in the wee hours, with the national anthem, on television sign-offs across the country. "My whole life has become the 'O Canada' clip," said Joy, in a 1995 interview with the CBC Radio program *Inside Track*. "In many people's eyes, that's who I am — Greg Joy the high jumper." But the hundreds of people who crowd into the Ottawa Food Bank daily could care less about Joy's medal. That isn't exactly going to put food on their plates. What is, is Joy's position as executive director of that food bank. "Finally in Ottawa now, people are beginning to say: 'Oh, that's Greg Joy from the Food Bank.' To me, that's who I am. I'm not the guy who jumped over the bar. That's a part of my life. My real life is giving to the poor and helping people and having a family." Joy was raised in Vancouver, where he used his lean and angular body and spring-like legs to get into track and field and star at the club and high school levels. He was talented, obviously good enough to make the national team, but nobody ever expected an Olympic medal out of him. However he set in his mind certain standards he wanted to achieve and went after them. "It's difficult to find another goal like that," said Joy, who ran for the Progressive Conservatives in the 1995 Ontario provincial election but lost. "That's the integral thing about my sport. There were no judges. Success was clearly defined. And there was nobody but yourself to define your own level of success. That doesn't happen in the real world. In my sport, you control your own destiny. You jump over the bar and either it falls down or it doesn't. That's a difficult thing to transfer into regular life."

Don Talbot, the brash Aussie hired to coach the Canadian swimmers, was appalled by what he saw and heard in the cavernous 10,000-seat Olympic Pool. He later had some pointed things to say about Canadians — basically, that they lacked a will to win. Happily winning the odd Summer Olympic medal and equally as happily finishing third in the

It's a real Olympic medal! Gary MacDonald of Mission, BC, admires his silver medal after the men's 4x100 medley relay at the Montreal Olympics.

Commonwealth Games behind England and Australia and third in the Pan-American Games behind the US and Cuba was a sort of Canadian habit accepted unquestioningly. Canadians were always the nice guys who were good but never quite good enough. According to Talbot, Canada doesn't compete at the international level, it merely participates. Talbot was especially miffed that Canada handed over "home pool advantage" to the Americans without so much as a whimper at Montreal. "Here were the Olympic Games right at home in 1976 and the Americans were in total psychological control of the pool," he said. "They had most of the tickets and their cheering for American swimmers was tremendous. Our team got none of this level of support from the Canadian public and we felt intimidated by the lack of it. Canadians have never had a national identity, particularly in sport. They just don't really care a great deal about themselves as a nation. That has never been the case with Australians and Australian athletes." But Talbot's Canadian splashers did manage to come through with a more-than-decent haul of eight medals, even though most of the flag waving in the Olympic Pool was being done by the Americans. While East Germany won eleven of the thirteen women's swimming events at Montreal, the US captured twelve of the thirteen men's races. Only David Wilkie of Scotland denied the Americans a clean sweep on the men's side. Stephen Pickell, Graham Smith, Clay Evans and Gary MacDonald managed an admirable silver medal for Canada in the men's 4x100 medley relay in 3:45.94, which clipped almost two seconds off the world record. But the superstar American foursome of John

Naber, John Hencken, Matt Vogel and Jim Montgomery destroyed the world record with a clocking of 3:42.22 to take gold. For once, the Canadians in the crowd got into a little flag-waving of their own and even tried to shout down the American supporters in the crowd. "The excitement of being a part of that race in Montreal is something I'll never forget," said Graham Smith. "It was exhilarating watching Pickell and the others chasing down the Americans. It was electrifying swimming in front of 10,000 people with all of them screaming." But the US swim team was so strong that Naber, Hencken, Vogel and Montgomery sat out all the heats and only raced in the final. Even without them, the American subs set a world record of 3:47.28 in the qualifying round. So the Canadians were more than pleased with their silvers and went out to celebrate that night. "We had a golden rule — we were like monks until after the competition," said Smith. But after that, let's mambo. The relay boys arrived back late to their dorm and were sent home for breaking curfew by the Canadian team's overly zealous team officials, who really needed to lighten up. "I remember my dad wasn't too worried about that when I got home," recalled Smith. "He was more concerned about me doing something goofy like getting drunk and breaking a leg." It had been an emotionally draining year for Smith. His father, Donald, was diagnosed with terminal cancer in February while Graham and sister Becky were training for the Olympics in Thunder Bay. Donald Smith, a former coach and manager of the national swim team, lived long enough to see his son and daughter compete in the Montreal Olympics and Graham win a silver medal and Becky two bronzes. "It's one of those moments that stays galvanized in the mind for the rest of your life," said Graham, about that year. Graham and Becky wanted to come home to Edmonton to be with their father during his final months. But he convinced them their place was in Thunder Bay with Talbot. "The range of emotions Becky and I went through while training for Montreal were incredible," said Graham. "I'm especially proud of Becky. She really hung in there during an extremely hard time for all of us." Becky Smith, almost angrily it seemed, crashed through the water to win bronze in the women's 400m individual medley in 4:50.48. Cheryl Gibson finished second in 4:48.10 — taking .69 seconds off the world record — to give Canada two of the three medals. But Ulrike Tauber of East Germany took an incredible 6.02 seconds off the world mark to win the gold in 4:42.77.

Shannon Smith of Vancouver held off Rebecca Perrott of New Zealand to win the bronze medal in the women's 400m freestyle swim final. Smith finished in 4:14.60 and Perrott in 4:14.76. Petra Thumer of East Germany won the gold medal in a world record 4:09.89 while the fuming American Shirley Babashoff took silver in 4:10.46. Babashoff, beaten into second place three times in individual races and once in the relays at Montreal by East German swimmers, was irate at what she expected was German drug use and made plenty of nasty aspersions about the "husky" and "male-like" look of the female East German swimmers. But she turned out to be right. "Shannon would have been the silver medallist and Babashoff the winner," said Canadian Smith's coach Ron Jacks, himself a three-time Olympian. "You have to look at what it [steroid use] has done to the honest performers who didn't win. Everybody said 'poor Ben Johnson' because of all he lost. But what about all the opportunities lost by the people he beat?" If that's the case, then Canada could very well be considered to have swept the medals in the women's 100m backstroke at the Montreal Olympics.

No race better exemplified the level of frustration the Canadians may have felt about the East Germans. World record holder Ulrike Richter (1:01.83) and her buddy Birgit Treiber (1:03.41) took gold and silver while Canadians stormed in for the next three placings — Nancy Garapick winning the bronze medal in 1:03.71, Wendy Hogg finishing fourth in 1:03.93 and Gibson fifth in 1:05.16. Garapick had held the women's world 200m backstroke record prior to the 1976 Olympics, but so had four of the other seven finalists at the Games. When the spray had settled, Garapick (2:15.60) had her second bronze medal of these Games. And in front of her again, as if in the rerun of a bad dream, were Richter (2:13.43) and world record holder Treiber (2:14.97). The Canadian squad of Hogg, Robin Corsiglia, Susan Sloan and Anne Jardin captured the bronze medal in the women's 4x100 medley relay in 4:15.22. Who else but the East Germans won gold in a world record 4:07.95, followed by Babashoff and the Americans in second place in 4:14.55. Gail Amundrud, Barb Clark, Becky Smith and Jardin of Canada took the bronze medal in the women's 4x100 freestyle relay in 3:48.81, just .01 of a second outside the old world record. Babashoff finally got to turn the tables on the East Germans, helping to relegate them to silver this time in 3:45.50 as the Americans won gold in a world record 3:44.82.

Montreal's very own twenty-two-year-old Michael Valliancourt, riding a $100,000 former pace horse from Winnipeg named Branch County, won the silver medal in equestrian Grand Prix individual jumping with only twelve faults over a wet and treacherous course as the skies glowered angrily over Bromont. Not having enough money to buy Branch County, Valliancourt and his team came up with about $15,000 to rent him for three months before the Olympics and train in Florida. Riding a horse he hardly knew, Valliancourt was perfect over the first fourteen jumps. With anticipation rising, Branch County faltered over the slippery ground but still managed to put his rider in medal position. Francois Mathy of Belgium and Debbie Johnsey of Britain also finished with twelve faults but Valliancourt secured the silver by recording four faults in a jump-off to Mathy's eight and Johnsey's fifteen. The winner was Alwin Schockemohle of West Germany, who recorded the first faultless ride in Olympic competition since 1928 in Amsterdam.

Even though the event is called the 500m Canadian singles, John Wood of Port Credit, Ontario, wasn't given much chance in the canoeing events dominated by the Eastern Europeans. But streaking into the lead from the start, Wood had the 5000 fans at the Olympic Basin cheering in pleased surprise. He hung on until the final five strokes when he was overtaken by the favourite, Aleksandr Rogov of the Soviet Union, in 1:59.23. Wood took the silver medal in 1:59.58.

The three unexpected silver medals by Joy, Vallaincourt and Wood were needed because one by one, the few pre-Games medal favourites that Canada was counting on had fallen. Debbie Brill in the women's high jump — boom, out in the qualifying rounds. Bruce Simpson in the pole vault — boom, out in the qualifying rounds. Jocelyn Lovell in cycling under the distinctive but very expensive roof of that very expensive velodrome — boom, out in the qualifying rounds. (Lovell years later courageously fought a far more important battle as a quadriplegic after being hit by a truck and dragged while road training on his bike.) With the Canadians in the crowd at the Big Owe anxiously cheering her every move, Diane Jones of Edmonton was fourth and a strong bet for a medal with only the 200m to run in the pentathlon. But she faded in the biggest moment of her life and finished sixth. Even though defending Munich champion Frank Shorter of the US was the clear favourite, Jerome Drayton of Canada was given a good shot of taking a medal in the marathon. With his signature, wraparound aviator sunglasses on even in the pounding rain on that dark and wet day, Drayton gave it all he had as he sloshed through the streets of Montreal with sixty-six other runners representing thirty-five nations. The former winner of the Boston Marathon came into the stadium sixth in 2:13:30.0 and the crowd gave him a rousing ovation. Minutes earlier, a totally unknown East German named Waldemar Cierpinski had baffled the experts by crossing the line first in 2:09:55.0. Shorter was second in 2:10:45.8. To show it was no fluke, Cierpinski won the Olympic marathon again four years later in Moscow. Canadian women's 400m star Joyce Yakubowich of Burnaby, BC, won two gold medals and a silver at the 1975 Mexico City Pan-American Games and could have been counted on for at least a spot in the individual final and to propel Canada to medals in the track relays at Montreal. But she was struck by a blood disorder just before the Olympics and felt terrible in Montreal. Advised it was pointless to even try, Yakubowich felt she had sacrificed too many years to simply just not show up for the Olympics. She gave it her best despite having little strength. The individual 400m was a write-off but Yakubowich managed to help get the Canadian foursome into the 4x400 final, where she and Margaret Stride, Rachelle Campbell and Yvonne Saunders finished eighth. But by the time the 4x100 relays rolled around in two days, Yakubowich was wasted. She was too sick to run and a spare had to be put in. "We had such a good medal chance and it was a hard decision to make," says Yakubowich, who suffered with the blood malady for three more years after Montreal before getting better. Even without their star, the Canadian team of Margaret Howe, Patty Loverock, Joanne McTaggart and Marjorie Bailey finished fourth in 43.17, just .08 seconds away from a bronze medal. East Germany won in 42.55, West Germany took silver in 42.59 and the Soviets the bronze in 43.09. "They [her relay teammates] still bug me about that, good-naturedly, of course," smiles Yakubowich. "They say my being sick cost them and me an Olympic medal."

Canada finished with five silver medals and six bronze at Montreal. Sport in Canada had received a big push in federal funding in order to prepare for the Montreal Olympics. But, like so many things bureaucratic, the program was started too late. In fact, two years too late, in 1973. The result was that the effects weren't really first felt until the 1978 Commonwealth Games in Edmonton, where Canada easily swept to its first — and only, to date — victory in the overall Commonwealth Games medals table.

Some said the guy from the tiny Vancouver Island community of Chemainus was a hot dog. Others said he was impossible to coach. But everyone marveled at Billy Robinson's fluid, natural instinct for the game of basketball that helped carry Canada into the 1976 Olympic men's semi-finals at the Forum against Dean Smith's mighty American squad, and then to the bronze medal game against the Soviets. Robinson — all five-foot-eleven of him — carried the Canadian Olympic team on his back for years. "When I first came to Canada, I would start Billy and the next four guys who happened to come out of the dressing room," laughs Jack Donohue, the transplanted American who coached Canada from 1972 to 1988. After the bizarre spectacle of the US-Soviet gold medal game at the 1972 Munich Olympics, basketball became a focal point at Montreal. And through it all, Robinson's flashiness led Canada to the semifinals with a 4–1 record in the preliminary round games played at

A basketball ballet as Canada battles Dean Smith's US team in the 1976 Olympic semifinals at the Montreal Forum.

Etienne Desmarteau Centre. When the venue shifted to the Forum for the semifinal match-ups, the Canadians were up against a team of US collegiate stars that included Phil Ford, Adrian Dantley, Walter Davis, Quinn Buckner, Ernie Grunfeld, Ken Carr, Scott May, Tom La Garde, Phil Hubbard and Mitch Kupchak. It was a virtual Who's Who of the NCAA under the tutelage of University of North Carolina Tarheels coach Smith. The Americans had received a huge scare in the preliminary round, beating Puerto Rico by just one point. But the US was a team on a mission — win back the gold medal that had been lost in such controversial fashion at Munich.

Canada answered with Robinson, Alex Devlin, John Cassidy, Derek Sankey, Robert Sharpe, Cameron Hall, Jamie Russell, Robert Town, Romel Raffin, Lars Hansen, Phil Tollestrup and a very young Martin Riley. With the exception of Hansen, the Coquitlam, BC post player who made it to the University of Washington Huskies and then the Seattle SuperSonics of the NBA, and the quirky but dangerous Robinson, it wasn't exactly a line-up to send shivers up American spines. But the packed Forum was still a carnival of noise and hope that night as Hansen tipped off against Kupchak. A team of Robinsons and Hansens might have kept it close. But with only two players of that calibre available in Canada, Ford and Dantley took control early as the Americans scored the first nine points and eventually won by nineteen. "It was like an NHL team playing a junior hockey team," sighs Robinson, putting it in a context Canadians could easily understand. In the other semifinal, Yugoslavia upset the Soviet Union to deny the much anticipated US-Soviet showdown. The Americans won the gold medal with an anti-climactic 95–75 win over the Yugos. For what it was worth, Canada had held the US to a nineteen-point margin in the semifinals.

But the Soviets, stung by their upset loss in the semis, took it out on Canada by thumping them 100–72 in the bronze medal game. Donohue and Robinson, both emotionally spent, tightly embraced after the bronze-medal loss. "Jack was good to me," said Robinson, who played professionally in Europe. "I was always the hot dog from Chemainus — the small-town kid. I didn't become a player until subjected to his coaching. Coaches didn't like me dribbling through my legs and behind my back and shooting fifty times a game. I was sure hoping to find someone to tell me what to do. Jack was that someone."

Hansen, meanwhile, felt Canadian athletes were and are poorly treated in return for giving up much of their early lives to represent the country. "I got nothing for it," said Hansen, the greatest post player Canada has ever produced and who played five years for the national team before a brief stint in the NBA. "You don't develop a life in the national team programs. I enjoyed Montreal and the Olympics and wouldn't trade that experience for anything. But it was time for me to move on in 1977. You take a personal risk playing for Canada. It's a risk to your career. You devote twelve months of the year to represent your country and forego other career opportunities. And you get stabbed in the back for doing it. I've known people who have dedicated their lives to representing Canada and then taken a back seat because of it in other areas of life."

Women's basketball was included in the Olympics for the first time at Montreal. The Canadian women were nowhere near the level of the men's team and were easily dispatched 0–5 in the tournament at Etienne Desmarteau Centre. Among the members of the Canadian team was the talented but prickly Sylvia Sweeney, the niece of Canadian jazz legend Oscar Peterson. Sweeney went on to become the most valuable player at the 1979 world championships, the first Canadian player ever to gain that honour; she was also the Canadian flagbearer for the opening ceremonies of the 1979 Pan-American Games in San Juan, Puerto Rico.

She later become the president of her own television production company in Toronto, producing an award-winning documentary on her piano-playing uncle. A band she managed won the $100,000 grand prize in NBC's *Star Search* program. She also become a CBC anchor and is the assistant *chef de mission* for the Canadian team to the 1996 Atlanta Summer Olympics. But Sweeney's greatest claim to fame as a nineteen-year-old at the Montreal Olympics was that she snubbed the Queen. Sweeney went to the Village dining room to eat and there was the Queen dining with some athletes, a favourite hobby of hers at Commonwealth Games that she was also indulging at the Olympic setting. When Sweeney took a picture of the Queen, the basketball star was quickly surrounded by security men who took her camera and exposed the film. It's apparently not cricket to snap the Queen while she she eating. Sweeney was irate at what she thought was rough handling by the forces of royal protocol. The next day the Queen again arrived at the Athletes' Village, this time to visit the Canadian women's basketball team. But only eleven of the players stood in line awaiting Her Majesty. One was missing. Sweeney stayed on her bed and fumed. "They ruined my film," she says. "I didn't want to meet that woman."

If there was a gold medal for persistence and longevity, it would surely have gone to Alex Oakley. Born the same pre-Depression year that countryman Percy Williams won two gold medals for Canada in the sprints at the 1928 Amsterdam Olympics, Oakley competed in the Montreal Games as a forty-eight year old. Daniel Bautista of Mexico won the 20,000m walk in 1:24:40.6. More than twenty minutes later Oakley strode into the stadium after walking the streets of Montreal. He was tired and exhausted — the thirty-fifth-place finisher in a field of thirty-eight walkers. But a very strange thing happened. The Canadians and others in the crowd, perhaps grown weary of the Stars and Stripes hype as well as the steady stream to the podium of Eastern Bloc athletes with unpronounceable names, stood as one to give Oakley a standing ovation as he duckwalked his final lap. Startled competitors in other events going on in the stadium couldn't figure out what the commotion was about. It was almost a way of saying: Okay, we surrender. We're the first Summer Olympics host country not to win a gold medal at its own Games, but we've still got some pride, dammit. For that one brief but shining moment, Oakley became a lightning rod for a lot of pent-up feelings. A standing ovation for a thirty-fifth place finisher who was nearly fifty years old? Why not? It felt good.

The Montreal Games may not have left a lot of good feelings among the Canadian public, but there were tiny, pin-prick moments like that where the hair stood on end and the magnitude of the whole thing became almost overwhelming. Soccer star Bob Bolitho held off turning professional with the Vancouver Whitecaps of the NASL just so he could play in the Olympics in his home country. Even though Canada was eliminated after losing a 2–1 heartbreaker to the eventual bronze medallist Soviets and then 3–1 to North Korea, the Games remain a highlight of Bolitho's life. He played ten years as a professional and earned more than forty caps for Canada during three World Cup qualifying efforts from 1973 to 1981. But the Olympics remain his most ethereal memory in sport. "The memories are still a thrill for me, even though we didn't make it past the first round," says Bolitho. "I remember the march from the Athletes' Village to the Olympic Stadium for the opening ceremonies. Who says Canadians aren't emotional? The people were lined twenty to thirty deep all the way along the streets leading to the stadium and they shook our hands and grabbed at us to wish us luck. And when we [Canadian athletes] marched into Olympic Stadium as the last team, the place just erupted. These were *our* Games. I still get goosebumps on my goosebumps just thinking about it. That's what the Olympics are all about. It was a special feeling."

Sixteen days later, Canadian trumpet great Maynard Ferguson wailed a soulful and sad farewell tune that brought a hush over the crowd at the closing ceremonies in the monstrous and controversial stadium. But he was just doing his version of a lip-synch. All the music coming over the loudspeakers was recorded earlier and canned. It wasn't a great closing, but it had its few moments. Huge tepees stood in the infield as Canadian children danced around them. Thousands of green glow-in-the-dark pen lights waved as darkness encroached. The fortnight of Olympic competition had been an athletic and artistic success. The financial fallout would have to wait until a later reckoning. This was not the day to worry about that. The crowd sang "Auld Lang Syne" and, perhaps tellingly, a low rumble started but got louder as the crowd chanted "Drapeau, Drapeau … " for the man with the great vision, if not the accounting skills. And then the crowd poured out of the stadium and onto the streets of Montreal to go home or walk wistfully down Sherbrooke Street as city workers took down the Olympic banners and bunting. At home, millions of Canadians watched and then switched the channel or went back to feeding the kids or fixing the bathroom tiles. Although the bills would seem never-ending, Canada's first and only Summer Olympics were over.

MOSCOW 1980

July 19 to August 1
5326 Athletes from 81 Nations

Graham Smith was born to be an Olympic champion. His destiny was to climb to the top of the podium. Swimming is just something the Smiths of Edmonton did. Lawrence of Arabia rode around the desert on a camel uniting the Arab tribes. The Smiths swam. Father Don was the manager of the Canadian swim team at the 1968 Mexico City Olympics and coach at the 1970 Edinburgh Commonwealth Games. Mother Gwen was the chaperon of the 1970 Canadian team and a poolside official at meets all over Canada. There were eight children in the Smith family and seven represented Canada internationally at either the Olympic, Commonwealth, Pan-Am or World University games. George Smith swam in the 1968 Mexico City Olympics, Susan Smith in the 1972 Munich Olympics and Beckie and Graham Smith in the 1976 Montreal Olympics, with Graham coming away with a relay silver as a seventeen year old.

Yes, Graham. He was the special one. There was no doubt about that. He was ten when he sat in the stands watching brother George finish fourth and seventh in relays at the 1968 Olympics and two years older at Edinburgh where he sat and watched George win two gold and two silver, sister Susan two silver and a bronze and sister Sandra make it to two finals at the 1970 Commonwealth Games. But everybody pointed to the little brother in the stands. He would be the real one to watch, the experts said. And they weren't wrong. Graham Smith was a teenager when he struck for relay silver at the Montreal Olympics. Building more strength on his rapidly burgeoning young body, he exploded to become a sort of Mark Spitz of the Commonwealth Games, winning six gold medals in 1978 at Edmonton in the Donald F. Smith Memorial Pool, named after his late father. His sister Susan, a Games hostess, carried out Graham's gold on a pillow during the medal ceremonies of the 400m individual medley. The medal was placed around Graham's neck by Queen Elizabeth. Eight years earlier at the Edinburgh Games, the Queen had placed the gold medal for the same event around the neck of his brother George. Watching at Edmonton, in that pool named after her husband, was Games swim official and proud mother Gwen Smith.

Graham had established himself as the leading Canadian gold medal threat for the 1980 Moscow Olympics. He was now a whirlwind, powerful and unstoppable. Was Canada about to have its first Olympic gold medallist in the pool since George Hodgson in 1912 at Stockholm?

The ringing of the phone still jangles in Smith's ears these many years later. It wasn't just anyone on the line, it was The Phone Call. It was ringing to tell him he wasn't about to become a Canadian sporting hero. It was ringing to tell him he would not join the roll call of Olympic champions that stretches back in antiquity to Greece. It was ringing to tell him his name would not be added to that list which includes Percy Williams, Jesse Owens, Johnny Weissmuller and Cassius Clay. It was ringing to tell him he wouldn't be signing any sponsorship deals. It was ringing to tell him the worst career news imaginable. Smith had devoted an entire year to prepare full-time for the 1980 Olympics. He was training in Nashville, Tennessee, when the phone rang. Smith and Bill Sawchuk, another Canadian swimmer getting ready for the Olympics, were outside their dorm tossing a football. They let the phone ring. And they let it ring. But the sound wouldn't go away. In his gut, Smith knew what it was about. This was the day Canada's decision was to be announced, one way or the other. Smith picked up the phone. It turned out to be a reporter from Canada asking for Smith's reaction to the fact Canada had announced it was going to the boycott the Moscow Games as a response to Russia's recent invasion of Afghanistan.

It was like first hearing about the death of a loved one. The initial reaction isn't what you think it might be. That all comes later, after your mind and body have sorted out the magnitude of the news. Smith just felt blank. "I have no comment," he said. That night at the pool, he stared at the water for an hour without going in. The news was starting to hit home. His coach, Don Talbot, convinced him to get in. But Smith only went through the motions. "I was devastated, to say the least," he says. "We were stunned. We went out that night to a bar for a sort of wake. We still couldn't get over what we heard that day. It had quite a depressing effect on me for quite some time. It's devastating to see your life change — everything you've ever worked for. And it had nothing to do with money. I was never mercenary about my swimming. I was never into it for the potential money or sponsorships. I just wanted to see what I could do at the Olympics in my prime. In swimming, that chance only comes once in a lifetime. I was very young at Montreal in '76 and too old for L.A. in '84."

Smith at first begrudgingly accepted that a boycott may have been necessary to send the Soviets a message but then became cynical about the whole thing. "At first, my reaction was, yeah, this is devastating, but I'll follow my government's lead. They have the wisdom. But you quickly saw the Soviets weren't budging and the boycott never made a difference. I remember some Canadian team members at the Winter Olympics that year [in Lake Placid] said we should boycott the Summer Games. I thought to myself, 'Yeah, well it doesn't affect them, does it?' It's quite easy to say when you're not making the sacrifice. Politics is politics and you always think sport should be different. That's what Pierre de Coubertin wanted when he started the modern Olympics. But you quickly find out that isn't the case. 1980 was going to be my big year. I put my life on hold for it. It was a real slap in the face. But it's part of life and I really learned from it. It taught me how to roll with the punches in life. At least I had one Olympics, in 1976."

The IOC knew it was taking a calculated gamble in awarding the 1980 Games to Moscow over Los Angeles, the first ever to go to a Communist country. There were stirrings of discontent as soon as the decision was announced in 1974, with forty members of the US Congress voicing their disapproval. Then the Cold War froze over totally on December 28, 1979, with a brief but ominous news flash on Radio Moscow. The Soviets announced they had rolled tanks and troops into Afghanistan at the bequest of the Afghan government — which the Soviets themselves had installed eight months earlier. American hard-liners viewed US president Jimmy Carter as ineffectual and weak on Cold War matters. With the American hostage crisis in Iran starting to drag on and the right-wing rhetoric of Ronald Reagan beginning to win converts, Carter knew he had to act decisively. Economic sanctions are costly and political sanctions difficult to arrange. But there was one low-cost and high-profile option staring Carter right in the face. Hosting the Olympics is the perfect opportunity to show off in front of the world. That is the main reason nations spend billions of dollars to do it. Jimmy Carter was about to rain on the Soviet parade. On January 20, 1980, he issued an ultimatum: The Soviets must leave Afghanistan or the US would boycott the Moscow Games. The proposal was easily passed in the US Congress and Senate. The appeal then went out to the US Olympic Committee to do the patriotic right thing. The USOC acquiesced and voted by a 1604–797 margin not to send a team to the Moscow Games.

The Carter administration next turned to its allies in the non-Communist world. The Muslim nations were happy to oblige to show solidarity with their Afghan brothers and were lockstep behind Carter. So were the Japanese, who had too much trade with the US to sacrifice over an ideal. Margaret Thatcher, hardly surprisingly, avidly and vociferously supported the boycott as did the Conservative-dominated British House of Commons. But unlike in the US, the British Olympic Association wasn't ready to bend its knees. With Thatcher so upset she could spit, the BOA voted 18–5 against boycotting. Aussie Prime Minister Malcolm Fraser trotted around the world proposing an alternative Olympics (while wool from his farm was still being sold to the Soviet Union). But the Australian Olympic Association also defied its government and decided not to boycott in a tight 6–5 vote. The AOA, however, left it up to each sporting federation to decide and four Aussie sporting groups voted not to send their athletes to Moscow. The New Zealand Olympic and Commonwealth Games Association voted 8–7 to snub Prime Minister Rob Muldoon's call for a boycott and named a full team of 106 athletes for Moscow. But it left the final choice to the individual sports federations. The federations in that small and conservative little country had other ideas, and only canoeing and modern pentathlon elected to go. New Zealand's team at Moscow — including doctors, managers and athletes — numbered eight. And they were subject to obscene phone calls and letter bomb threats before leaving home.

Canada's and West Germany's teams were destined to number zero. The German Bundestag voted overwhelmingly to boycott and the West German National Olympic Committee reluctantly also agreed in a fifty-nine-to-forty vote. Canadian Prime Minister Joe Clark laughed at the idea of a boycott in early January. But on January 27 he changed his tune and said Canada would not attend unless the Soviets pulled out of Afghanistan. When Pierre Trudeau's Liberals and Ed Broadbent's NDPers brought down Clark's minority PC government, it was thought the song might change once again. The Liberals were hardly bloodthirsty Red haters on the world stage. But then, neither was Clark. The pressure from the American government, however, was too intense to ignore. The Liberals too, upon returning to power, agreed with Clark's policy that Canada should boycott. The Canadian Olympic Association, which knew all too well on what side its toast was buttered, voted 135–35 on April 26, 1980, in favour of a boycott. It was by far a greater margin than the much tighter vote West Germany's Olympic committee took and also by a wider margin than the 2–1 pro-boycott ratio of the US Olympic Association vote. It also pointed out how closely tied with government policy the COA, Sport Canada and the entire Canadian amateur sport infrastructure was. From the late 1960s to the time of the 1980 boycott call, national amateur sport and also culture had become almost entirely reliant on government for funding and support in the great Canadian move to the left. While that had obvious benefits for amateur sport in Canada, it also meant that an organization like the COA was hardly in a position to do anything but follow the government lead when the boycott drama was unfolding. The federal government was calling in its chips and the COA knew it. The reason Olympic committees in Britain, Australia and New Zealand (although the Kiwi sports federations fell in line) were able to resist their governments' strenuous calls to boycott is that amateur sport in those countries is mostly privately funded.

The final tally was sixty-two nations boycotting and eighty-one attending, with the 5326 athletes the fewest at a Summer Olympics since 1964 in Tokyo. The morning of July 19 dawned cloudy with rain in the forecast for the opening ceremonies. But already in the wee hours there were planes over Moscow trying to break up the clouds with a chemical spray. This is how far the Soviets were willing to go to make their show a success. It still rained during the opening and it certainly rained on the Soviet regime. Hosting the Olympics meant a lot to them. It was later reported Brezhnev was so offended and infuriated by the boycott he told some of his most trusted Communist Party cronies that opening day that the decision had already been made to gain revenge by boycotting the 1984 Los Angeles Olympics. Strangely, in the years leading up to 1980, it never occurred to the Soviets that a political or military action of theirs could have any bearing on the Games. Many party officials later admitted to being stunned at the reaction of the West. There actually was a Canadian presence at Lenin Stadium during the spectacular opening ceremonies of the 1980 Games. Stephane Prefontaine and Sandra Henderson, who lit the flame four years earlier at the Big Owe to begin the 1976 Montreal Olympics, carried in the Olympic flag. This was an IOC-mandated responsibility of the previous host and one the Canadian government had to allow. Russians dressed in Greek tunics sprinkled rose petals on the track in front of each of the marching teams. More than five thousand card holders put on a flashcard and pictogram display that would put any Super Bowl to shame. Unbelievable human pyramids, each containing hundreds of tumblers and gymnasts at their base, built layer upon layer until one beautiful woman rested at the top of each with her arms reaching to the heavens. Thousands of peasants from the fifteen states of the Soviet Union danced in national costumes. The final torch-bearer, basketball star Sasha Belov, was lifted to ignite the Olympic cauldron on the backs of hundreds of Red Army soldiers who acted as a staircase.

The opening was stunning and powerful. But evidence of trouble was everywhere. Sixteen teams refused to carry their national flags, instead opting to march behind the five-ring Olympic banner. The British team decided only to have a token representation at the opening ceremonies and a lone official marched and carried the Olympic flag instead of the Union Jack. Soviet television cameras turned away every time a team marched in with an Olympic flag and no mention was made of it on air. When the competition began, the Eastern Bloc — hardly surprisingly — dominated and captured the top four spots on the medals table. Reports of the Games were sparse in the North American media. The only time anything was reported with any zeal was when allegations of Soviet "cheating" were hatched. For example, the Finns complained that every time a Soviet javelin thrower was about to toss, the huge end zone doors of Lenin Stadium would mysteriously open, allowing for a strong tailwind. But when other javelin throwers stepped up, the doors would magically close.

The most-anticipated events of the Games (and among the most anticipated in Olympic history), however, came not from Soviet athletes but courtesy of two British running superstars. And they didn't disappoint. Steve Ovett was viewed by the media and track fans as surly and unresponsive. Sebastian Coe, on the other hand, was the white knight on a white horse — everybody's hero. That they were the two best middle-distance runners of their generation and hadn't raced against each other since 1978 was just icing on the track. For one tremendous week these two great warriors battled each other in a game of hide and chase. Ovett shocked the world-record holder Coe to take the 800m and leave the silver to Seb. And then, characteristically, Ovett failed to show for the post-race press conference. Ovett hadn't been beaten in the 1500m or mile in forty-two races over three years and shared the world record with Coe. But it was Coe, frail but dedicated, who rebounded from the setback in the 800m to come home first at Lenin Stadium to take gold in the 1500 as Ovett faded to bronze. Too bad hardly anyone in North America saw those battles. Alexsandr Dityatin of the Soviet Union won eight medals in gymnastics, the most ever in any sport by one person in a single Olympics. The British kept the Western Bloc flame flickering at the Moscow Games in the face of the Eastern Bloc wildfire of medals, with the notable victories by Ovett and Coe and also Alan Wells in the men's 100m and Daley Thompson in the decathlon.

The 1980 US Summer Olympians were invited to the White House and presented with special Congressional Olympic medals by Jimmy Carter. Among those Americans affected by the boycott were basketball star Isiah Thomas, later a star guard with the Detroit Pistons of the NBA and the first general manager and also vice-president of the Toronto Raptors, and world champion gymnast Kurt Thomas. Canada honoured its 1980 Summer Olympians with a mock Olympic opening ceremony at that year's Canadian National Exhibition in Toronto. Graham Smith was asked to be the headline speaker but refused to attend the CNE recognition ceremony. "I didn't want any part of it," he said. "If I accepted the invitation to be the main speaker, I would have just condoned what happened [the boycott]." It's anyone's guess what heights people like Smith could have reached in Moscow. One strong indication came in the 100m breaststroke final at the 1978 Edmonton Commonwealth Games when Smith out-fought Duncan Goodhew to win gold in a Games record 1:03.81 to the bald Englishman's silver medal time of 1:04.24. Goodhew won the gold medal in the men's 100m breaststroke at the Moscow Olympics, the event in which he finished second to Smith two years earlier at the Commonwealth Games. It is unlikely Goodhew would have become the Olympic champion if Smith had been there. "Goodhew never beat me at a major meet — the Olympics, Commonwealth, worlds or NCAAs," noted Smith. "But I'm happy for him and I don't begrudge him his [Olympic] gold medal. I've learned to accept what happened and not go through life worrying about 'What if?'"

Jack Donohue's Canadian men's basketball team had just finished qualifying for the 1980 Moscow Games at the Americas regional tournament in Puerto Rico when Canada's boycott announcement came down the next day. The basketball squad was a potent mixture of backcourt savvy with the gifted veteran point-guard Martin Riley of Winnipeg and the slick, emerging young shooting guard Jay Triano of Niagara Falls; they also boasted front-court size and talent through Leo Rautins of Toronto via the Syracuse University Orangemen and tall Jim Zoet. It was the only Canadian squad to qualify for the Moscow Olympics in a team sport. But a grim-faced Donohue called the team together. The players could hardly believe the words coming out of their coach's mouth. Could this be true? It was. "It was devastating to hear," admitted Triano, a legendary player and coach at Simon Fraser University in Burnaby, BC, and later the head of community relations for the NBA's Vancouver Grizzlies. "It was a hard pill to swallow. You always grow up thinking politics and sport don't mix. But they do. And it's not a great mixture."

Up to 1980, Philip Delesalle of Victoria was Canada's greatest male gymnast of all time. While that may not be saying much, considering Canada's stature in the sport, Delesalle revolutionized men's gymnastics in his country in terms of approach. "Philip was ahead of his time for Canadian men's gymnastics," notes Brad Peters of Brampton, Ontario, who competed for Canada at the 1984 Los Angeles and 1988 Seoul olympics. "No one before him in Canada trained the way he did. He was at it seven hours a day for six days a week. That's the type of dedication you need at the world level. He set the example for those who came after him." Beginning at age eight, Delesalle trained so long and so strenuously that he had no time for regular school like other kids and basically had to get his education by correspondence. Commitment like that is hard to comprehend for most youngsters and Delesalle became a bit of an outcast — a kid who didn't go to school like the others, but who trained unmercifully all day long in a sport only foreigners cared about. "My whole early life was spent training — that's basically what it amounted to," said Delesalle. He won five consecutive Canadian men's championships from 1976 to 1980 and went from twenty-second overall at the '76 Montreal Olympics to two gold medals at the 1978 Edmonton Commonwealth Games to twelfth-place overall at the 1979 world championships in Fort Worth, Texas — the highest finish ever by a Canadian up to that time. Delesalle was bitter about the boycott of the Moscow Olympics, where a top-ten overall finish was almost certain and a run at some medals possible. "I worked much too long and much too hard not to have hard feelings," he said. "The boycott accomplished nothing. We [athletes] were just pawns being used. I retired after 1980 because I was mentally tired after all that. I had about as much as I could take. But life goes on and you put it behind you and move on, which is what I did."

Graham Smith dropped out of the University of California at Berkeley for 1979–80 to pursue his Olympic dream. It turned into a nightmare. But it doesn't bother him that swimmers Alex Baumann and Mark Tewksbury became national heroes after him in subsequent Summer Olympics — an accolade denied Smith. "I'm happy for both those guys

— in fact I coached Mark when he was a kid," said Smith. "It doesn't upset me that they got something I didn't have the opportunity for. Actually, it was nice to see swimmers getting name recognition like they got. It was good for the sport and that's the thing that really counts. As a swimmer, you really only get a few chances to be in the limelight. I was more disappointed than I was bitter about missing my big chance at the Olympic Games. But I've exorcised those demons and left 1980 behind. I can't change it. You can really get bent out of shape by worrying about the past and living your life wondering what might have been. You just have to refocus your energies on something else." Smith floated around Edmonton, Calgary, Victoria and Vancouver coaching and working before finally finding himself back at Berkeley in 1995 finishing off the economics degree he abandoned in 1979–80 to train for Moscow. But his new textbooks showed there is no longer a Soviet Union; and the Cold War rhetoric that counted for so much in 1980 means absolutely nothing now.

LOS ANGELES 1984

July 28 to August 12
7078 Athletes from 140 Nations

On the same day — September 2, 1937 — that Baron Pierre de Coubertin died almost penniless in Geneva, Switzerland, a baby named Peter Ueberroth was born in Chicago, Illinois. Those who like their Olympic symbolism drawn in broad and emphatic strokes, need look no further than that fact. De Coubertin's family fortune had been eaten away and all that was left was the title of Baron and his fading fame as the founder of the modern Olympic movement. He was an unhappy man that day he died of a stroke at age seventy-four while walking through a public garden in Geneva. He died broken and distraught, privately disillusioned by how the movement had been subverted at Berlin by the 1936 hosts (although he was publicly accommodating to the Germans). But de Coubertin still believed, or at least wished, the Olympics he founded would one day become a vehicle for world peace and racial tolerance. It was his desire, and it was carried out, that his body be buried near the IOC headquarters in Lausanne but his heart be taken out and entombed in a marble column in front of the eternal Olympic flame in Olympia, Greece.

What would de Coubertin — who gave his heart, quite literally, to the Olympic ideal — think of the baby Ueberroth born across the sea on the very same day the good Baron died? What would de Coubertin have thought of Ueberroth's unabashed and unapologetic mercantile approach to the 1984 Los Angeles Games that took in a windfall profit of $222.7 million? What would he have thought of the almost grotesque, flag-waving display of American chauvinism the hosts displayed in 1984? What would he have thought of the glitzy, but hardly heartfelt, David L. Wolper opening and closing ceremonies, which featured everything from a man jettisoning into the stadium 007-style with a back powerpack to eighty-four baby grand pianos playing Gershwin to laser displays?

That's hard to say. What isn't is the Canadian athletes didn't care if it was pure capitalist greed or other more enlightened business motives that fueled the L.A. Olympics. The national record of ten gold medals, eighteen silvers and sixteen bronzes and sixth-place standing in the overall medals table was a Summer Olympics high-water mark for this country. Ask Alex Baumann if he cared one way or another that his Olympic venue at USC was called the McDonald's Swim Stadium or that the hamburger chain spent nearly $30 million on television commercials during the Games. After the debt debacle of Montreal, there were no other takers for de Coubertin's now-not-so-little pet project when bidding for the 1984 Games culminated in 1978. There was initial interest from Tehran (wouldn't that have been fun) but it faded as the political/religious situation in Iran escalated. L.A. won by default and it dictated the terms. Where else could the IOC turn? The city of Los Angeles, faced with a municipal referendum in which only 34 percent of voters supported the Games if it cost them *any* tax dollars, refused to accept the Olympic Charter's mandated fourth rule which declared that the host city must assume responsibility for any deficit.

So for the first time, the Games were given not to a city but a private organizing committee. That committee — in a 9–8 vote on March 26, 1979, with 1960 decathlon champion and ultimate 1984 cauldron lighter Rafer Johnson casting the deciding ballot — elected the unknown forty-one-year-old Ueberroth as CEO and president over favoured department store chairman Edwin W. Steidle (who would likely have won had he not been entangled in a contract/severance dispute with his former company). You have to hand it to the Americans, of which Ueberroth is a certain archetype. Capitalism is their game and they are good at it. And for only the third time since 1932, the Games did not run a deficit. But that's like saying a hill is not like Mount Everest. In terms of money, L.A. '84 obliterated all that came before it. The Los Angeles Games boasted an unheard of return of 31 percent on investment when most past Games not only couldn't earn a thin dime but almost always lost money. ABC made a profit of $430 million *after* spending $225 million to secure the domestic US television rights and millions more on production. It cost up to $500,000 to air a one-minute commercial during the Games in prime time.

The Greeks were so outraged when Ueberroth planned to make money from the torch relay, they initially refused to allow the traditional lighting of the torch by the sun's rays at Olympia. Under pressure from the IOC, they acquiesced and 10,000 of the relay legs winding 19,000km through fifty states were "sold" for $3,000 each with the money going to youth sport in the United States. Even left-wing Olympic commentators were being won over by Ueberroth's ground-breaking approach. Why should the state pay for circuses when there is such a crying need for funds elsewhere? "One can understand the anger of Montreal taxpayers over their billion-dollar deficit, or the related fear of taxpayers in Los Angeles," wrote University of British Columbia professor Rick Gruneau, former Canadian champion in water-skiing and author of *Class, Sports and Social Development*. "Working people tend not to benefit from the Olympic circus, except in some passive, spectatorial way. Indeed, if funds spent on the Montreal Olympics had been directed to other areas, the effects could have been stunning. For example, Montreal's investment in the Olympics could have provided low-rent housing for 120,000 citizens, free public transport for ten years, or free recreational programs for a generation of young people."

Ueberroth, who in his past career had started his own company and turned it into the second-largest travel agency in the US, was so pleased with his Olympic effort he gave himself a $475,000 bonus. Get over yourself, Pete. But if Ueberroth and Big Macs are what it took now to keep the Olympic flame burning, de Coubertin's old heart would just have to learn to stand the heat in its marble tomb in Olympia.

Canada's medal total was, without doubt, padded because of the Soviet-bloc boycott of the Los Angeles Games — which was cunningly announced on the day the Olympic torch reached the US on May 8, 1984. The official smoke screen for the no-show was security concerns but the real reason was revenge for the US-led boycott of the 1980 Moscow Olympics. But many of the Canadian athletes would have won their medals, boycott or not. Foremost among those was Alex Baumann, the sleek and streamlined part-human, part-fish from Sudbury, Ontario, who as a fresh-faced sixteen-year-old was named to the Canadian swim team for the '80 Moscow Games before the boycott was announced. He had to wait until the 1982 Commonwealth Games in Brisbane to make his mark for the first time on the world stage with a world record 2:02.25 in the 200m individual medley and a second gold medal in the 400m IM.

Alex Baumann of Sudbury looks to the heavens after winning gold in the 200m individual medley at the 1984 Los Angeles Olympics.

When he was two years old in 1966, Baumann's family left for a stint in New Zealand. That's where they were two years later when Soviet tanks rolled into Prague. There was no going back to their homeland for the Baumanns. They emigrated to Canada and settled in the northern Ontario nickel mining community of Sudbury, which was most famous for a giant nickel that greeted people as they entered town along the main highway; residents were less boastful of its slag heaps, which created a moonscape so real that NASA astronauts trained there before lunar missions. Sudbury now has become a pleasant city which has reclaimed and replanted its barrenscape outskirts. And oh, by the way, it's best known now as the home of Alex Baumann, who celebrated his adopted country with a tiny but heartfelt red maple leaf tattoo on his left chest over his heart. Above the maple leaf is the word "Sasha," his nickname.

Baumann entered the 1984 Los Angeles Olympics with the most pressure on a Canadian athlete since Elaine Tanner in 1968, who also did a star turn at her Commonwealth Games two years before in Kingston, Jamaica. Tanner's so-called Olympic silver medal "failures" at Mexico City and the subsequent reaction back home shattered her emotionally and have affected her life ever since. It's not something Baumann was forced to endure. He burst through at L.A. to win Canada's first Olympic swim gold medal since George Hodgson in 1912 by taking the 400m IM in 4:17.41 to eclipse his own world record. Even though twenty, he was still below the California legal drinking age of twenty-one. But it was only after three beers were given him in doping control that the mistake was realized by organizers, who made him switch to pop. But by that time, Baumann was feeling pretty happy in more ways than one.

Five days later, he was even happier with his second Olympic gold medal in world record time. And he hadn't had a beer all day. He won the 200m IM in 2:01.42 to smash the old world record he set at the Commonwealth Games two years before. The sight of the lanky and grinning Baumann tossing frisbees into the outdoor stands as he walked to the victory podium is one of the more glorious memories in Canada's history at the Summer Games and a striking counterpoint to the humiliation that awaited on the track four years later in Seoul.

Victor Davis of Guelph, Ontario, was as heated and explosive a personality as Baumann was cool and placid. Together, they were the fire and ice of Canadian swimming in the first half of the 1980s. In 1981, Davis was but tenth in the world in the 200m breaststroke and thirteenth in the 100m breaststroke. But a year later, he was world champion and world record holder in the 200 (2:14.77) and world silver medallist in the 100 behind world record holder Steve Lundquist of the United States. He repeated that gold-silver combination later that year in Brisbane at the Commonwealth Games but not before showing his explosive temper in an incident that dogged him for years. Davis flew into a tantrum and tossed and trashed a few chairs poolside after one of his Canadian relay teams was disqualified.

The trouble was this took place just when the Queen happened to be in the Chandler Pool. She, however, wasn't too perturbed and may not have even seen the incident very clearly. Even if she had, she's probably seen worse in Buckingham Palace. The media had a heyday with the incident and it followed Davis, who wore his emotions too close to the surface at the best of times. But he also had a sense of humour. After he won his third medal of the 1984 Los Angeles Olympics — a silver in the 4x100 medley relay — he quipped: "No chair kicking this time." Davis settled for another Olympic silver in the 100m breaststroke when his American arch-rival Lundquist set a world record of 1:01.65 to win the gold. Davis was close behind in 1:01.99.

But Davis reached the top podium in the 200m breaststroke by eclipsing his own world record to take gold in 2:13.34, well ahead of silver medallist Glenn Beringen of Australia (2:15.79). His relay silver in the 4x100 medley was won with Mike West of Waterloo, Ontario, Tom Ponting of Calgary and Sandy Goss of Toronto in 3:43.23. The US squad, which included Lundquist, Pablo Morales and Rowdy Gaines, won the gold medal in a world record 3:39.30. Davis' hometown was so pumped by his three Olympic medals that Guelph mayor Norm Jary announced

The fiery Victor Davis reacts to his gold medal victory and world record after the 200m breaststroke final at the L.A. Olympics.

that a sign would be erected in Davis' honour on the outskirts of town and that a street and an Olympic-size pool would be named after him. Davis died tragically in 1989, hit by a car after a scuffle outside a Montreal night club. On the way to the 1990 Commonwealth Games in Auckland, New Zealand, some of his close swim friends stopped in Los Angeles and scattered his ashes in the USC pool in the lane in which he set the world record to win his Olympic gold medal.

Joe Ottenbrite used to pretend he was a shark and chase his three-year-old daughter Anne around their backyard family pool in Whitby, Ontario. That's when Anne first developed her strange whip kick that would give her so much power fifteen years later. She went from using that nifty little manoeuvre to elude her daddy in the pool to eluding her international competition. "Her coaches didn't like it [the whip kick] at first," recalled Joe. "But they began to love it and recommend it." Olympic medals will do that. Anne Ottenbrite became Canada's first-ever female swim gold medallist when she splashed to victory in the 200m breaststroke in 2:30.38. When he watched his daughter on the victory podium on television in Whitby, Joe Ottenbrite cried. "I just couldn't contain myself," said Joe, who owned a sporting goods store. "To think that's my daughter up there getting the gold medal." Ottenbrite followed that up with silver in the 100m breaststroke in 1:10.69 behind Petra van Staveren of Holland (1:09.88). Ottenbrite was sixth at the halfway mark and then rallied, just failing to catch the Dutch girl at the wall. And it was bronze for Ottenbrite in the 4x100 medley relay with Pam Rai of New Westminster, Reema Abdo of Belleville, Ontario and Michelle MacPherson of Toronto in 4:12.98. West Germany got the silver in 4:11.97 and the superstar American team of Theresa Andrews, Tracy Caulkins, Mary T. Meagher and Nancy Hogshead the gold in 4:08.34.

A ten-foot sign was erected outside the Whitby Tourist Information Centre heralding its most famous citizen: "Olympic Gold 84: Anne Ottenbrite." That sign actually should have been installed outside the trauma ward of the Durham Region hospital. The injury-prone Ottenbrite survived a few accidents to get her medals. She once walked through a plate glass window and also gashed her arm in an encounter with a food processor. She dislocated her right kneecap while showing off some high heels in May of 1984. She had to miss the Canadian trials but was given a spot on the Olympic team anyway. In Los Angeles, the van in which she was travelling rear-ended a car and gave Ottenbrite minor whiplash. Back in the Athletes' Village, she strained a thigh muscle while playing a video game. The latter two injuries, luckily, occurred after her two individual swims but just before her relay bronze. Her gold-silver-bronze represented the best-ever performance at the Olympics by a Canadian female swimmer.

"We [the swim team] wanted to do it for ourselves, not for the history books," responded Ottenbrite. Other Canadian swim medals came through a pair of bronzes won by backstrokers Cam Henning of Edmonton (2:02.37 in the 200m) and Mike West of Waterloo (56.49 in the 100m). But the Albatross, Michael Gross of West Germany, was the only non-American swimmer at the 1984 Olympics getting any real ink or broadcast coverage in the United States. ABC swim commentator Mark Spitz rarely referred to Baumann and once when he did, he labeled him "excitable and temperamental." Exactly what Olympic swim competition Spitz was watching is anybody's guess. In his only interview on ABC, Baumann was asked just one question by Spitz: "Why did your family escape from Czechoslovakia." In fact, Baumann's family didn't "escape" but was in New Zealand when Soviet tanks rolled into Prague and so never went back. Swim Canada officials were so irate at what they saw as an attempt to weasel out of Baumann an anti-Soviet comment, they stopped giving ABC access to Canadian swimmers. As if ABC cared.

If there is one group of modern athletes de Coubertin would have been proud of, it is the rowers. They still perhaps best exemplify the ancient amateur ideals of sport for sport's sake. Except for a select few like Canada's Silken Laumann, there is absolutely no money to be had from rowing in appearance fees or endorsements. It's not that rowers wouldn't take it if it were there. They are, after all, no different than anybody else. But they willingly persist in a sport they know full well offers few financial rewards. And in this age, that in itself is worth admiring.

That is what compelled celebrated Pulitzer Prize-winning American journalist and author David Halberstam to choose rowing when he decided to write a book that would mark the coming of the Summer Games to the United States for the first time in fifty-four years. He could have picked 1984 US Olympians such as Carl Lewis or Michael Jordan, but he chose instead four anonymous scullers as they prepared for the US trials. Fittingly, he titled the book *The Amateurs*. "Brad Lewis enjoyed immensely the grand tour of the United States with the other [1984 L.A.] American Olympic medallists, even though being a gold medallist in a sport as eccentric as rowing did not increase his fame very much," wrote Halberstam. "The other rowers knew that he had won a gold, and some local papers paid attention. Other than that, the feeling of pleasure came entirely from within."

It was from within that Canada's most heart-pounding gold medal from the 1984 Olympics came. For just under six stomach-wrenching minutes on a hazy Sunday morning on a lake about 150km north of downtown Los Angeles in Ventura County, eight Canadian athletes exerted themselves into near physical and emotional collapse. An Olympic gold lay in the balance. The great seize such moments; the near-greats let them slip away. For Pat Turner and Paul Steele of Vancouver, Dean Crawford, Kevin Neufeld and Grant Main of Victoria, brothers Mark and Mike Evans of Toronto, Blair Horne of Kelowna, BC, and coxswain Brian McMahon of St. Catharines, this was to be a time for greatness.

Crawford remembers the last few moments of the Olympic men's rowing eights final with a kind of horror that makes you wince. His mind was going blank and his arms and legs were nearing numbness. "I can't explain it," he said. "Something inside me just said, 'keep stroking, keep stroking.' We would have spent a lifetime regretting it if we had listened to our bodies and let up. Something inside me kept pushing on although my body was completely spent near the end. Emotionally, I just wasn't there. My mind went blank near the end. I couldn't think. There was no blood left in my brain. But something inside me made my arms pump." If that race had been ten metres longer than the 2000m distance, the hard-charging US boat, which had taken huge bites into the Canadian lead, would surely have pulled out a win. But the race wasn't longer and Canada held on in 5:41.32 to the Americans' 5:41.74.

For all nine Canadians in the boat, it was a dream come true. Crawford remembered an elementary school project where he had to chart the medal winners of the 1968 Mexico City Olympics and thinking what an incredible thing it would be to win an Olympic gold medal. But even a grade-schooler with a vivid imagination would have sense enough to know it is pure folly to harbour any dream of ever getting to the top level of an Olympic podium. But sixteen years after that school project, a dream came true on Lake Casitas near Los Angeles.

Because of something that happened earlier in 1984 at Lucerne, Switzerland, the Olympic win carries added significance for the Canadian eights. "Any victory at Los Angeles will be hollow without the East Germans," Crawford said at the time the Eastern-bloc boycott was announced. (At the last previous Summer Olympics in which the Eastern and Western blocs competed together — Montreal in 1976 — the nations which boycotted L.A. accounted for 58 percent of the gold medals.) "The winners will spend the rest of their lives wondering how they would have done if the East German crew was there," added Crawford. But at the regatta in Lucerne, with the best of the Western and Eastern blocs racing, the Canadian eights swept to victory over the top-ranked East Germans. So the 1984 Canadian eights can stop wondering. Their win at Lucerne gives their Olympic championship greater depth and meaning. Their gold medals aren't sullied by the boycott. Unlike many of the gold medals from Moscow in 1980 and Los Angeles in 1984, theirs aren't so hollow.

Besides the gold in men's eights, there were five other rowing medals for Canada at Lake Casitas — in all, a handy haul. Bob Mills of Dartmouth, Nova Scotia, won bronze in the men's single sculls; Doug Hamilton of Toronto, Mike Hughes of St. Catharines, Phil Monckton of Vancouver and Bruce Ford of Victoria bronze in the men's coxless quad sculls; Silken and Danielle Laumann of Mississauga, Ontario won bronze in the women's double sculls; Betty Craig of Brockville, Ontario and Tricia Smith of Vancouver earned silver in the women's coxless pair oars; and Marilyn Campbell of Victoria, Angie Schneider of Toronto, Barb Armbrust and Jane Tregunno of St. Catharines and coxswain Lesley Thompson of Nepanee, Ontario, also struck for the silver medal in women's coxed fours.

Linda Malcolm of Hamilton was eight years old when her father, Neil, taught her how to handle a gun and instilled in her a lifelong love of the sport. Neil Malcolm had shot at the prestigious Bisley meet in England. The sport had been handed to him by his father and now he wanted to pass it on to his daughter. Linda Malcolm learned by shooting at tin cans in a Hamilton quarry. Under her married name of Linda Thom, she became good enough to make the national team but quit in 1974 after becoming discouraged by a poor showing at the world championships. She moved to Paris with her husband and got a cooking diploma from the esteemed Cordon Bleu School and started a catering business back in Ottawa. Thom cooked for many of the ambassadors and high commissioners stationed in the national capital and also the leader of the opposition, Joe Clark, at Stornaway. After learning women's shooting events would be included for the first time in the Olympics at Los Angeles, Thom began practising again in 1982. Part of her problem before was she would get too excited, so she worked with a psychologist to keep her anxiety level down in competition and thus give a boost to her control and concentration. That's why her husband and children didn't fly down to Los Angeles until the day before her competition in the sport pistol event. On the first day after the 1984 opening ceremonies, Linda Thom — a forty-year-old mother of two — won Canada's first gold medal at the Summer Olympics since the Gayford-Day-Elder equestrian victory on the last day of the 1968 Mexico City Games. Trailing by four points and in fourth place among the thirty competitors representing twenty-one nations, Thom made it up over the final ten shots to force overtime against Ruby Fox of the United States. Thom then pulled out the gold medal by squeezing for thirteen bull's-eyes in fifteen shots. It was the first Olympic shooting medal ever won by a woman and Canada's first in the sport at the Olympics since Gerald Ouellette in 1956 at Melbourne. Her eight-year-old daughter, Samantha, had bragged to her school chums that her mommy was going to win the gold medal. And she did. "I hope a lot of forty-year-old housewives will see what I've done and decide to try something themselves," Thom told reporters after her victory.

Larry Cain's baseball team went winless the summer before so he turned to something else to do the next summer when he turned thirteen. He and two pals signed up with the Oakville Canoe Club in 1975 for recreational paddling. So while most Canadians remember only high jumper Greg Joy's silver medal from the 1976 Summer Olympics, Cain was inspired by one of Canada's two other individual silver medallists at Montreal. He remembers shouting in front of his television set as John Wood of Port Credit, Ontario, paddled his way to a canoeing silver medal. "Other kids had NHL heroes; I had John Wood," said Cain, who became inspired to canoe more than just recreationally. With his blond hair, Hollywood looks and muscular build, Cain emerged as a powerhouse on the canoeing scene. As it happened, Wood was the canoeing colour commentator at Lake Casitas for CBC during the 1984 Olympics and helped describe Cain's gold medal victory in the 500m C-1 in 1:57.01 and silver medal performance in the 1000m C-1 in 4:08.67. Cain wished he could have tested his medal against a full Olympic field. "It was a bit disappointing to me that the East Germans and Russians weren't there," he told reporters. "It's sad for them and sad for us. I might have won with them here — I might not have. The hard part is that we'll never know. It just isn't the way it should have been." Regardless, Cain celebrated his medals by going for a quiet canoe trip in Algonquin Park after the Games.

Alwyn Morris, a Mohawk from the Kahnawake Reserve near Montreal, became the first Canadian native Indian to win an Olympic medal in an individual sport and first ever to win gold (the Mohawk lacrosse club took a bronze in 1904 at St. Louis). The closest a Canadian Indian came before in an individual sport was Tommy Longboat, who led the marathon at the 1908 London Olympics before dropping out. Morris became only the third North American native Indian to win an Olympic gold medal after Jim Thorpe's belated decathlon victory at Stockholm in 1912 and Billy Mills' 10,000m upset win at Tokyo in 1964, both for the United States. Morris competed despite his small five-foot-four and 120-pound build. Ironically, his Indian name is Tall Standing Pine. Morris, with Hugh Fisher of Burnaby, BC, won gold in the kayak pairs 1000m at Lake Casitas in 3:24.22 and bronze in the kayak pairs 500m in 1:35.41. Women's kayaking provided two medals for Canada as Alexandra Barre of Jonquiere, Quebec and Sue Holloway of Ottawa won silver in the doubles 500m in 1:47.13 and Barre, Holloway, Lucie Guay of Montreal and Barb Olmstead of North Bay bronze in the fours 500m in 1:39.40.

On the water across the way in Southern California at Long Beach harbour, Canada's yachtsmen were both helped and hindered by the whopping seventy-eight protests that marred the 1984 Olympic sailing competitions. Terry McLaughlin of Toronto, who skippered *Canada I* at the 1983 America's Cup at Newport, led going into the final race of the Flying Dutchman class after winning three of the first six races. It looked as if only a disaster would prevent him from taking the gold medal. That's exactly what happened as a worst-case scenario unfolded for McLaughlin and his crewmate Evert Bastet. In the jockeying for position at the start among the seventeen boats, McLaughlin and Bastet went over the line and had to go back and start again. McLaughlin, feeling the antics of some other boats had led him over the line, immediately hoisted his protest flag. The Canadians finished the final race eighth because of having to go back and re-start and saw the gold medal slip away to Jonathan McKee and William Carl Buchan of the United States at 19.7 points. McLaughlin's and Bastet's protest was not upheld and they settled for the silver medal with 22.7 points on the reverse-scoring system.

Hans Fogh won his first Olympic medal, a silver for Denmark in Flying Dutchman, way back at the 1960 Rome Games as a brash twenty-two year old. A protest helped him win the bronze medal in soling twenty-four years later at L.A. as a forty-six-year-old Canadian. It was the sixth Olympics for Fogh, who moved to Canada in 1969 to start a sailmaking business. After Rome, the hard-luck Fogh had twice again been in Olympic medal positions going into the final day before fading to fourth place — in 1964 at Tokyo for Denmark and in 1976 at Montreal for Canada. He finished fourth again at Los Angeles in 1984 but was bumped up to the bronze medal after the third-place Norwegians were disqualified for rocking their boat to gain momentum. "I don't feel altogether happy about winning a medal this way but I don't feel ashamed, either," said the veteran Fogh, who shared the bronze medal win with his Toronto crewmates John Kerr and Steve Calder. After sailing in polluted waters, Terry Neilson of Toronto got a fungus infection that caused painful blisters on both his thumbs. His thumbs were really aching, but he managed to hang on for the bronze medal in Finn class with 37.7 points. John Bertrand, who skippered Australia to its landmark America's Cup victory the previous year, slipped in just ahead for the silver medal with 37.0 points. Russell Coutts, a New Zealander headed for future America's Cup fame, won the gold medal with 34.7 points.

One of the most electrifying moments of the 1984 Olympics occurred when Steve Bauer of Fenwick, Ontario, legs churning madly, stormed the final 100m toward the finish line of the 190.2km cycling road race. More than 300,000 people — hey, it was free — lined the Olympic course. After nearly five hours of huffing and pumping, it came down to the final sprint. Bauer had taken the lead from Alexi Grewal of the US with 10km left and Grewal looked to be history. But the American made up the difference and he and Bauer were neck and neck with just metres to go. The sprint is Bauer's specialty. But, unfortunately for him, the final few metres were at an incline, which was his soft spot. It happened so lightning quick. Watching tapes of that final sprint to the finish is still thrilling. Bauer cranked it up for all he was worth at 100m and took the lead. Grewal, however, came up from behind in the final 40m to nip the Canadian at the line. Both riders were listed at 4:59:57.0.

Grewal was lucky to even be in the race. He had apparently taken a Chinese herbal pill earlier in the year and when that showed up in his urine as the illegal substance phenyethylamine, he was suspended from the US Olympic team. But he fought the suspension and was reinstated less than a week before the Olympic race. Bauer, who went on to a pro cycling career of some note, left Los Angeles immediately after the race. When he showed his silver medal to airline workers at the airport, he was upgraded to first class and given champagne to drink all the way home. Elsewhere, Curt Harnett of Thunder Bay looked on his way to victory in the 1000m cycling sprint time trial at the Games velodrome at Carson City with a time of 1:06.44 until the last rider, Fredy Schmidtke of West Germany, came along with a 1:06.10 to snatch the gold medal.

Harnett was only nineteen and a junior rider the year before. Nobody on the international scene had heard of him, which made his Olympic silver medal all the more surprising. "I was getting a lot of strange looks from the other riders, like 'who are you?'" laughed Harnett. In 1995 at the world championships, Harnett set the world sprint record at altitude with such an amazing time that many predict it will stand for fifteen to twenty years.

While Bauer and Harnett both swept to silvers in 1984 for Canada's first Olympic medals in cycling since the 1908 London Games, the nation's biggest riding medal hope — Alex Stieda of Coquitlam, BC — was blanked as he faded in the 4000m pursuit and placed tenth in the 50km points race. With Stieda wobbling out of the picture, the winner of the 4000m pursuit was Steve Hegg of the United States, who while living in Edmonton won four gold medals at the Canadian closed junior championships in 1980 as Steve Ingram. Hegg/Ingram was born in the US but lived in Alberta from age eight to sixteen and began cycling in Red Deer in 1979. As one of Canada's rising young cycling stars, great things were expected of him. But when he applied for a passport to compete in international events, it was found that Steve Ingram didn't exist. His father was known in Alberta as Charles Ingram. But he was actually Charles Hegg, who was wanted in the US by the FBI for a fraud charge in South Carolina involving $47,000. The elder Hegg was given a two-year sentence in Edmonton for impersonation. His son was deported to the United States, which is the country he won a gold medal for at Los Angeles. In the post-race press conference, Hegg broke down and wept when he mentioned how influential to him former Canadian cycling star Jocelyn Lovell had been when Hegg was a Canadian junior cycling star. "He's the reason I'm standing here today," said Hegg, who had been coached on the Canadian junior team by Lovell. "My hero and mentor is Jocelyn Lovell." Lovell was then a paraplegic and confined to a wheelchair after being hit by a truck in 1983 while training near Milton, Ontario. "I love Canada, but I don't know if I would have won today if I had remained there," said Hegg. "The Americans are the best. We have the technique." You could call it technique, or you could call it something else. It was later learned many members of the 1984 US Olympic cycling team used "blood boosting" to enhance their performances.

Sylvie Bernier of Montreal won Canada's first gold medal ever in diving when she stunned experts by taking the women's springboard title. She never looked at the scoreboard, watched anybody else dive or talked to anyone during competitions to avoid becoming tense — which was long a problem for her. Instead, the tiny Bernier listened to the

Flashdance soundtrack between dives on her headset. It wasn't until after her last dive that coaches informed her she was in the lead and could only be overtaken if American Kelly McCormick had a sensational final dive and scored more than seventy points. McCormick — daughter of four-time Olympic gold medallist diver Pat McCormick — came mighty close with an excellent last dive that got her 67.20 points. But it wasn't enough as Bernier won gold with 530.70 points and McCormick settled for silver with 527.46. Irene MacDonald, the only other Canadian to win a diving medal at the Olympics with a bronze at Melbourne in 1956 behind Kelly's mom Pat McCormick, was the diving colour commentator for CBC and described Bernier's performance for the national television audience. Synchronized swimming, which turned out to be an annual easy touch for medals for Canada, made its Olympic debut and three Calgarians splashed, whirled and twirled in the pool for two silver medals. Carolyn Waldo collected 195.300 points to finish second behind American Tracie Ruiz of Seattle (198.467) in solo while Sharon Hambrook and Kelly Kryczka got 194.234 points to finish second to Ruiz and Candy Costie of the US (195.584) in duet.

To the outside world, the most famous Canadian athletes at Los Angeles '84, weren't Baumann, Ottenbrite or Davis but instead were two boxers: Willie Dewit of Grande Prairie, Alberta and Shawn O'Sullivan of Toronto. They went into the Olympics with tremendous reputations. Boxing promoter Don King predicted during the Games that as a white heavyweight contender, DeWit "held the keys to Fort Knox" when he turned pro. DeWit was such a celebrity he didn't stay in the Athletes' Village but instead at a rented private residence with personal security guards. He had come a long way since getting hooked on boxing when just fooling around with a punching bag at a health club in 1978. The American interest in the two Canadian boxers was keen enough that the British Olympic boxing team coach Kevin Hickey alleged O'Sullivan and DeWit had an "unfair advantage" because they were being "packaged by American television as part of the promotion for when they turn professional" and the two Canadians were getting "hometown decisions in Los Angeles."

O'Sullivan and DeWit were fairly erratic at the Games, showing devastating power at times and then looking less than super at other times. The rowdy and sometimes downright ugly crowd in the Los Angeles Sports Arena, which thought it was at Friday Night at the Fights and not the Olympics, booed when O'Sullivan won a controversial and highly suspect light middleweight semifinal victory over Christophe Tiozza of France. "This crowd booed Muhammad Ali when he was intro-

Willie DeWit of Canada and Henry Tillman of the US duke it out for the gold medal at the 1984 L.A. Olympics.

duced," shrugged the twenty-two-year-old O'Sullivan, a reflective young man who read Thoreau. "They're pretty hard to please." O'Sullivan admitted, however, he wasn't sure himself which way the decision was going to go. The judges actually gave the 3–2 decision to Tiozza. But new rules instituted before the 1984 Games said all 3–2 decisions had to go to a five-man jury. That jury overruled the judges and voted 4–1 for the Canadian.

O'Sullivan, feisty but likable, had grown up tough. He practically lived in the Cabbagetown Boxing Club, soaking the tough and sweaty atmosphere through his pores for seven years and compiling an 87–5 record with sixty knockouts heading into the Games. His Toronto bus-driver father, Michael, was a top amateur fighter in Ireland. There was a decent and gentle quality in Shawn O'Sullivan that even the roughness of his sport couldn't extinguish. He looked to have the gold medal bout against Frank Tate won, twice staggering the American for standing eight counts in the second round. But the 5–0 decision went to Tate. That, too, was booed lustily by the crowd. O'Sullivan charitably called it "an unfortunate decision." Dewit also fought his way into his final, where he met Henry Tillman of the US for the heavyweight gold medal. DeWit had twice before beaten Tillman, who learned to box while in jail for armed robbery. DeWit could have met a young Mike Tyson in the Olympic final but Tillman twice beat Iron Mike at the US trials to win the Games berth. Tillman scored a 5–0 upset over DeWit to hand Canada a second disappointing silver medal in the ring. Boxing experts said that loss probably cost DeWit "$1 million off the top" for when he turned pro. Both DeWit and O'Sullivan turned professional with much fanfare and hype after the Olympics. But after initial successes, both of their pro boxing careers fizzled and their great early promise was never realized. DeWit suffered an incalculable tragedy later when several members of his immediate family were killed in a plane crash.

The real Canadian surprise in the ring was bantamweight Dale Walters, whose amateur boxing career was sponsored by three pubs in Burnaby. Walters was 158–11 heading into the Olympics. His father, Len, fought in the 1952 Helsinki Olympics and won his first two bouts before breaking his hand in the quarterfinals and losing. His son almost didn't make it to his second bout. Because of road closures due to the women's marathon, the bus driver started going the wrong way and was heading away from the arena before an alarmed Dale Walters told him to turn around. Walters got to the venue just twenty minutes before his bout. "If I hadn't spoken up, we'd still be driving and I would have been out of the Games," sighed Walters, an aspiring actor who had already appeared in a couple of CBC television productions before the Olympics. Walters survived that scare and made it to the semifinals, eventually ending up with a bronze medal. Lightweight Asif Dar of the Cabbegetown club didn't make the Canadian team after losing a hard decision in the Olympic playdowns. But he came up with $4,000 and his coach Ken Hamilton took out a bank loan for another $3,000 to go to Karachi and fight in the Pakistan Olympic trials. Dar had been born in Pakistan and had dual citizenship. He won a berth into the Los Angeles Games but wore the light green and white of Pakistan and not the red and white of Canada. "All my boxing life I wanted to fight for Canada at the Olympics," he sighed to reporters. "But it wasn't to be. But my mother is happy to see me fighting for Pakistan and I'm glad God gave me this second chance." Dar, who won his first bout but lost his second at Los Angeles, went on to fight for Canada at the 1988 Seoul Olympics.

Canada hasn't won a medal in a team sport at the Summer Olympics since the silver in basketball at the 1936 Berlin Games. It stayed that way at Los Angeles despite three teams making it to their bronze medal games, another finishing tied for third but awarded fifth place on tie-breakers and yet another going down in a quarterfinal heartbreaker. US men's team basketball coach Bobby Knight said: "Canada was one of the teams that could win gold." Canada had a good team. But not that good. "It's a psyche job," responded Canadian coach Jack Donohue, under whom a much younger Knight had once worked as an assistant at a basketball camp. Since then, Knight had gone on to become Mr. Terrible of US college hoops at Indiana University — a ranting, raving, crazed person who roamed the sidelines like a not-so-benevolent dictator. "Compliments aren't Bobby's style," deadpanned Donohue, who is no stranger to humour or the telling understatement. Canada finished 3–2 in the round-robin at the Great Western Forum and then stunned European champion Italy 78–72 in the quarterfinals to earn a berth against Knight's boys in the semifinals. Here's a partial list of just who those American guys were: Michael Jordan, Patrick Ewing, Chris Mullin, Sam Perkins, Alvin Robertson, Wayman Tisdale, Jon Koncak — then college stars on their way to the NBA with a bullet. Mullin had twenty points and Jordan thirteen as the US dumped Canada 78–59 in the semis. Ewing shut the Canadian offence down almost singlehandely after Canada led 6–4. Canada played the US almost even, 35–33, in the second half. The trouble was the seventeen-point deficit the Canadians faced at halftime. But things were looking good for the bronze medal. Canada met Yugoslavia, a team it had beaten twice just before the Olympics. But thirty-two-year-old Drazen Dalipagic of Zagreb, who had a tryout with the Boston Celtics way back in 1976, had a career night with thirty-seven points and was virtually unstoppable. Canada — paced by Jay Triano of Niagara Falls, Howard Kelsey of Vancouver, Dan Meagher of Duke via St. Catharines, Karl Tilleman of Calgary, Tony Simms of Toronto, Bill Wennington of St. John's University in New York, Eli Pasquale of Sudbury and Gerald Kazanowski of Victoria — led 49–48 at one point. It was just 81–80 for the Yugos with 1:09 left but Canada fell short 88–82 to finish fourth. The Canadian players went back to the dressing room and, to a man, wept. "It was quite a disappointment," said point guard Pasquale, the Sudburite who, with Kazanowski, led the University of Victoria to five CIAU championships in his five years of university basketball. "We were the second best team, physically, in the Olympics and should have won a medal. And we came so close to winning one, which is why it hurt so much." Even future NBA player (most recently with the Chicago Bulls) Bill Wennington was in tears. "It's going to be hard to say goodbye to these guys," said the big forward, who was born in Montreal but raised in the United States. "In that dressing room, we realized it was our last time together and this wasn't the way we hoped it would end."

Canada put forth one of its greatest performances ever on the soccer pitch. Pros were allowed to play in the Olympics for the first time, just as long as they had never competed in a World Cup. That was no problem for Canada since its first World Cup appearance was still two years away at Mexico '86. The team was thrown together just days before the Olympics because obstinate American-based clubs in the North American Soccer League were hesitant to release their players to play for Canada. The releases finally came but not before a lot of rancour and ill will. But the Canadian side, captained by the reliable Bruce Wilson and coached by Tony Waiters, had talent and played well in the preliminary round at Cambridge, Mass. (Olympic soccer games are held far and wide in the host country.) A key 3–1 victory over Cameroon gave Canada a quarterfinal berth at Stanford Stadium in Palo Alto, California against Brazil — a country whose soccer history needs no introduction. The game was tied 1–1 and Canada looked to take the lead when Gerry Gray scored in the sixty-seventh minute. The goal was called offside but replays show it should have counted. The game ended 1–1 and went to a shootout. Dale Mitchell of Vancouver and Ian Bridge of Victoria — both future World Cup players in '86 — were stopped by the nimble Brazilian netminder in the key latter stages of the shootout. Brazil, the eventual silver medallist behind France, escaped with the victory and went on to the Olympic semifinals and final in front of massive crowds at the Rose Bowl.

The Canadian men's volleyball team was favoured for a medal at Long Beach Arena but lost the heartbreaking bronze medal game to Italy and finished with a 3–3 record. The women's basketball team also made it to their bronze medal game but lost 63–57 to China in a game it should have won, considering the talent on the Canadian team through the likes of Bev Smith, Sylvia Sweeney, Misty Thomas and Debbie Huband. The team performed below par and finished with a disappointing 2–4 record behind the top three — the Cheryl Miller-led US (6–0), South Korea (4–2) and China (3–3). In women's field hockey at Monterey Park, hopes were high after Canada's silver medal performance in the 1983 World Cup (the talented team would also win a bronze medal at the 1986 World Cup). But Canada finished in a third-place tie at the '84 Olympics with the US and Australia at 2–2–1 behind gold medallist Holland (4–0–1) and silver medallist West Germany (2–1–2). The US was given the bronze medal and Australia fourth place and Canada fifth on tiebreakers. The Americans and Aussies both had nine goals for and seven against while Canada had nine goals for and eleven against. "Failing to win an Olympic medal was the biggest disappointment of my career," said Lynne Beecroft of Duncan, BC, a starter for Canada for eight years with fifty-eight caps. "But why dwell on that when you can remember walking into that huge coliseum for the opening ceremonies? I had to pinch myself. I couldn't believe this was happening to me."

It was mostly through the relays that Canada's track and field contingent shone at that Memorial Coliseum bowl in a seedy area of town near USC. A rising young Toronto sprinter named Ben Johnson won bronze in the men's 100m in 10.22 behind Americans Carl Lewis (9.99) and Sam Graddy (10.19) and then tumbled to the track after crossing the line. He rubbed his arms as he got up. Prime Minister John Turner, a former sprinter, sent Johnson a congratulatory telegram. We would be hearing more of this shy, stuttering young man in the years ahead. He also led Canada to a 1984 Games bronze in the men's 4x100 in 38.70 behind the US (a world record 37.83) and Jamaica (38.62). The all-Toronto Canadian team consisted of Johnson, Tony Sharpe, Desai Williams and Sterling Hinds, the latter also a star football player with the University of Washington Huskies. Angela Bailey and Angela Taylor (later Issajenko) of Toronto, Marita Payne of Concord, Ontario, and late-addition France Gareau ran for silver in the women's 4x100 in 42.77 behind the Evelyn Ashford-powered American squad (41.65). Gareau was only seventeen years old. The year before, she had been running for Franco-Cite High School in Verner, Quebec, population about 1000. "This is like a dream," said Gareau. Canada struck for silver again in the 4x400 in 3:21.21 through the always personable and sunny Charmaine Crooks of Vancouver, Jillian Richardson of Calgary, Molly Killingbeck of Toronto and Payne. The Americans, paced by Valerie Brisco-Hooks, won gold in 3:18.29. Lynn Williams of Vancouver survived the crash heard around the world in the women's 3000m final — when running giants Mary Decker of the US and South African-turned-Brit-for-a-day Zola Budd bumped. As a fallen, sobbing and finger-pointing Decker fell to the track and a frightened Budd was booed, three lesser lights stormed through for the medals — Maricica Puica of Romania for the gold in 8:35.96, Wendy Sly of Britain for the silver in 8:39.47 and Williams for the bronze in 8:42.14.

Jacques Demers of Brossard, Quebec, won Canada's first Olympic weightlifting medal since Gerard Gratton took silver in the same middleweight class at the 1952 Helsinki Games. Lifting at Loyola Marymount University, Demers snatched 147.5 kilos and jerked 187.5 for a 335 total and the silver medal behind Karl-Heinz Radschinsky of West Germany (340). Demers faced a charge of smuggling after being caught with a large quantity of steroids at Montreal's Mirabel Airport in 1983. "I don't use steroids," said Demers flatly, when asked. Most of Canada's top wrestlers are produced by the Burnaby Mountain/Simon Fraser University wrestling centre in the basement of the rather sterile SFU athletic building in Burnaby, BC. They come under the stern eye of national team coach Jim Miller, who wrestled for Canada at the 1976 Olympics. "This is not a normal cross-section of the population," he once told a reporter. "We have a bunch of gifted people who work very hard and really care about something." I guess that doesn't say much for the normal cross-section of the population. Out of the SFU basement emerged two Olympic medallists at Los Angeles — Bob Molle and Chris Rinke. Molle, who came to the Burnaby centre from his native Saskatchewan, won the silver medal in the super heavyweight class at the Anaheim Convention Centre. Gold was the virtual domain of US superstar Bruce Baumgartner, who defeated Molle 10–2 in the gold medal bout. Chris Rinke of Port Coquitlam, BC, who Miller described as being "fast and powerful but too self-conscious for his own good," got over the affliction to win bronze in the middleweight class behind Mark Schultz of the US and Hideyuki Nagashima of Japan.

Mark Berger of Winnipeg did well to win Canada's second medal ever in Olympic judo after Doug Rogers' silver at Tokyo in 1964. Fighting in the same heavyweight class in which Rogers competed, Berger took bronze. Gold medallist Hitoshi Saito was virtually unbeatable and Berger had the misfortune of meeting him in the semifinals, lasting only seventeen seconds against the Japanese typhoon. And then there was lovely Lori Fung of Vancouver in a sport nobody in Canada had heard of before, one where you actually lose points if your bra strap is showing. Ranked seventeenth in the world, Fung seemed to surprise everybody but herself when she came out of nowhere to win the gold medal in rhythmic gymnastics at Pauley Pavilion, better known as the home of John Wooden's old UCLA basketball dynasty. Even with the boycott, Fung stood little chance. But she was committed, even going so far as leaving school for a year to study in Bulgaria under those terrors of the rhythmic gymnastics mats, the Bulgarians and Romanians. She studied under Doina Staiculescu of Romanian, the gold medal favourite for the Olympics. When the last ball had been thrown, last hoop spun and final ribbon twirled, Fung stood atop the list of thirty-three competitors from twenty countries with 57.950 points. The student had become the master. Staiculescu finished second with 57.900 points.

Canadians didn't seem to know how to react to this torrent of 44 medals, more than all the Summer Olympic medals combined for Canada since the last Los Angeles Games in 1932 and 29 more than at any previous Summer Olympics. Canada was fourth in overall medals won, behind the United States' 174, West Germany's 59 and Romania's 53. It tied for sixth with Japan in gold medals won with 10. The flag-waving US had 83 gold, Romania 20, West Germany 17, China 15 and Italy 14. Based on

10–5–4–3–2–1 scoring for top six finishes, Canada finished fourth on points with 333, behind the United States' 1363, West Germany's 470 and Romania's 378. Most important, based on world rankings, the estimates are Canada would have won between 20 to 30 medals if there hadn't been a boycott. Even if the East Germans (who had been picked by some to win as many as ninety gold medals) and Soviets had attended, this would still easily have been Canada's best performance ever at a Summer Olympics. A banner front page headline in the *Toronto Star* during the Games screamed: "It's Time To Strut Canada; We've Got Olympic Gold Fever." Was this actually Canada doing this? "In the bad old days, a Canadian would come to the Summer Olympics disguised by a false beard and mustache," wrote veteran Toronto sportswriter Jim Proudfoot, who has covered many an Olympics. "You were hoping nobody would recognize you. Internationally, Canada was always the team to beat — and everybody invariably did. Embarrassing? You said it. That's why these '84 Games present us with an exhilarating change. This is what triumph feels like. It's really quite wonderful. Don't say anything to spoil it."

"I think Canadians feel good enough about being Canadians today that they will think the investment is worthwhile," Sport Canada director Abby Hoffman told reporters after the closing ceremonies. She was talking about the $100 million that had been spent on amateur sport in the previous four years. But that kind of money was just chump change for Ueberroth and his gang, who spent many of their millions on all the wrong things in the closing ceremonies, which included such artificial "highlights" as a laser show and a glorified Lionel Ritchie concert. James Lawton of the *Vancouver Sun* was horrified by the glitz of it all and compared it to the closing ceremonies of the 1980 Moscow Olympics, which had "No laser shows, just peasant girls dancing and tears on a summer night." But Los Angelenos didn't care because this was definitely more their style, there not being too many dancing peasant girls within hollering range of Sunset Boulevard. And the denizens of La La Land didn't have to shell out any tax dollars for their extravaganza. It was bought and paid for by McDonald's and Coke. As the final lights dimmed in the Los Angeles Memorial Coliseum on August 12, 1984, the sound of a cash register closing could be heard.

SEOUL 1988

September 17 to October 2
8465 Athletes from 159 Nations

Oh Ben. How you brought a nation to its feet. Oh Ben. How you made a nation weep.

There are but a few instances in the history of a country where the people are transfixed by a single moment and transformed by it. And it's remarkable how many times those moments are provided by sport. Federal elections or referendums rarely, if ever, have that sort of defining power where a nation sees in a fleeting instance a reflection of what it believes it is or can become. Paul Henderson provided such a moment in 1972 with his historic goal that gave emotional, if nominal, proof we were still tops in a game that represents the very soul of this nation and which is one of the few things in the world we do better than anybody else. But that's ice hockey, a game played well by maybe just six to eight countries. The reason the 100m dash is considered one of the true glamour events of the Olympics is that it's so basic. It's less than ten seconds of chase across a flat piece of earth. Nothing much in the way of equipment is needed and hot, dusty weather isn't a deterrent. It's so easy and simple — and yet, as we were to quickly learn — also more complex than we could ever have imagined.

Ben Johnson was born the fifth of six children to Ben Senior and Gloria Johnson on December 30, 1961 in Falmouth, Jamaica, just months before the country would win its independence from Britain. He was a sickly little lad in his first year and had to be nursed constantly through a malarial illness that killed several children in the Johnsons' northern coast port village. Ben survived and grew to challenge neighbour kids in barefoot races around the block for a few cents. He didn't show too much early promise but managed to win occasionally. He was fourteen when he emigrated in 1976 to join his mother in Toronto. A year later at junior high school and still weighing less than 100 pounds, he was challenged to a race by a group of boys who thought the skinny Johnson was just a little too cocky in gym class. He smoked them in the challenge sprint. They never bothered him again. Ben was introduced by his brother Edward, himself an okay sprinter, to coach Charlie Francis of the Toronto Optimist Track Club. The rest, sadly enough, is the most famous story in Canadian Olympic history.

Francis was embittered by what he saw as an absolutely lame Canadian attitude in the face of fierce Games competition from European athletes. "We got there and lined up against some of the best-trained, competition-sharpened running machines in the world," Francis told Jim Christie in *The Fastest Man on Earth*, Ben Johnson's pre-Seoul authorized biography. "And Canada just said: 'Go out and run, kids. It's the Olympics.' I saw how Canadians were getting kicked around, how everybody was saying that somehow we couldn't do anything. 'Why can't we run? Are we genetically inferior?' You take a bunch of Canadian athletes, who had no meets, no competition, no preparation, no program ... " As a twenty-three-year-old, Francis ran the 100m at the 1972 Munich Olympics but pulled out just before the 200m because of injury. Canadian team officials howled their disapproval and tried to punish him for his move, which convinced him even further that the proper technical support was sadly lacking for Canadian track athletes. You can see where Francis was coming from and there is a degree of empathy that goes out to him. His thoughts are echoed by Don Talbot, the hard-driven Aussie who was fired as the Canadian Olympic team swim coach just weeks before the Seoul Games because of differences with Swim Canada over national team philosophies. "I established [tough] standards for 1988 and they thought it was fine until a month before the Olympics and they changed their minds," he said. "I believed the athletes could have done the standards but they said they couldn't. I felt they quit on me. The program in Canada was more athlete-driven than coach-driven. In Australia, it's more coach-driven and that's more likely to succeed. I vowed to be Number One with Canada and I'm sure I was the only one who thought that way. Australians are doers, Americans are doers and Canadians are, well, I won't say it ... " Talbot, who went back Down Under to lead the Aussie swim team to tremendous success at the 1992 Barcelona Olympics and 1994 Victoria Commonwealth Games, believed in doing it through hard work. Francis had other ideas. A nation that has always been too willing to accept fourth and fifth rate in the Summer Olympics needed a kick in the butt and somebody to administer it. Francis thought he could be that person. But he knew what few Canadians back then knew, or at least were willing to admit: there was a price to be paid for winning in the sprints. Call it a loss of innocence, perhaps. Francis believed or knew, and rightly so, that many of the top sprinters in the world were using steroids to build up muscles and thus explosive speed.

And so Ben's rise began. There was the silver medal in the 100m at Queen Elizabeth II Stadium at the 1982 Brisbane Commonwealth Games in 10.05 seconds behind the 1980 Moscow Olympics champion Alan Wells of Scotland and another silver in the 4x100 relay. There was bronze in the 100 at the 1984 Los Angeles Olympics in 10.22 seconds and bronze in the 4x100. After that, Johnson got a personalized Ontario licence plate for his Corvette that read "Ben 84." That was followed by gold at Meadowbank Stadium in the 1986 Edinburgh Commonwealth Games 100m in 10.07, bronze in the 200m in 20.64 and gold in the 4x100. Queen Elizabeth presented the Commonwealth 100m gold medal to Johnson. Getting off to his patented quick start in Lenin Stadium, Johnson recorded the fastest time ever at sea level in winning the 1986 Moscow Goodwill Games gold medal in 9.95 seconds. Then he truly exploded onto the pages of the record books at the world track and field championships in 1987 at Rome's Olympic Stadium. Boom — 9.83 seconds — a world record watched by a television audience of nearly 600 million and which took a tenth of a second off American Calvin Smith's old world mark of 9.93 set at altitude in 1983. The fastest human being ever over 100m was a Canadian. How's that for a national jolt?

All of a sudden Canada had the most prized, most talked about, most photographed Olympic athlete going into Seoul. This was the big time. The red of the Canadian singlet no longer stood for embarrassment. It had been a long time in coming for a nation that managed to let flag-waving American fans overtake the Olympic stadium and pool during its own Games in 1976 at Montreal and whose greatest Olympian in many people's eyes, Percy Williams, had done his thing sixty years before. With all respect to Alex Baumann's accomplishments at Los Angeles in 1984 — which were drowned out in the international media by those of fellow swimmers Michael Gross of West Germany and Rowdy Gaines of the US — six decades is a long time to wait for another performer whose name alone shines above all the rest on the Olympic marquee. Most small and medium countries never get such a hitter. But Canada had one — not bad for a nation founded by a department store.

Johnson had looked sluggish and indifferent in his heats — in fact he let up to finish third in the quarterfinals but advanced anyway to the semis based on time. Bothered since February by a pulled hamstring, Johnson's fitness had been a question of much national speculation, especially in light of two third-place finishes at Zurich and Cologne in the month before the Olympics. It had also been the cause of much speculation in the Johnson camp and was the reason his doctor, George Mario (Jamie) Astaphan, made the infamous decision to administer a dose of Winstrol-V (a stanozolol steroid that is a synthetic form of the male hormone testosterone used to fatten cattle) to the sprinter just twenty-six days before the Olympic final. Steroids spur muscle growth, which is a big advantage for those in events needing explosive starts. Another key attribute of steroids is they speed up recovery time from injury. It was a display of panic and fear by men who regarded Johnson as one of the greatest potential meal tickets in sports. An unnamed source told *Sports Illustrated* that Astaphan treated Johnson "like a race horse, a commodity." The injury was touch-and-go, as were Johnson's August results. The time it takes for stanozolol-compound steroids to flush completely out of the body is twenty-eight days. Francis and Astaphan felt it was worth the gamble of the extra injection. It was the fudge heard around the world.

The day and time of the 100m final — Friday, September 24 (Saturday in Seoul), 1:30 P.M. Pacific and 4:30 P.M. Eastern — seems burned in the memory. Canadians rushed home or to televisions in bars and restaurants. This kind of attention to one event was unheard of outside of hockey. Johnson appeared to be on form in the semifinals on the morning of September 24 and motored to a 10.03 victory despite becoming irate after being charged with one false start. Less than two hours later, Johnson took off his sweats and stared down lane six with his yellow eyes — which very few Canadians at that point knew the significance of. Carl Lewis of the US was in lane three for the final, Linford Christie of Britain, who would become the 1992 Olympic champion, in lane four and former world record holder Smith of the US in lane five. The other finalists were Desai Williams of Canada, Ray Stewart of Jamaica, Dennis Mitchell of the US and Robson da Silva of Cuba. Johnson was off like a flash. He had a patented start that tested the nerves of the official race starters. Johnson loved playing chicken with the gun. He had a knack of anticipating the start and this time he timed it perfectly. He was in his stride and charging like a runaway locomotive before his great American arch-rival Lewis, who had cast aspersions about Johnson's drug use during the world championships the year before in Rome, could do anything about it. Just before the finish, Johnson looked disdainfully to his side and this put his hand up with index finger held high to indicate he was No. 1. Was he ever. Lewis glanced over at Johnson with a hurtful look. Lewis' father died in 1987 and the son had put his 100m gold medal from the 1984 Los Angeles Olympics into his dad's hands to be buried with him and made a promise that he would win another one in this glitter event of the Games. "It's over Dad," Lewis recalls thinking to himself as the muscular Johnson, his gold chain dancing around his dark neck, sped across the line in the almost superhuman world record time of 9.79 seconds. It was not only one of the most fabulous feats in the history of the Olympics, but in the entire history of human sporting endeavour.

Back in Canada, an entire nation exploded with joy. Watching the race was a strange experience for a country not exactly hooked on track. Until now. The singular national reaction over those 9.79 seconds seemed to be almost orgasmic, flying in the face of the normal flat Canadian response to even great events. "Go, go, go, yes, yes yes, yeeeees …!" followed by high fives and clenched fists punching the air in celebration in front of television sets from Victoria to St. John's. Johnson had re-corded one of the all-time great moments in Olympic history. The ancient Greeks could not have envisioned a man running anywhere near this fast. But one had. And he was a Canadian. It was dizzying. It was joyous. It was glorious. It lasted three days.

While Canada celebrated — unified for a rare moment as it had been in 1972 when Paul Henderson's dramatic goal lifted us to hockey victory over the Soviets — Johnson's urine was being routinely tested. Prince Alexandre de Merode of Belgium, the head of the IOC medical board, was alerted that steroids were found in the "A" sample of a yet-unknown athlete. He checked the sample with his coded list of numbers and up popped the name Ben Johnson. He checked again. Again, Ben Johnson. De Merode took a deep breath. It was true. And he knew what a storm this discovery was about to create. Carol Anne Letheren, the Canadian team *chef de mission* and soon-to-be IOC member and head of the Cana-dian Olympic Association, was awakened at 2:00 A.M. Seoul time Monday morning to accept a letter sent by de Merode. With sweaty palms she ripped open the envelope, knowing any letter delivered urgently at that hour of the morning could only bring horrible news. It did. About five hours later, she told Johnson what had transpired. Three hours after that, quiet and ashen-faced Canadian team officials sat in witness as the "B" sample was tested. It too contained steroids. Ben Johnson had become the thirty-ninth athlete caught for drug use at an Olympics since testing began in 1968 but the biggest name, by far, ever to be nabbed. Then came the IOC press conference that confirmed the swirling rumours: "The urine sample of Ben Johnson, Canada, 100m athletics, collected on Saturday, September 24, 1988, was found to contain metabolites of a banned substance — namely the anabolic steroid stanozolol ... "

The rest was like a bad dream. After one of the worst days of hand wringing in the history of Canadian sport, a bleary-eyed Letheren went to Johnson's posh downtown suite at the Hilton (he didn't stay in the Athletes' Village) at about 3:00 A.M. Tuesday to retrieve the gold medal, which the next afternoon was presented to Carl Lewis in a quiet ceremony in a dressing room under the stands of the Olympic Stadium. The sinking feeling many Canadians felt when they first heard the news of the positive drug test is hard to describe to outsiders. The reaction of many headline writers was less than admirable. Quick to elevate Johnson as the King of Canada over the weekend, they were busy tearing him down as one of the biggest bums in history a day later. The Canadian team was also split, along noticeably racial lines. The mostly white Canadian middle-distance runners at Seoul had long suspected drug use among the mostly black Toronto Mazda Optimists sprint group. A big bedsheet hung from one of the windows of a Canadian dorm. On it was the hand-printed message: "From hero to zero in 9.79 seconds." Lynn Williams, who had won a bronze medal in the 3000m at the Los Angeles Olympics, yelled angrily to Francis that he had disgraced the entire Canadian team. Sprinter Angela Issajenko shot back with an angry obscenity. Emotions were seething beneath the surface and often bubbled over the top. Some Canadian athletes in the Village began referring to Johnson as "Jamaican Ben." A British weightlifter at the Seoul Games, Welshman David Morgan, wasn't so quick to criticize. "If you were offered $20 million US [Johnson's endorsement contracts if he won gold] you'd seriously think of taking something that might improve your performance," said Morgan. "There are people who'd shoot or blow your kneecaps off for £300 and yet Ben Johnson is considered a big criminal."

Johnson's agent, Larry Heidebrecht, an American and former University of Toronto track coach, estimated Johnson would have earned US$10 million to $15 million from 1988 to 1992 with an Olympic gold and world record. After Rome in 1987, Johnson charged $30,000 per meet. It is estimated he made US$2 million between 1986 and 1988, although not all of it had been paid out by the time of Seoul. He bought seven cars during that time, including a Ferrari and a Porsche at a total cost of about $315,000 and a piece of property in Markham, Ontario, for $350,000. He had $500,000 in a trust account administered by the Canadian Track and Field Association.

But what he had paled in comparison to the future wealth that slipped away as lucrative deals with Diadora, Mazda, Toshiba and Purolator all fell through. *Sports Illustrated* even reported Johnson was looking forward to getting off steroids after Seoul. But it was too late for that. The new federal sport minister, Jean Charest, said Johnson had "embarrassed Canada" and would never run for the country again. But Charest had overstepped himself and angry words flew across the floor in the House of Commons. Even Prime Minister Brian Mulroney was apparently irate about what his minister was saying. Ironically, Johnson outlasted Charest in the sporting field. While the sport minister tearfully resigned during the 1990 Auckland Commonwealth Games over a letter of clarification he had sent to a judge hearing a case brought by a disgruntled athlete, Johnson was back at the Olympics in 1992. The International Amateur Athletic Federation's automatic ban then for drug offenders was two years, and Johnson was indeed back racing his way into the semifinals of the 1992 Barcelona Games.

The Canadian public, which by and large still simply referred to Johnson as "Ben," wanted to believe in conspiracies or any explanation but the truth. They wanted to believe his initial assertion that he never took steroids or Francis' far-fetched theories of Johnson's drink possibly being spiked. Even fellow drug-using sprinters from Johnson's Toronto Mazda Optimists Club were shocked by this astounding reversal of fortune. How could the timing of Johnson's last injection have been screwed up on this of all occasions?

Angela Issajenko was a Los Angeles and Seoul Olympian, Commonwealth Games gold medallist and one of Canada's best female sprinters ever. She had personally stuck the needle in Johnson's behind many times. "Members of our team had been taking anabolic steroids and other drugs for years," she wrote in her autobiography, *Running Risks*. "We knew how long they took to clear out of the system, so we knew when to stop taking them before we had to attend meets and submit to doping tests. I couldn't understand how Ben had blown it so badly. He knew about these clearance times as well as any of us."

The Johnson affair led to the Dubin federal inquiry into drug use by athletes. Charles Dubin, then an associate chief justice of the Ontario

Supreme Court, conducted an exhaustive $3 million investigation that laid bare drug use by Canadian athletes. What is clear is the best way to combat it at the elite competitive level is through random, surprise, out-of-competition testing. Even at that, with masking agents and new substances being developed illicitly (you can't test for something if you don't know it exists), the men in the labs are always one step ahead of their pursuers. And at lower levels of sport among those who don't have to worry about being caught, the use of steroids appears to be staggering in Canada. Three years after the Dubin inquiry, a national student survey in 1993 found the use of steroids to be overwhelming. The study indicated up to 30,000 Canadian males between the ages of sixteen and eighteen were actively using anabolic steroids in 1993. The study also suggested up to 83,000 Canadian youngsters between the ages of eleven and eighteen had used steroids over the previous twelve months. The survey involved 16,169 elementary, junior high and high school students from all ten provinces and had a margin of error of less than plus or minus 1 percent and was deemed accurate ninety-nine times out of a hundred. Johnson tearfully told Canadian youngsters during the Dubin inquiry to "be honest and don't take drugs." But the Johnson scandal at Seoul seems to have had little effect on Canadian youth. "There's a major problem out there of bigger proportions than I ever even imagined," said Tom Nease, chairman of the federal Fair Play Program, after the national student survey results were released in 1993. "There is an acceptance level of drugs in sport that is just scary."

Johnson was stripped of not only his Olympic gold medal but also his world records created at Rome and Seoul. Not to defend Johnson or justify his actions, but what about the East Germans and Soviets who all got to keep their medals and records despite documented proof of widespread drug use among their ranks? If Johnson was the king of the Olympic track at Seoul, at least for a couple of days, the queen of the pool was Kristin Otto. The East German swam to six gold medals at Seoul and was hailed the female Mark Spitz. But the December, 1994, issue of *Swimming World* quotes a chemist familiar with the East German sporting system and also documents from the secret police (Stasi) indicating every top East German athlete used performance-enhancing drugs that were administered at scientifically charted intervals that enabled them to avoid being caught by testing at events such at the Olympics. In between events, when no international testing was going on, the Stasi documents show Otto had a testosterone to epitestosterone level of seventeen-to-one. Anything over six-to-one is considered illegal by the IOC. "Otto had more testosterone in her than the entire starting team of the

Dallas Cowboys," said Phillip Whitten, editor-in-chief of *Swimming World*. "It's no wonder she was able to win six gold medals at the Seoul Olympics." Otto said she was put totally into the hands of her coaches and trainers and trusted them completely when they said the pills, medications and injections being administered were nothing more than vitamin supplements and the like. She said that, unlike Johnson, she never knew she was taking steroids. Otto's is a suspicious denial, to be sure, but a plausible one. So the world leaves her medals to shine, although with a great deal less luster, while Ben Johnson's hangs from the neck of Carl Lewis — a man that millions of people witnessed being run into the track by the Canadian. "Okay, I took drugs," Johnson told the *Nice Matin* newspaper in 1994. "But everyone did it. Doping existed before me in all countries and in all sports. I didn't do anything more than the others. But I became too strong. I bothered too many people."

One of the great urban folk legends of modern sport is that with NBC paying so much for the rights to the Olympics ($300 million for the Seoul Games), there are secret stipulations written into the agreements that any positive Americans drug results will be suppressed. Issajenko alludes to such suspicions in her autobiography and some people still believe Olympic officials were looking to "frame" the most significant non-American and non-Soviet athlete they could find at Seoul to show the world they were doing something about drugs.

The urban legend continues that NBC threatened to withhold millions of dollars from IOC coffers if any star-attraction Americans were caught. "I can guarantee you if I was American and not Canadian, nothing would have happened to me," said Johnson. There were ten steroid users caught at Seoul and none of them American. But tales of some sort of conspiracy seem fanciful, at best. "There was no conspiracy," sighs Robert Stinson of Britain, the treasurer and honourary secretary of the International Amateur Athletics Federation and one of its most influential administrators behind president Primo Niebolo. "No blind eye was turned to any nation, no matter how much television money they were putting into the Games."

What is factual is that Johnson was caught again for taking performance-enhancing drugs in 1993 and banned for life. By this time, most Canadians had had enough. Most felt a second chance was warranted for Johnson. But he blew even that. But Johnson said people are naive if they think he was the only one. He lost probably between $10 million and $15 million in contracts and endorsements and said abuses will occur when the stakes are so high. "It was what you have to do at competition at that level," he said in 1994. "It is not a little girl's game.

Ben Johnson and the elusive moment of glory.

But it's all hypocrisy. The IOC makes millions of dollars from the Olympics and no one would pay to see a 100m run in ten seconds." Johnson doesn't believe his time of 9.79 will ever be bettered legally. The official record is held by American Leroy Burrell at 9.85, set in 1994. But Johnson loves reminding the world he *did* cover 100m of earth in 9.79 seconds. That is a fact, regardless of legality or illegality. It can't be disputed. It actually happened. A man did run 100m in 9.79 seconds. "Although it has been scrubbed from the list, I still look upon my 9.79 from the '88 Olympics as the world record," Johnson told the tabloid *News of the World* in 1995. "I didn't fly that day. I ran 100m on my own two feet and the world saw it. They are desperate to beat it. They all want to say: 'I did it clean, not like Ben Johnson.' But it still goes on. The only way they will beat my time is if they only run ninety metres or if there is a wind speed over the limit. There is no way they will beat it legally."

The steroid issue inevitably leads to one question: Why does the IOC even bother banning drugs? Why is it okay to take vitamins in training and eat a chocolate bar for energy but not steroids? It's a question of semantics. Why should a chocolate bar be okay? Isn't that little sugar rush an unfair advantage over a competitor who didn't eat one? Why not open the Olympics to anyone who wants to compete in any fashion they wish? After all, if there are health risks, these people are not hurting anybody but themselves. Out of the question, bellows the IAAF's Stinson. "First of all, it would tacitly encourage people to do it," he said. "Then there's the whole health issue, which has never been properly chronicled. I believe Russian athletes have died quite young with liver problems. Opening the doors to let anyone take what they want into their bodies and then allow them into the Olympics is not a responsible position to take for any sport official. Plus, it's cheating. I know there's a fine line between taking vitamins and the like and drugs. But it's a fine line we have to hold. It's like attaching a helium balloon to a javelin and floating it out of the stadium and calling it a record."

Lynn Williams of Vancouver finished a creditable fifth in the women's 1500m in 4:00.86 at Seoul and then accused the runaway gold medallist, Paula Ivan of Romania (3:53.96), of hiding a condom filled with drug-free urine in her vagina during the race. The basis of Williams' accusation was an anonymous handwritten letter in poor English she received in the Athletes' Village. Williams' coach Doug Clements, the team doctor for the Vancouver Canucks and a former Olympic track athlete for Canada, said he noticed Ivan taking an extraordinarily long time in the cubicle to produce a urine sample after the 1500 final. "Nonsense and stupid," was Ivan's response to the aspersions. It was all getting to be too much. "I can't wait until they extinguish this flame," said Paul Dupre, the president and CEO of the Canadian Track and Field Association. Most Canadians agreed with him.

But just when this worst of all Olympics for Canada seemed in an irreversible tailspin, a few things happened to soften the crash. Canada won ten medals at Seoul, most of them late in the Games. While Johnson showed all that had gone so drastically wrong with Canadian track and field, twenty-eight-year-old Dave Steen epitomized all that was right with it. He had always taken a public stance against drugs in sport. The Olympic decathlon champion is habitually given the label of the greatest athlete in the world. In 1988, Steen became the third-best athlete on the planet. His bronze medal in the decathlon at Seoul is one of the greatest achievements in Canadian Olympic history but is little remembered or talked about because the Johnson scandal totally overwhelmed it in the media. And the two East Germans who finished in front of him could very likely have been "dirty," based on later revelations about Eastern

Bloc steroid use. Steen, now a fireman in Windsor, Ontario, and who was eighth at Los Angeles in 1984, is philosophical about both those issues. His line has always been: "Patience is the answer, not shortcuts." Steen needed every ounce of patience he had at Seoul. He wasn't exactly an unknown, having finished second to the brilliant 1980 Moscow and 1984 Los Angeles olympics champion Daley Thompson of Britain at both the 1982 Brisbane and 1986 Edinburgh Commonwealth Games. But Steen entered the final day of the ten-event decathlon in eleventh place at the Seoul Olympics and the situation seemed hopeless. He was eighth heading into the final event, the 1500m, but then jumped five places with a magnificent effort. Slimmer and less bulky than most of the other decathletes, he was a naturally better runner and needed every bit of that advantage in the 1500 to squeeze in for the bronze medal. Christian Schenk and Torsten Voss gave East Germany a one-two finish with 8488 and 8399 points, respectively. Steen was next with 8328. And the man he edged out for the bronze medal by just twenty-two points? None other than Daley Thompson.

The Canadian fireworks that were supposed to explode in the Olympic boxing ring at Los Angeles in 1984 through Willie DeWit and Shawn O'Sullivan were, quite unexpectedly, saved for the Chamshil Students Gym in Seoul. Lennox Lewis was born in East London and moved to Canada when he was twelve. Raised in Kitchener, Ontario, he started boxing at age thirteen and remembers being motivated by the desire to have book cases full of trophies so he could impress all the kids on the block. He ended up impressing more than just his neighbourhood. He elevated himself in Seoul to a title that was won in 1964 at Tokyo by Joe Frazier, in 1968 at Mexico City by George Foreman and in 1972 at Munich, 1976 at Montreal and 1980 at Moscow by Teofilo Stevenson. The strapping Lewis, all 6' 5" and 220 pounds of him, stormed through the 1988 Games super heavyweight class by easily dispatching his three opponents (he had a walkover in the semifinals because Janusz Zarenkiewicz of Poland pulled out due to injury) in a total of 5:16 to lift Canada's first Olympic boxing gold medal since bantamweight Horace "Lefty" Gwynn at Los Angeles in 1932. In 1988, Gwynn was a seventy-five-year-old pensioner in Midland, Ontario, and watched on television as Lewis pounded his way to glory. The Olympic super heavyweight class was known as the heavyweight division from 1904 in St. Louis to 1980 in Moscow and produced celebrated champions such as the Americans Frazier and Foreman and Cuban Stevenson. Muhammad Ali won his Olympic gold as Cassius Clay in the light heavyweight class at Rome in 1960. He threw that medal into the Ohio River after being refused service at a whites-only restaurant in his hometown of Louisville.

Lewis wasn't expected to have a gold medal to toss around anywhere since he wasn't supposed to survive his quarterfinal duel against World Cup champion Ulli Kaden of East Germany. But he hammered the German to the canvas in just thirty-four seconds for a lightning knockout. Lewis marched into the final against the fancied future big-time professional Riddick Bowe. At the end of the first round, his coach Adrian Teodorescu asked why he was fighting Bowe inside when everybody knew Lewis was the better boxer and the American favoured a close-range, clutch-and-grab dance. Teodorescu, the head coach of the Ontario Boxing Institute at Rexdale, was Lewis' personal coach and knew him well. But the Canadian boxing team had been riddled with dissension before the Games and Teodorescu had been left off the coaching staff despite being personal coach to both Lewis and Egerton Marcus, Canada's top medal prospects. Teodorescu took out a bank loan to go to Seoul on his own but was added to the national team coaching staff a day before the team left for Korea. Lewis listened carefully to what his mentor said between rounds of the final. "So I switched to more of a boxing style," he said. "I got tagged a couple of times by Bowe in the first round. But do you know what those shots were? They were wake-up calls."

Bowe had bragged about taking Aleksandr Miroshnichenko of the Soviet Union "to school" in the semifinals and promised to do the same to Lewis. But in the second round it was Lewis who did the teaching with three looping lefts that stunned Bowe and caused a standing eight count. That was followed by a brutal right that staggered the American before the referee stepped in to end it. All the other Canadian boxers, and overall Olympic team *chef de mission* Carol Anne Letheren, stormed into the ring to mob Lewis. "This is better than a Stanley Cup in Toronto or the Blue Jays in the pennant race," said Canadian team boxer Asif Dar (in typical Toronto-centred fashion).

Lewis, a stand-up puncher, was humble in his golden moment. "This victory was for my mother, first of all, for the Canadian people and for all the guys on the boxing team," said Lewis. Both Lewis and Bowe became well-known professional fighters, with Lewis winning the WBC heavyweight championship. But after fighting as an amateur for Canada, Lewis decided to pursue his pro career in his native England. He said boxing isn't popular in Canada and there are few avenues in which to exploit an Olympic gold medal here. But even at that, he wanted to take advantage of his gold on his own terms and so turned his back on the US as well. "I was an Olympic champion turning pro and I didn't want to get caught up in the US hype of all that," he said. So he went back to Britain, which hadn't produced a world heavyweight champion in the twentieth century. "I wanted to go back because of my background," said Lewis. "I wanted to make people where I was born proud. I wanted to be the best British heavyweight." And that's what he became — this century's best Brit boxer — when he took the first world heavyweight crown won by a Briton since Bob Fitzsimmons knocked Gentleman Jim Corbett senseless in 1896.

Canada won a silver medal in boxing at Seoul through another Commonwealth-born fighter who emigrated to the Great White North. Charlie Arnos represented Guyana at the 1968 Mexico City Olympics. His nephew, Egerton Marcus, did the same for Canada at Seoul in 1988 and became the most successful Guyana-to-Canada Olympic transfer since the great runner Dr. Phil Edwards won five medals over three Games. A crowded field of thirty-three competitors took to the canvas in the middleweight division at Seoul. It would have been thirty-four but Tony Hembrick of the US, in an echo of the 1972 Munich 100m fiasco for the Americans, arrived late for his first bout because coaches misread the schedule. Marcus, whose mother, believe it or not, was also a boxer, proved to be a natural. He smoked every opponent as he moved steadily to the Olympic final.

But all that punching came at a price. Marcus' achilles heel isn't a heel but a hand — a right hand that seems made of glass. Marcus broke it on the way to the final and met the favoured southpaw Henry Maske of East Germany for the gold medal with basically only his left hand operational. Although the decision in the final went 5–0 for Maske, leaving Marcus with the silver medal, it was much closer that the unanimous decision indicates.

"I still look at that Olympic tape and I still don't know how he got the decision, even though I was fighting with one hand," laments Marcus, whose hand was so swollen it was virtually round with all the knuckles invisible. "It's impossible for a guy to win without his right hand," said famous trainer Angelo Dundee, who has handled Muhammad Ali and Sugar Ray Leonard. "It's like going to work without tools or an astronaut trying to go up without the capsule. You've got to give the Canadian kid [Marcus] a lot of credit. He could have easily quit."

Despite breaking his right hand four more times after Seoul, Marcus amassed a 14–0 record as a professional before he finally got his long-awaited rematch with Maske. But the German was even better, not having to worry about hand injuries and going 24–0 as a pro during that same stretch. Seoul was very definitely on Marcus' mind when he met Maske in 1995 for the world IBF light heavyweight title in Hamburg,

Germany. "If you think about something like that [losing the Olympic gold] for that long a time, you sure don't want to miss the chance to make up for it," Marcus told reporters before his second fight against Maske. "My goal is to be a great champion. I know the sport isn't too good right now in Canada, but I really want to win a title for the Canadian fans. When I started boxing, my goal was to win an Olympic gold medal and now I have the chance to right that wrong." But seven years after the duel for Olympic gold, it was another unanimous decision for Maske as the quicker and technically superior German defended his IBF world title against Marcus.

Ray Downey of Halifax took third place in welterweight as Canada hit for the cycle in boxing at Seoul with a gold, silver and bronze. Downey was a victim in the semifinals to Park Si-hun of South Korea, who has been labeled by many as the most undeserving boxing gold medallist in Olympic history. Park rode to the victory podium on the backs of five highly controversial "homer" decisions. He defeated Downey on a unanimous decision in what was actually a very tight semifinal bout. But what happened next was scandalous. Roy Jones Jr. of the US easily outclassed and outhit Park, but the 3–2 decision went to the South Korean in probably the worst decision ever in a judged sport at the Olympics. The media and millions of fight fans were incredulous. Rumours ran rampant the South Koreans had bribed the judges to get even with some blatant "homer" decision for the US at the 1984 Los Angeles Olympics. Even Park himself admitted Jones had won the fight and apologized to the American.

After this fiasco, a computerized scoring system was introduced into amateur boxing with the count displayed. The boxing at Seoul was a sick joke on many fronts. After a South Korean lost a close decision, referee Keith Walker of New Zealand was punched and kicked in the ring by irate South Korean boxing officials and security guards in a shocking display of boorishness. The boxer in question, bantamweight Byun Jong-il, staged a sit-in and refused to leave the ring. To make his protest more comfortable, a chair was brought out for him. He finally left after more than an hour.

Adding to the bizarre nature of the 1988 Olympic boxing tournament was the saga of Jamie Pagendam, Canada's featherweight representative. In his first fight, the twenty-two-year-old Pagendam of St. Catharines knocked Tserendorj Awarjargal of Mongolia to the canvas three times in the second round for an apparent automatic win as stated in the rules of amateur boxing. But the referee, Marius Lougbo of the Ivory Coast, thought there had been only two knockdowns in that round and mistakenly let the bout continue. As fate would have it, Awarjargal floored Pagendam in the third round and Lougbo stopped the fight and declared the Mongolian the winner. The Canadian team filed an immediate protest that was upheld. The decision was overturned and Pagendam was given the win.

But there was a catch. Pagendam received a month-long medical suspension because of the blow he took in the third round that sent him to the canvas — a hit he never should have received because he should have been declared the winner in the second round. Regardless, the twenty-two-year-old machine operator was unable to advance. Referee Lougbo didn't advance, either. He was suspended for the rest of the Olympics. Despite the high farce in the boxing ring, it turned into a source of much needed precious metal for Canada in this disgrace-plagued Olympics. Ironically, the Canadian boxing team had been riddled with dissension and was suffering from low morale before Seoul.

Carolyn Waldo of Beaconsfield, Quebec, wore four dozen hairpins beneath her sparkling, sequined bathing cap and what seemed like eighty pounds of make-up on her face. Not that she needed the latter. Waldo is appealing in or out of make-up. But this is the world of synchronized swimming, where bright, shining faces and those never-ending smiles are the kinds of things that impress judges. But is it a sport? That has been debated until sports fans are as red in the face as the lipstick that sparkles on the lips of the synchro girls. It is a sport; the IOC says so. And that should be good enough for Canada, which invented it and has produced its best practitioners. Canada is a synchronized swimming world power. Don't complain. Don't be embarrassed. Just take the medals and run. They're not that easy to come by at the Olympics.

Waldo became only the fourth Canadian after swimmer George Hodgson (Stockholm 1912), sprinter Percy Williams (Amsterdam 1928) and swimmer Alex Baumann (L.A. 1984) to win two gold medals in the same Summer Olympics and the first woman to do so. Tracie Ruiz-Conforto of the US had shunted Waldo to the silver medal position in the solo event at the 1984 Los Angeles Games and had also beaten her Canadian rival in a pre-Olympic meet in Seoul before the '88 Games. But Waldo turned the water tables during the Games themselves, churning almost flawlessly through the compulsory portion of her routine to build a lead that couldn't be breached by anyone during the free swim. Waldo took gold with 200.150 points, Ruiz-Conforto silver with 197.633 and Mikako Kotani of Japan bronze with 191.850. There was a bit of an insult during the medal ceremony when only about twenty seconds of "O Canada" was played. Even shorter than Waldo's stay on the podium was the time it took reporters to ask her about Johnson, as if she had

Lennox Lewis of Canada outduels Riddick Bowe of the US for ring gold at the 1988 Seoul Olympics.

anything to do with the affair. "What happened to Ben Johnson was unfortunate," said Waldo, who later become a sports reporter for an Ottawa television station. Then came the inevitable question, asked in jest, about the hilarious notion of synchronized swimmers on steroids. But after what had already transpired at Seoul, who knows? "Oh yes, I'll pass it [drug test]," laughed Waldo. "I'm not on anything."

Waldo and Calgary's Michelle Cameron later combined to win a controversial gold medal in the duet event, again building an almost insurmountable lead in the compulsory figures and hanging on in the free swim for a tight victory over the silver medallist Josephson twin sisters, Sarah and Karen, of the United States. The scoring system was weighted in favour of the compulsory portion, which accounted for 53 percent of the final score compared to 47 percent for the free swim. Waldo and Cameron lost the free swim to the Josephsons 99.6 points to 98.8 but it didn't matter. It was perhaps fitting that the distinguished and long-serving COA and IOC official Jim Worrall presented the gold medals to the Canadian girls, giving them a kiss on the cheek. A huge Canadian flag was draped over the balcony by some fans and this time "O Canada" was played in its entirety. But after that bit of glory, there was a firestorm of synchro fury awaiting Waldo and Cameron courtesy of the irate Josephson twins, who felt judging robbed them of the gold. Canadian Joyce Corner was the only judge to give Waldo and Cameron a higher mark than the American twins in the free swim. If that hadn't happened, the Josephsons would have taken gold and the Canadians silver. Corner gave Waldo and Cameron a 10.0 in the free portion and the Josephsons 9.8. American judge Dawn Bean had it reversed with 10.0 for the Josephsons and 9.8 for the Canadians. The controversy clearly upset Waldo, who shot back: "You can't worry about the judges. All you can do is go out and do your best and have fun." Instead of going for the bait, she then thanked the whining Josephsons for pushing her to the limit and won another gold medal for class.

American swimmer Matt Biondi's assault on Mark Spitz's legendary seven golds from 1972 fell just short in the pool at Seoul with five gold, one silver and one bronze. Biondi paced the US men's 4x100 medley relay team to a world record victory in 3:36.93. Left in the wake, but picking up the silver medal, was the Canadian foursome of Mark Tewksbury, Victor Davis, Tom Ponting and Donald "Sandy" Goss. American David Berkoff began with a torrid 54.6 backstroke leg. Tewksbury challenged him stiffly but just couldn't match that. The race was in the bag for the Americans after the first leg. Calgary's Ponting had a fourth place finish in the tight men's 200m butterfly final in 1:58.91. West Germany's "Albatross", Michael Gross, took gold in 1:56.94 while Benny Nielsen of Denmark (1:58.24) and Anthony Mosse of New Zealand (1:58.28) shaded Ponting for the silver and bronze medal placings. Jon Cleveland of Calgary, whose father Reggie pitched in the 1975 World Series for the Boston Red Sox, was seventh in the men's 200m breaststroke in 2:17.10 to Hungarian winner Jozsef Szabo's 2:13.52. The defending champion, Victor Davis of Canada, failed to make the final. He did in the 100m breaststroke, though, but was unable to duplicate his silver medal in that event from the 1984 Los Angeles Games. Davis, fourth at Seoul in 1:02.38, was pipped for the bronze by the Soviet Union's Dmitri Volkov (1:02.20). The winner was Adrian Moorehouse of Britain (1:02.04), who himself was fourth at Los Angeles. Canada churned for bronze in the women's 4x100 medley relay as Lori Melin, Allison Higson, Jane Kerr and Andrea Nugent clocked 4:10.49 behind the Kristin Otto-fueled winning East Germans (4:03.74). Kathy Bald, Patricia Noall, Nugent and Kerr gave Canada a sixth-place finish in the women's 4x100 freestyle relay in 3:46.75. The winners again were the East Germans (3:40.63), who it was later learned were propelled by more than just Otto's natural abilities.

Canada's persistent equestrian community again put forth a decent Olympic effort in 1988 and it was perhaps fitting that Tom Gayford of Toronto, an Olympic gold medallist twenty years earlier at Mexico City, was the *chef d'equipe* of the Canadian team. Cynthia Ishoy, aboard Dynasty, Ashley Nicoll on Reipo and Gina Smith on Malte won bronze in team dressage with 3969 points. Ishoy just missed out another bronze by sixteen points, finishing a close fourth in individual dressage with 1401 points. Swiss rider Christine Stuckelberger, who won gold in this event all the way back at the 1976 Montreal Olympics, took third with 1417 points and Nicole Uphoff of Germany gold with 1521.

The sailing course off the port city of Pusan was windy, wet and wild. Frank McLaughlin and John Millen, who began sailing as tykes off Ward's Island near Toronto many years before, decided to join the Dane and Norwegian Flying Dutchman crews in training off northern Jutland, Denmark, in the summer of 1988 because the rough conditions there matched what lay ahead in Pusan. It turned out to be a wise move as the Danes, Norwegians and Canadians finished 1–2–3 among the twenty-two Flying Dutchman crews entered in the Olympics. McLaughlin and Millen won bronze with 48.4 points compared to 31.4 for the winning Danes and 37.4 for the Norwegians on the reverse scoring system. McLaughlin's and Millen's situation appeared hopeless until they won the final race to scrape through for the bronze. But their timing couldn't have been worse. They won their medal on the day the Ben Johnson test result was announced. How's that for having the wind taken out of your publicity sails?

But for every action there is an equal and opposite reaction. The laws of physics somehow got translated onto the field, or in this case ocean, of sporting endeavour in Seoul. While Johnson provided the stunning low point for Canada, Larry Lemieux of Edmonton may have given the nation its high point of the 1988 Games. Oddly enough, it wasn't through a medal win. It's trite to say how this or that athlete showed the true Olympic spirit. But Lemieux deserves special mention. When the non-medallist was inducted into the Canadian Olympic Hall of Fame in 1995, there was a good reason. Lemieux was in second place during the fifth race of the Finn competition off Pusan when he noticed that Joseph Chan of Singapore was in the water flailing away and trying to keep afloat in the churning waves. Chan's boat had capsized and he injured his back and was being swept away by the rolling and punishing waves. Lemieux immediately turned around and went to Chan, who was too hurt and exhausted to pull himself into the Canadian's boat. Lemieux managed to reel him in. The IOC presented Lemieux with a special award for his actions. He was shocked that everybody was making such a big deal out of it. Chan would likely have drowned. What would anybody have done, Olympic race or not? "I'm not *that* intense," was Lemieux's classic one-sentence response to all the attention.

And if you're in the camp which believes *that* is the true Olympic spirit, then there were plenty of other Canadian stories to counterbalance Johnson's. Lori Strong of Whitby, Ontario, suffered a broken ankle and Phillippe Chartrand of Laval, Quebec, a torn knee ligament but both stayed in their gymnastics competitions until the end despite excruciating pain. But let's face it, no amount of gallantry or courage was going to eclipse what Seoul will always be remembered for by Canadians and millions of others. A pall descended on these Games for Canada after the Johnson scandal and refused to lift. After the women's track 4x400 relay team, which was in the hunt for a medal, lost its chance when the baton went flying out of Molly Killingbeck's hand in the final, teammate Jillian Richardson lamented: "I don't think anything worse can happen unless the plane crashes." Perhaps in order to make the $3.2-million cost of sending and outfitting the Canadian team look like money well spent, federal sports minister Jean Charest went groping for minor league championships and boasted Canada would at least be the top Commonwealth nation at Seoul. But he was wrong even at that. Canada placed behind Britain, Kenya (which won every men's distance race from 800 to 5000m), Australia and New Zealand in the medals table. A *Toronto Star* headline said it all: "Gloomy Games Couldn't End Too Soon." Don Talbot, the outspoken and hardly shy Aussie swim coach who was brought in to shore up Canada's team but then was let go just before Seoul, said Canadians lacked a will to win. He said Canadians don't compete internationally, they participate. But there was a group of sprint people in Toronto who set about to change that. A mild-mannered nation of participators was about to be catapulted to centre stage. Such shifts in attitude can be good for a nation. But we found there is a dark obverse side to the golden medal. Canada reaped the bitter fruit of life in the fast lane.

BARCELONA 1992

July 25 to August 9
10,632 Athletes from 171 Nations

Of all the haunting buildings and statues by Spain's famed Antonio Gaudi that dominate parts of Barcelona, one towers magnificently above the city. And it's the one that's not finished. The fanciful Sagrada Familia cathedral, started in 1883, was to be Gaudi's crowning achievement on the face of the city he loved. But he never got it completed by the time he died in 1926. Even as it almost magically seems to shimmer and hover above the city's skyline today, it remains incomplete. To this Spanish Mediterranean city with the unfinished cathedral came a team with some unfinished business of its own. For a country badly in need of Summer Olympic heroes after the Ben Johnson nightmare at Seoul, Sylvie Frechette, Mark Tewksbury and Silken Laumann couldn't have come at a more opportune time. It didn't hurt to throw in four gold medals for Canada from those almost anachronistic rowers — maybe the last of the true amateurs and the antidote to the commercial excess of Michael Jordan, Charles Barkley and the rest of the 1992 US Olympic men's basketball team. The rowers rowed just for the sake of their sport with few financial rewards in the offing beyond the $5000 worth of their golden medals.

But even in glory, there was a dark side to that medal for some. The sunny Barcelona Olympics seemed perfect. Almost too perfect. South Africa was back, the horror of apartheid put behind it. Lithuania, Latvia and Estonia were finally there as teams in their own right and not under the iron Soviet umbrella. Germany was one team again. Canada started slowly amidst grumblings back home of another lackluster Summer Games display but then exploded for a sparkling performance of seven gold, four silver and seven bronze medals — the second-best showing for Canada at the Summer Olympics behind only the boycotted 1984 Los Angeles Games. Canadians suddenly scrambled back to their television sets after a disheartening first five days in which their nation's squad was derisively named Team Terrible. "This is the best Canadian Olympic team performance ever," beamed Ken Read, the former Crazy Canuck skier who was the *chef de mission* of the Canadian squad at Barcelona. And there was the matter of finally burying Seoul. "We proved that Canadians can play well, play fair and play clean," said Read. Then there was Barcelona itself, glowing and radiant in its Olympic moment. If there was a more spectacular Olympic sight in history than that of the divers leaping atop Montjuic, with the entire city spread out below, I've yet to see it. But Mark Tewksbury proved you can get too much of a good thing, even in that outdoor pool in that glorious setting.

Although little-known, twenty-year-old science student Nicolas Gill of Montreal gave Canada its first Barcelona Games medal, a bronze in judo, the medal parade was really kick-started by Tewksbury's dramatic swimming gold medal in the men's 100m backstroke. A kid who would eat fast food "until he got sick," Tewksbury began swimming every day after school in Calgary from age eight on. He mended his wayward junk food ways and even swore off red meat but then lost his energy. He got back to hamburgers, but more sensibly, and slowly regained his form — so much so he became a spokesman for the Beef Information Council. He finished an individual fifth at Seoul and won a silver medal in the medley relay. With a huge smile and the personality and drive to go with it, he was the perfect person to lift Canada out of the Games funk in which it had been mired since Seoul. He was the all-Canadian boy whose father owned a photography business and mother was a bookkeeper for Shoppers Drug Mart in Calgary. A natural leader, he radiated a love for life and people that was catching. And he had the energy to lift others with motivational speeches. When he put on a tremendous spurt to edge, at the wall in 53.98 seconds on the final stroke, the American world record holder Jeff Rouse — who looked to have the race won — the Canadian public eagerly lapped it up. "I didn't think of mom and dad watching ...

A jubilant Mark Tewksbury of Calgary celebrates his gold medal victory in the 100m backstroke at the 1992 Barcelona Olympics.

I didn't think of the people back home watching," noted Tewksbury. "I just thought: 'This is my moment.' I tried to sleep after the morning heats but I couldn't. But I kept picturing the race and I could picture myself winning." The immediate and overwhelming nature of the Canadian response to the gold medal started to really sink in on the medal podium. "I lost it — I can't remember the last time I heard 'O Canada,'" said Tewksbury. "I've never had it played for me. I tried to sing and I got about two lines through and couldn't. It was all too much ... "

It was all too much, all right. Canada couldn't get enough of Mark Tewksbury. He gave more than two hundred speeches in less than a year after Barcelona but was struggling internally. "The thrill of being in the public eye wore thin after Christmas and I found myself really lost," he told the CBC Radio show *Inside Track*. "I realized I was taking no steps forward. I was just reliving the past over and over again. But then people would say how much I moved them and motivated them and that would perk me up again. But so as not to get big-headed or arrogant, I handled it strangely. I would say to myself: 'Oh, you're not that great.' But that became the only voice I began listening to. I would just feel like the biggest loser in the world." It got so bad Tewksbury took to sitting in his hotel room in the dark with the lights off. He was headed for a crash. It occurred one night when he blacked out and couldn't remember the speech he had delivered hundreds of times before. "I had absolutely no self esteem, which was strange because I had to have a lot of it to get to the top," he said. Mark Tewksbury the personable, funny and affable guy from Calgary was having a hard time being Mark Tewksbury, the Canadian Olympic Hero. He saw a psychologist and then decided to move away from Canada for his own mental well being. Studying and teaching at Sydney University in Australia, it felt good to be out of the Canadian limelight. "If I had stayed, I would still be referred to and defined as the Olympic swimmer," said Tewksbury.

Sylvie Frechette admits to being "in a state of shock" at Barcelona. The ambiance of the city, and those strolls along the Ramblas the citizens take until the small hours, meant little to her. Neither did Gaudi's unfinished masterwork nor the sunshine. Barcelona was a blur after Frechette found her fiance, Sylvain Lake, dead of a suicide in their Montreal condominium just days before she left for the Games as the favourite for gold in solo synchronized swimming. The memory still haunts her and Frechette saw a psychologist for more than two years. The life she thought awaited her after Barcelona was no more. And it shattered her, even though she didn't let on through her pasted-on smile at the Olympics.

"Sylvain was an athlete," Frechette told the *Victoria Times Colonist*. "He knew how important it is for an athlete to compete at the Olympics. We were looking forward to sharing that. There are a lot of questions I don't have the answers to. And I'll just have to go on without those answers." Frechette remembers going through the motions but was devoid of her usual competitive emotions: "I don't remember a lot of things that happened at Barcelona. Then, after my performance, [the suicide] all came back. I didn't have a home anymore. I didn't have a fiance anymore." Probably the last thing Frechette, then at her most fragile, needed was the farce that followed her brave and brilliant performance. Brazilian judge Anna Maria da Silveira inadvertently punched in 8.7 instead of 9.7 to grade one of Frechette's compulsory figures. Da Silveira quickly tried to rectify her error but it was too late. The computerized scoring system wouldn't record the correction. The head referee and assistant referee then disallowed a Canadian protest and ruled the mark had to stand at 8.7, which meant the difference between gold and silver for Frechette. Because of the mistake, the gold went to American Kristen Babb-Sprague, the wife of Toronto Blue Jays third baseman Ed Sprague.

"I thought: 'Why Sylvie?'" Canadian coach Julie Sauve told reporters. "Why not one of the swimmers who is in twenty-fifth spot? Why the top swimmer in the world and one with a chance at a gold medal?" Sauve was understanding when it came to the Brazilian judge but irate about the actions of the American referee and the Japanese assistant referee. "As a human being, I can accept that she [da Silveira] made a mistake so I know it's not her fault," noted Sauve. "It's those who made the decision not to make things right." But they eventually were made right after a long and tortuous route to get there. After sixteen months of lobbying and pleading with FINA, the world governing body of aquatics, Frechette was finally awarded the Olympic gold medal. Babb-Sprague, however, wasn't dropped to the silver position. That remains vacant with both Frechette and Babb-Sprague listed as the gold medallists. Frechette received her gold medal in an emotion-laden ceremony at the Montreal Forum on December 15, 1993. It was a lot colder than Barcelona outside that night but a lot warmer inside. Frechette is extremely popular in Quebec and hosted a television program called *Simply Sylvie*. Her book, *Sylvie Frechette: Gold at Last*, sold more than 25,000 copies in Quebec. Smooth and refreshingly honest, Frechette decided to give it another go for the 1996 Atlanta Summer Olympics, where the team event will be the only synchronized swimming event contested.

Silken Laumann handled her fame from Barcelona with all the dexterity of a Madison Avenue marketing whiz. In fact, the nation's most famous bronze medallist turned her persona into a cottage industry. The female world single sculls rowing champion in 1990 and 1991, the powerful Laumann was almost assured the gold medal at the Barcelona Olympics. Then just less than two months before the Games, at a regatta in May at Essen, Germany, the unthinkable happened. The course was poorly supervised and a men's German doubles crew, which was warming up for its race, sliced broadside through Laumann's shell and through her right leg. The injury was horrendous. The first German doctor at the scene said that not only were the Olympics out, but Laumann might not walk again. Transported back to Victoria, where five operations were performed by a team of doctors headed by sports-medicine specialist Richard Backus, things looked grim. With less than six weeks to go before the Games, and most experts predicting at least eight months of rehabilitation ahead, the golden dream seemed over. But what Laumann did next shocked the sporting world and made her a Canadian national hero. Not only did she get out of her wheelchair long before most people thought possible, but she got to Barcelona.

Hardly able to walk and hobbling badly, she would get to the dock at

As smooth as Silken: Canada's Silken Laumann composes herself after her amazing comeback bronze medal performance at the Barcelona Olympics.

Elk Lake on Vancouver Island with the help of others who placed her in the boat. Once on the water, it was up to her and her steely will to some-how propel that shell no matter how bad the pain. Her doctors said that an average person couldn't possibly heal such an injury and be doing such physical activity for at least a year, if that. But Laumann was some physical specimen and living proof that tissue and muscle fibre heal faster the more physically fit and active a person was before an injury. If she hadn't been in such magnificent shape, her body could not have responded as it did. And there was her inner spirit and drive. "I enjoy how purpose-ful sport is," says Laumann. "A lot of people's lives aren't clearly defined. But sport takes care of that for you. It sharpens your focus. Here are the Olympics. This is your goal. And you focus on that and go after it. Sport has a way of forcing sharply defined goals on you because it's often just a one-shot chance. But I love the pressure, the challenge and the daily process that all go into not letting that one chance slip away."

To most Canadians, she was a winner just getting to Barcelona. And when she captured third place, coming up from behind in a last-gasp last stroke, that was one bronze medal that was as good as gold. Laumann was now more than just a symbol of what a superbly conditioned human body could overcome with the will and determination. She had under-gone five operations with a sixth to come later in 1992 and full recovery still about a year away. She had become a marketer's dream and speaking engagements and sponsorship offers flowed her way. A new flower, the Silken Laumann Rose, was named in her honour. The CBC was filming a made-for-TV movie about her, to be aired just before the 1996 Atlanta Olympics, where she will be one of the most watched Canadian athletes in Games history as she tries to complete her story by finally winning the gold medal.

Hans and Seigrid Laumann, he from what was then West Germany and she from the partitioned East, met in neutral Berlin shortly after the Second World War. A successful salesman, and later the owner of a thriving window-cleaning business in Mississauga, Ontario, the outdoors-loving Hans got his family involved in sports at an early age. "The whole family was active," says Laumann. "It was a big part of our lifestyle. I was always a big kid. Our family cycled together and ran together. That's the way it should be, instead of everybody in the house watching television all the time."

It was in her Grade 12 year at Lorne Park that Laumann took to rowing to help recover from a track injury suffered in the 800m. Two years later, she won the bronze medal in the double sculls at the Los Angeles Olympics with her sister, Danielle. What most people don't recall is that Laumann had almost packed it in in 1989. She took her bachelor of arts degree in English and tried her luck in the Toronto publishing industry with an eye to making it permanent. She became publicist for Penguin Books but felt frustrated.

Then came the opportunity in 1990 to row under national men's team coach Mike Spracklen at Elk Lake in Victoria. Laumann flowered under the exhausting volume-training method preferred by Spracklen and went from seventh in the world to two-time world champion. Laumann was inadvertently at the centre of a drug story in 1995 when she tested positive for a banned stimulant at the 1995 Pan-American Games in Mar del Plata, Argentina. Because of a mix-up in communication between herself and Dr. Backus, she had accidentally taken the wrong medication for a cold she was suffering in Mar del Plata. It was an honest mistake and ruled as such, even though the Pan-Am medal was taken away. Laumann, who is so drug-free she refused to take pain killers after her accident in 1992, was cleared of any wrong doing. But her finger-pointing at Backus and other Canadian team doctors was unfortunate considering all that the medical community, especially Backus, had done to get her ready for Barcelona after her accident.

Like Laumann, Spracklen's Canadian men's eights were also subjected to volume training under the stern former Brit. They rowed more than sixty thousand kilometres on Elk Lake — and responded with silver medals at the 1990 and 1991 world championships. But that was never good enough for them. Hard driven, they had just one goal. And they achieved it at Barcelona with a furious tenacity in the water that led to the Olympic gold medal.

A key member of that crew was Laumann's then-boyfriend and now-husband John Wallace. The ultimate irony is that Wallace's gold medal probably means less to the Canadian public than Laumann's bronze. In the weeks after Barcelona, Wallace usually just stood to one side, ignored by the groups of people that crowded around Laumann in airports or shopping malls to shake her hand or get her autograph. "I have no concern or trouble with that," Wallace said. "What she accomplished was incredible. To many people, she represents the true spirit of the Olympics." Wallace grew up in Burlington, Ontario, and became an exceptional rower at the University of Western Ontario and the University of Victoria. Laumann also rowed at those schools but their paths never crossed. While Laumann was at UVic, Wallace was at Western. The year Wallace decided to head west and row for UVic, Laumann went back east to row for Western. Although they knew each other in passing at national team camps, it wasn't until the 1988 Seoul Olympics that they really noticed each other. "We just started talking one day in Seoul and haven't stopped since," smiles Wallace. While Canadian dreams crashed and burned at Seoul, their love rose from the ashes. The rowers had more than a little to do with the Phoenix-like rise of Canada at Barcelona from the emotional rubble of Seoul. With four gold medals and Laumann's famous bronze, the Canadian rowers were a sort of water-skimming cyclone.

"In many ways, it was just a fluke of some sort," said men's coach Spracklen, who had been recruited from England. "Club rowing in Canada is far behind that of Britain but the top few rowers in Canada just happened to be so much better than almost anywhere else. It was just a dream situation to stumble into." He admitted to being thunderstruck to find "right out of the blue, it seemed, these magnificent six or seven men sitting atop the heap and rowing at Elk Lake — this very small group which turned out to be among the best in the world." And Spracklen drove them hard. They spent thousands of hours and rowed thousands of kilometres. That seemingly endless prepping paid off handsomely at the 1992 Olympic rowing course at Lake Banyoles, eighty kilometres north of Barcelona. With about 200m left in the men's eights final, Andy Crosby remembers thinking that he would remember the next forty-five seconds for the rest of his life. But that didn't turn out to be true. He remembers nothing of that gold medal sprint to the line to end the gripping 2000m Olympic final. His mind had gone blank but his arms kept pumping — perhaps as a natural reflex response after more than sixty thousand kilometres of practice. "I don't know how we got across the line," recalls Crosby. "I asked my body to somehow keep going. I had essentially passed out with about 200m to go and I think it was pure adrenalin or something that kept my body moving. I don't even remember crossing the line or the people telling us we had held on to win. I came to about a minute after the race ended and I remember our cox, Terry Paul, just whooping and hollering." Peterborough's Paul was about the only one of the nine Canadians who had the energy left to muster a yell after Canada held off the hard-charging Romanians to win the Olympic gold medal by 14/100ths of a second. The members of the victorious eights crew were Wallace, Crosby, Mike Forgeron of West Vancouver, Bob Marland of Mississauga, Darren Barber of Victoria, Mike Rasher of Fernie, BC, Bruce Robertson of Calgary, stroke Derek Porter of Victoria and coxswain Paul.

The Canadian women's crews, coached by Al Morrow of London, Ontario, were even more impressive than the men at Barcelona and came away with a remarkable three gold medals. The eights crew of Kirsten Barnes of Victoria, Brenda Taylor of Sidney, BC, Megan Delehanty of Vancouver, Shannon Crawford of Toronto, Marnie McBean of Toronto, Kay Worthington of Toronto, Jessica Monroe of Victoria, Kathleen Heddle of Vancouver and coxswain Lesley Thompson of London, Ontario, won gold. The Canadian pairs also won gold to make McBean and Heddle double gold medallists. Barnes, Taylor, Monroe and Worthington stroked to victory in the fours to also finish with two gold medals each. "We started from scratch," said Morrow. "I said, 'We don't have a lot of money in our sport but that's okay because all I need is some shells and some strong athletes. That's all.' I separated the need-to-do's from the it-would-be-nice-to-do's. We didn't waste our time with unimportant things like fancy offices. We simply put our money in shells and went out to find the best athletes possible to fill those shells.

Over the years, Canadian rowing has taken kids the other sports wouldn't take and turned them into world-class rowers. We have an incredible work ethic. And look what we accomplished at Barcelona. It's amazing what you can do when you just focus on what the bottom line is — athletes on the water." Canadian rowing isn't fancy. Just focused. Just good. Just simple. But Laumann's huge persona and comeback bronze almost swamped the achievements of the other rowers who brought Canada four gold medals. "It was a little bit frustrating," admitted Brenda

Taylor, owner of two Olympic gold medals. "When people think rowing, they think Silken and sometimes forget about the other Olympic medallists we had in our sport. But we recognize that in a crew event, it's hard to get the kind of recognition one gets in an individual event. We put as much work into it as Silken but it's understandable that she has gotten so much of the attention because her story is amazing." Taylor supported herself by cleaning houses. "I was essentially rowing full time and cleaning allowed me at least to set my own hours," she said. Bettering 1992 would be almost impossible for McBean, Heddle, Barnes, Taylor, Monroe and Worthington. Most elite athletes toil for years without ever making it to an Olympics, never mind winning two gold medals. "There was an incredible amount of time and effort involved and I just don't know if I could ever do it again," said Barnes.

Canada got two unexpected medals on the mats through a couple of students. After a quiet first five days of the Barcelona Games for Canada, big-eared twenty-year-old Montreal science student Nicolas Gill finally broke the ice with a bronze medal in the 86-kilo class of judo. Gill enrolled in his first judo class at age six. It's safe to say few Canadians had ever heard of him. But he provided the nation with its first medal after a hugely disappointing start to the Games. And it felt sweet. "Half an hour ago I was completely unknown; and now here I am with twenty reporters in front of me," Gill told those very same reporters. "It was a hard day. But I finally finished well to get the bronze. If I'm the first Canadian or the last to get a medal at these Olympics, it doesn't matter. It's the medal that counts." Jeff Thue, a student at Simon Fraser University in Burnaby, BC, and a native of Saskatchewan, is as big as Gill is tiny. Wrestling in the 130-kilo class for the big boys, Thue came away with an Olympic silver medal to cap his career. But after Barcelona, it was time to move on to other things for the self-effacing giant of a man and father of two young children. "There's not a lot of money in amateur Olympic wrestling and I've got a family to support," said Thue, who pursued a career in sports medicine.

On the canvas, in another combat sport, Chris Johnson won a bronze medal for Canada in the boxing middleweight class. And Mark Leduc of Kingston, Ontario, stuck his well-bludgeoned nose into the middle of the ring again. In ten years of fighting as an amateur boxer for Canada, Leduc took his share of cuts, scrapes and blows. But nothing quite prepared him for the Big Hurt of Barcelona. He ran a high fever because of an insect bite and had his right shoulder frozen to dull the pain from a ripped tendon. But in his last appearance for Canada, the twenty-eight-year-old light welterweight fought like a man possessed. He pounded his way through the opening bouts and landed in the semifinals, where he outscored Leonard Doroftei of Romania 7–0 in the third and final round to rally for a 13–6 victory. Leduc lost to heavily favoured Hector Vinent of Cuba in the gold medal bout, but the Canadian won a lot of admirers for his sheer grit. His was a hard-earned Olympic silver and the last medal won by Canada on the last day of the Barcelona Olympics. "I've done a lot of travelling, been to roughly forty countries, seen a heck of a lot and experienced a heck of a lot," Leduc told reporters, while clutching his medal. "Now it's time to settle down and get a life."

Angela Chalmers, of half-Sioux and half-Scottish ancestry, was given the Indian name of Walks Fast Woman by her Manitoba tribe because of her ability to run. The native of Brandon won the women's 1500 and 3000m titles at the 1990 Auckland Commonwealth Games and then seemed to fall off the face of the earth. Hampered by mononucleosis and a leg injury, she had a tough time living up to the stardom predicted of her after Auckland and fell out of sight. But she fashioned a comeback story at Barcelona that was surpassed only by Laumann's. It was only as the world turned the corner into the 1992 Olympic year, that Chalmers recovered enough to personally turn that same corner. She started coming on in January and had several strong runs in the spring and summer, culminating with a tremendous kick in the final 200m to take the Olympic 3000m bronze medal at Barcelona. "You can't compare my comeback with Silken's," said Chalmers. "Hers was over such a short period of time and my problems stretched over a couple of years. But I like to think that both cases showed that desire and commitment are a big part of sports — Silken's case most of all. There are hundreds of comeback stories at the Olympic Games, and they all deserve to be recognized. But I guess we personalized the whole thing to Canadians more than some of the other stories that also deserve to be told." Before her father died, Chalmers promised him she would win an Olympic medal or give that goal the best shot she could. "Crossing that line at Barcelona was indescribable," she said. "It was such a sense of relief, such a sense of joy. I was choked up, feeling everything at once."

Sprinter Mark McKoy bolted from the Seoul Games after the Ben Johnson scandal blew open. But before leaving, McKoy scored probably the most significant track and field medal for Canada since Percy Williams' two sprint golds at the 1928 Amsterdam Olympics. He stunned his great friend and the eventual world record holder, the favoured Colin Jackson of Wales, to take gold in the 110m hurdles at Barcelona in 13.12 seconds. McKoy bolted from the blocks like a cannonball and continued to build up speed over each hurdle as he blasted to the lead and left the field behind. He was as magnificent and unstoppable as he was aloof. Jackson faded out of the medals as Americans Tony Dees and Jack Warren took the silver and bronze in 13.24 and 13.26 seconds. But the joy for the Canadian public was really taken out of that landmark win by McKoy's attitude, which the public could sense. It was a gold medal won by a dissident. McKoy had soured on Canada — he was bitter at how his friends in the former Toronto Mazda sprint club had become objects of scorn to the public and had been treated harshly in the Dubin inquiry — and his resentment was palpable. The great hurdler then emotionally and physically bolted from Canada as well, eventually giving up his Canadian citizenship and moving to Europe.

Guillaume Leblanc, a thirty-year-old engineer with the Quebec Telephone Company, had finished fourth at the 1984 Los Angeles Olympics and tenth at the 1988 Seoul Games in the 20km racewalk. The walker from Rimouski was a mild threat for a medal in 1992. But his hopes really began to rise at the 13km point when he was in the leading group and noticed many of the favourites were struggling with the heat and mugginess along the streets of Barcelona. But with two cautions already for lifting both feet off the ground, Leblanc knew he had to be careful. A third caution would have meant disqualification. Two Spaniards were leading him and one, Valentin Massana, drew his third caution and was out of the race. As the patriotic stadium crowd atop Montjuic erupted in a carnival of noise when Daniel Plaza of Spain entered the stadium first, almost forgotten in the commotion was the sweat-drenched figure of Leblanc as he followed in second to take the silver medal in 1:22:25 to winner Plaza's 1:21:45. Pass the glass slipper. Team Terrible was on its way to becoming Team Terrific.

But some ghosts from the past just wouldn't go away. Ben Johnson was back and looked good in the early rounds of the 100m. But he stumbled coming out of the blocks in the semifinals and couldn't recover to make it to the final, in which Britain's ageless Linford Christie won the gold medal in 9.96 seconds. But Johnson's efforts on the track conflicted with the men's cycling sprint races at the velodrome and guess which story the media found more attractive. Cyclist Curt Harnett of Thunder Bay wasn't impressed and he let the Canadian media know in an icy blast. Harnett was irate that only a small number of reporters showed up to watch him win the bronze medal in the cycling sprints. "All we hear is Ben Johnson this and Ben Johnson that," said Harnett, to the few Canadian reporters there to listen to him. "All the time it's Ben Johnson. It's a disgrace he gets more attention than other Canadian athletes. I'm proud to see you guys wasting time out here rather than drinking Coke at the stadium. It's too bad one individual has to take away the attention from other people who are performing. It's too bad steroid use is such a focus in sport." Harnett, who would set the sprint lap world record in 1995 at the world championships, continued to be bedeviled by his nemesis Gary Neiwand of Australia. Neiwand had beaten Harnett in the sprint gold medal final at the 1990 Auckland Commonwealth Games. The two met again in the semifinals of the Barcelona Olympics. The result was the same. The hard-working and likable Harnett rebounded to defeat Roberto Chiappa of Italy 2–0 for the bronze medal while Jens Fiedler of Germany edged Neiwand 2–1 in the gold medal final. Harnett and Neiwand locked spokes again in the gold medal final of the 1994 Victoria Commonwealth Games. The outcome was as predictable as clockwork. Neiwand first and Harnett second.

Eric Jespersen of Sidney, BC, left Barcelona before the closing ceremonies. With a child on the way and a family boat-building business to attend to, fun and ceremony weren't exactly high on his list of things he really needed at that point. He had seen enough of sporting circuses as a *Canada I* and *Canada II* crew member at the 1983 and 1987 America's Cups. He got what he came for at Barcelona — an Olympic medal in Star class yachting with Ross MacDonald of Vancouver. MacDonald and Jespersen needed a near-miracle to move from seventh to a medal position in their final race. They got one. They needed to beat the Dutch by at least two places, the Swedes by at least fifteen and the Germans by at least ten. All these improbable things happened on the last race to allow the two Canadians to capture the bronze medal. "I had trouble getting to sleep the night before the final race," said Jespersen, who knew the odds were stacked against them. "I was disappointed with the way things had gone up to then. But then you wake up and get out there and look what happens." Jespersen's parents had never owned a television prior to 1992 but they gave in and bought their first one to watch their offspring perform in the Olympics. "We did things outdoors as a family when I was growing up," said Eric Jespersen. "I know people find it strange in this day and age, but I didn't miss having a TV at all. We had no time for TV. We did other things."

A pair of twin sisters put on one of the better aquatic battles this side of *Crimson Tide*. Penny and Vicky Vilagos of Montreal ended a comeback after a five-year retirement by taking the silver medal in synchronized swimming doubles. The gold medallists were American twins Sarah and Karen Josephson. Backstroke swim gold medallist Tewksbury added a bronze medal to his collection by carrying the Canadian men's 4x100 medley relay team of himself, fellow-Calgarian Jon Cleveland, Marcel

Gery of Toronto and Stephen Clarke of Brampton, Ontario, to the podium in 3:39.66. The Americans set the world record in the final of 3:36.93 to win gold. Cleveland is the son of former major leaguer Reggie Cleveland, who pitched for the Boston Red Sox in the 1975 World Series. Gery had defected from Czechoslovakia before the Iron Curtain fell apart and fought a long battle to get his citizenship to swim for Canada. He was denied that chance for the 1988 Seoul Olympics but got the paperwork in time to win medals for his adopted country at Barcelona and the 1990 Commonwealth Games.

Among the biggest Canadian disappointments was Michael Smith of Kenora, Ontario, the decathlon star with the Hollywood good looks. The 1990 Commonwealth Games gold medallist and 1991 world championship silver medallist withdrew because of an injured hamstring. That came before Canada had any medals and the nation's Barcelona Olympic enterprise seemed headed to oblivion fast. After another disastrous outing at the 1993 world championships in Stuttgart, Smith was turning his peak-valley career around with gold at the 1994 Victoria Commonwealth Games and bronze at the 1995 world championships in Goteborg, Sweden. Instantly likable and highly telegenic, Smith will find the sponsorship world is at his feet if he can medal at the 1996 Atlanta Olympics. But as he probably knows by now, it is also a fickle world that will drop "losers" faster than hot coals. The potent Canadian men's 4x100 track relay team, led by Ben Johnson and rising star Bruny Surin, would probably have medalled at Barcelona if not for a dropped baton between Glenroy Gilbert and Atlee Mahorn. Canada took the bronze in the 4x100 at the 1993 world championships and then exploded for spectacular gold medal wins at the 1994 Commonwealth Games and 1995 world championships. Canada's 7 gold medals (including the belated one for Frechette) left it tied for tenth place with Australia in the gold medal parade at Barcelona, behind the Unified Team's 45, United States' 37, Germany's 33, China's 16, Cuba's 14, Spain's 13, South Korea's 12, Hungary's 11 and France's 8. Canada tied for fifteenth place with Romania in overall medals with 18, behind the Unified's 112, Americans' 108, Germany's 82, China's 54, Cuba's 31, Hungary's 30, South Korea's and France's 29 each, Australia's 27, Spain's and Japan's 22 each, Britain's 20, and Italy's and Poland's 19 each.

But despite the euphoria over Canada's fine display at Barcelona, there remained basic problems. *The Status of the High Performance Athlete in Canada Report*, which came out just before the Barcelona Olympics, showed that only 10 percent of Canada's international athletes were identified as "upbeat, satisfied or positive." The report, done by Ekos Research

Associates Inc., showed serious flaws in the system due mainly to chronic underfunding and having to live hand-to-mouth. The report, which polled 942 Canadian international-level athletes, showed that summer-sport athletes averaged $7,876 yearly from sports income but had $22,063 in annual sport-related expenses for an average shortfall of $14,187. Sixty percent of Canada's carded athletes — those who received small monthly stipends from the federal government — held jobs in 1992 and 37 percent got scholarships and bursaries. More than one in three national team athletes received direct monetary support from parents and relatives. But an Olympic medal can take care of some of those financial headaches when sponsors come knocking. Laumann, Frechette and Tewksbury would no longer have to be among those sleeping on floors and mooching off parents. Yet even when a so-called amateur sport athlete does well financially because of endorsements, it's all relative. They're still making hundreds of thousands of dollars less than journeymen NHL, NBA or major league baseball players.

Smith was Canada's flagbearer during the opening ceremonies but Laumann was selected to carry the Maple Leaf during the closing. She fought back tears as the announcement was made. Either Laumann, Frechette or Tewksbury would have been popular choices. It is estimated Barcelona spent more than $9 billion on its Olympic preparations, if things like road construction and other civic infrastructure improvements are taken into account. Yet despite the money and technology involved, the 1992 Summer Games had a refreshingly honest, simple and heartfelt air about them. The city of Barcelona had been trying since 1936 to get the Games and was a gracious and sunny host when it finally did. The closing ceremony was an eclectic swirl of popular culture and ancient Catalan legend as Spanish super-tenor Jose Carreras and Sarah Brightman sang Andrew Lloyd Webber's "Amigos Para Siempre (Friends For Life)" and mythical devils carrying torches darted and whirled. Barcelona mayor and Games organizing committee chairman Pasqual Maragall — the first to try that kind of double-sided control of a Summer Olympics since the Jean Drapeau disaster at Montreal in 1976 — handed the Games flag to Atlanta mayor Maynard Jackson. The 100th anniversary Games of the modern era were now just four years away. Many had predicted along the way that the movement would never see that anniversary. There have been many prognostications of demise after a rocky early start and poor outings at Paris in 1900 and St. Louis in 1904, the cancellation of the 1916 Games due to war, the Nazi propaganda Games of 1936, the cancellation of the 1940 and 1944 Games due to war, the 1972 Munich Massacre, the multi-billion-dollar Montreal deficit and the boycotts of

1980 and 1984. But somehow this five-ring circus survives despite its flaws. And they are many.

Take, for instance, the choice of Atlanta as the site to celebrate the Centennial Games. Excuse me, but Atlanta? Anyone with any sense of romance or history realizes the 1996 Summer Olympics should have gone to Athens. That the IOC picked a second-tier US city of little international repute speaks volumes for what the Olympics really are — a business fueled by American greenbacks. It's not hard to see why the Games often create a civil war within a city. Toronto bid for the 1996 Summer Olympics. In one corner, representing big business and the movers and shakers, was bid chairman and former Olympic yachtsman Paul Henderson. In the other corner was self-styled anti-Games crusader Michael Shapcott and the Bread Not Circuses Coalition, apparently representing the halt, the lame and the downtrodden. These unfortunates, so the party line went, would have suffered horrible harm as the city was bulldozed and billions of dollars diverted to the Olympics from more pressing social needs. It was an epic battle as Henderson and the bid committee tried to present Toronto the Good to the IOC members who would be voting. Bread Not Circuses, meanwhile, lauched its own lobbying campaign, going so far as to sending videos to each IOC member saying they wouldn't be welcome in Hogtown and capping their protest by setting up a tent outside the ballroom of the Tokyo hotel where the vote took place in 1990.

Seven cities began the race. As four fell by the wayside, only Toronto, Atlanta and Athens remained on the penultimate ballot. The Centennial Games were now clearly a battle between the historical and centennial allure of Athens 1896-1996 and the money and advantageous-for-advertising television time zones of North America. That meant the second-to-last ballot, for all intents and purposes, was going to be a North American run-off between Toronto and Atlanta — with Athens likely to hold its support. That's exactly what happened. It's probably giving too much credit to the motley assortment of anti-establishment types who made up Bread Not Circuses to say that they blocked the Summer Olympics from coming to Canada for the second time in twenty years. But their anti-Games rhetoric certainly didn't help Toronto in the latter stages when the choice was clearly to see which of two North American sites would face Athens on the final round.

Things were close between Toronto and Atlanta in many IOC members' minds, but the scale was tipped to the American city. And Athens was all but doomed when Toronto's support predictably went to Atlanta on the last ballot and the Georgia capital easily outpolled the Greek capital to win the right to host the Centennial Games of the modern era. Dumbfounded Greek bid committee officials and politicians left the ball-room looking as if they had just been kicked in the groin. In a way, they had been. When the words " ... city of Atlanta" came out of IOC president Juan Antonio Samaranch's mouth, there was a hesitation to even believe that it was true. Maybe old Juan was just having a little fun before announcing the real winner. Athens officials couldn't comprehend that the IOC would pass up the opportunity to hold the Centennial Games in Greece, site of the ancient Olympics and home to the first modern Games in 1896. The thought that they wouldn't win the 100th anniversary Games hadn't even seemed to have occurred to them. But they underestimated the power of money, advertising and television. For his part, Henderson was seething and said he hoped Bread Not Circuses was happy at passing up the opportunity for ten thousand Athletes' Village dorms that would have been turned into low-cost housing after a 1996 Toronto Summer Olympics. And so it came to pass that Atlanta mayor Jackson accepted from Barcelona mayor Maragall, on a blissful summer night on the Mediterranean, the flag whose five rings represent the most famous non-religious symbol known to humankind. The Olympics, in their way, hold up a mirror to world society and reflect its values. And its values are that North America counts. History and Athens don't. The Olympic Games' faults are everybody's faults. But the same can be said of their virtues. The Olympics present the human pageant in all its full glory and gaudy folly — which is why they are a worldwide magnet for critics and boosters alike and why they remain so utterly irresistible and endlessly fascinating.